Philosophical Fragments

or

A Fragment of Philosophy

Philosophical Fragments

or

A Fragment of Philosophy

BY *JOHANNES CLIMACUS*

Is an historical point of departure
possible for an eternal consciousness; how can
such a point of departure have any other
than a merely historical interest;
is it possible to base an eternal happiness
upon historical knowledge?

RESPONSIBLE FOR PUBLICATION
S. KIERKEGAARD

ORIGINALLY TRANSLATED AND INTRODUCED BY
DAVID F. SWENSON

NEW INTRODUCTION AND COMMENTARY BY
NIELS THULSTRUP

TRANSLATION REVISED AND COMMENTARY TRANSLATED BY
HOWARD V. HONG

PRINCETON · NEW JERSEY
PRINCETON UNIVERSITY PRESS

Printed in the United States of America
by Princeton University Press, Princeton, New Jersey

ACKNOWLEDGMENTS

Thanks are due to Ejnar Munksgaard Forlag, Copenhagen, for permission to issue in English the substantial Introduction and detailed Commentary by Niels Thulstrup which appeared in their Danish critical edition of *Philosophical Fragments*, 1955.

The translator wishes to express his gratitude to Niels Thulstrup for reading and correcting the typescript of the translation of his work, to Henrik Rosenmeier, William Narum, Charles Magel, Paul Holmer, and Homer Mason for insights on translation of the text, to Gary Overvold and the St. Olaf College Library staff for bibliographical assistance, and to Liselotte Zwettler and Edna H. Hong for extraordinary help in preparing and typing the copy.

CONTENTS

Foreword

BY HOWARD V. HONG

THIS new edition (the second) of *Philosophical Fragments* is marked primarily by the addition of Niels Thulstrup's Introduction and Commentary from the latest critical edition in Danish (Copenhagen: Munksgaard, 1955). Inasmuch as David Swenson's earlier Introduction presents *Fragments* in the setting of the entire Kierkegaard canon and the Thulstrup Introduction is confined to *Fragments* itself, both are included as complementary in the present edition.

In addition to these changes from the first edition, there is the minor difference of occasional revisions of the Swenson translation. Two expressions in particular have been changed throughout for the sake of fidelity to the meaning and terminology of the text: *Guden* (beginning with p. 6 of the translation) and *Tilblivelse* (primarily in the Interlude).

The expression *Guden* ("the God") rather than *Gud* ("God") is used throughout *Philosophical Fragments* (except in seven places and in a footnote on pp. 32-33 concerning Spinoza's and Leibniz's discussion of "the existence of God"). This *consistent* usage of an extraordinary Danish expression is unique in Kierkegaard's authorship. Elsewhere in his writings the expression is found almost exclusively in works of intentionally esthetic character (more particularly in connection with Greek-Socratic-Platonic allusions)[1] and in the portions of *Concluding*

---

[1] *The Concept of Irony, with constant Reference to Socrates* (sv xii, 149, 188: references to Agathon and Socrates), *Either/Or* (sv i, 52f., 345: references to Eros and Nautch girl), *Fear and Trembling* (sv iii, 146,

Unscientific Postscript to the Philosophical Fragments[2] bearing directly on *Fragments* or relating to Socrates. It is noteworthy that *Guden* does not appear in the volume published four days later (June 17, 1834): *The Concept of Dread* on the concept of original sin.

In *Postscript* the expression *Guden*, "the God," appears in another way consistent with *Fragments*, but with a difference. In *Fragments*, in accordance with the hypothesis of making an advance upon the Socratic by way of the decisive importance of the Teacher and the Moment in time, *Guden* comes to mean the Eternal in time, the God in history, the Incarnation. In *Postscript* the expression *Guden*, in addition to the use mentioned in the paragraph above, is employed frequently in the phrase *Guden i Tiden*, "the God in time," or in the clear sense of Christ as the Incarnation, God in time (sv vii, 231f., 258,

---

179: references to Agamemnon and Socrates), once in an article in *Faedrelandet*, Dec. 27, 1845 (sv xiii, 467: "The Activity of a traveling Aesthetician . . ."), *Stages on Life's Way* (sv vi, 70, 82, 85, 132ff., 152, 160f., 168, 308, 318, 473: references to the God of love in the banquet speeches in the manner of Plato's *Symposium* and in "Observations about Marriage," to a Greek God in "Quidam's Diary," and finally to Quidam's "holding fast to the God in faith," according to the view of Frater Taciturnus, who has just said, "I am concerned about this in a thoroughly Greek way"), in the last of the esthetic pieces, *A Literary Review* (sv viii, 14f., 20, 81f., 96: references to Socrates, literary productivity, wit, and enthusiastic reformers; p. 117 contains both *Gud*, with regard to the concrete individual relationship, and *Guden* and *Guddommen*, meaning the God and the deity). Apart from these esthetic works and *Postscript*, apparently only two works use the expression *Guden* and only once each: *The Gospel of Suffering* (sv viii, 423: reference to Socrates) and *Training in Christianity* (sv xii, 85: in a discussion of contemporaneity with Christ and following an allusion to Socrates, although the expression is not required by the allusion).

[2] *Concluding Unscientific Postscript* (sv vii, 30, 73, 75ff., 133, 137, 156, 166f., 168f., 196, 231f., 234, 258, 265, 312, 314f., 343, 393f., 459, 480f., 563f., 565, 567, 569, 575, 607: *Guden*, "the God," used in direct reference to *Fragments* or in connection with Greek-Platonic-Socratic thought or with German Idealism).

312, 314f., 343, 393f., 561, 569, 575, 607). In *Postscript* Lowrie and Swenson translate *Guden* and *Guden i Tiden* variously as *God, the Deity, God in time, the Deity in time, God-man, the God.*

For the translator, fidelity alone requires adherence to Kierkegaard's careful discrimination in terminology. But why did Kierkegaard employ an expression which is very unusual in both Danish and English? The answer clearly seems to be that in writing of Greek thought and religion he made use of the term closely associated with Socrates and Plato. Therefore also in *Fragments*, which is cast in the language and thought of Idealism (with Socrates as representative), the language at this crucial point is Socratic-Platonic. It is important to note that the first use of the expression in *Fragments* (p. 13 in present translation) is accompanied by quotations from Plato's *Apology* and *Theaetetus* in both Greek and in translation: ὁ θεος, *Guden* (*the God*, as in the standard Jowett translation of Plato). After this clear announcement of Socratic-Platonic terminology, Climacus uses it with almost one hundred percent consistency throughout the work. Thulstrup emphasizes this in the *Commentary* and reaffirmed it in correspondence with the translator. Emanuel Hirsch also emphasizes this Platonic cast and corresponding formulation of the hypothetical character of the *Fragments* as he chides Schrempf for falsifying the text by substituting *Gott* for *der Gott*.[8] If a reader does not know that "the

[8] "And now two points become clear. First, Kierkegaard has made it as apparent as possible that he is not speaking in the manner of traditional Christianity. Instead of developing a project of thought, he could have taken the second alternative and simply made a dialectical analysis of Christianity. Why did he not do this? Simply because in a comparison with the Socratic theory of knowledge a purely scholarly, theoretical

God" signalizes the Platonic background of the work, the unusualness of the expression should help prevent his forgetting the hypothetical character of the work ("a project of thought") and keep him from slipping readily into customary categories of theological discourse and religious edification.

Also on p. 13 is one of the second cluster of terms which have been amended for the sake of consistency with the authorship and clarification of meaning. *Tilvaerelsens Modsigelse* was and remains translated "contradictions of existence." Throughout the work *Tilvaerelse, vaere til, Tilblivelse,* and *blive til* have been amended, unless the special context calls for a variant, to read *existence, to exist, coming into existence,* and *to come into existence.*

Throughout the authorship these terms, particularly (a) *Tilblivelse* and (b) *bliver til,* have been variously translated by Lowrie and Swenson: (a) *coming into existence, creation, birth, genesis, process of becoming, coming into the world,* and *coming into being,* with the first and the last most frequent; (b) *to come into existence, to become* (with predicate), *to exist, to come into the world,* and *to come into being,* with the first and last again most frequent. A certain variation is at times more faithful to the particular meaning in a given sentence. In the *Fragments,*

---

viewpoint is dominant, a viewpoint entirely unsuited to grasping a living relationship to the God of Grace in adoration and prayer in the inwardness of one's existence. If the reader does not understand this warning-sign and then takes the schematic construction on the basis of a theory of knowledge as Christian discourse—what responsibility should Kierkegaard have for such stiff-necked stupidity? . . .

"The German reader, of course, is at a disadvantage because of Schrempf's translation, which falsifies Kierkegaard's frequently used expression *der Gott* (which continually emphasizes the character of the entire work as a dialectical hypothesis) by changing it to *Gott." Kierkegaard-Studien,* III, 2, pp. 95-96.

however, particularly in the Interlude, the simplest, most ordinary translation, some form of *to come into existence*, is most appropriate to the meaning. *Tilblivelse* here refers not to becoming or the process of alteration but to something's "coming into existence," and not to "coming into being" (for all possibilities have a kind of being and the Eternal is eternal being) but to the spatial-temporal actualization of any possibility and the individual, historical incarnation of the Eternal. The ultimate "contradiction of existence" is the Eternal in time, not the Eternal as coming into being but as coming into temporal-spatial existence with its particularity and contingency: the Incarnation. "God does not exist, he is eternal" (*Gud existerer ikke, han er evig*) writes Climacus in *Postscript* (sv VII, 321); and he continues later (sv VII, 570) in the language of *Fragments*, "the historical is that the God, the Eternal, has come into existence at a particular time as an individual human being (*"Det historiske er, at Guden, den Evige, er bleven til i et bestemt Tidsmoment som et enkelt Menneske"*). These lines point to the central problem of *Fragments*, not the essence and being of God but the God-in-time, the entry of the Eternal into human existence.

It is of little use to take a clue from the English translation of Aristotle's various uses of κίνησις (motion and change in general), because (except for possibility-actuality) these do not fit the basic categories (time and the Eternal) of the Interlude. Furthermore, κίνησις (motion, change) is not specific enough. In the Interlude κίνησις is in apposition to "change" and not to the *coming-into-existence kind* of change, an important detail handled inaccurately in all the early translations of *Fragments* in German, French, and English. In *Begrebet Angest* (sv IV, 388-90) there are two very important footnotes on Aristotle (possibility and actuality) and on Plato (the instant, being and non-being). Here Lowrie translates *bliver til* as *comes into existence* or *brought into existence* (*The Concept of Dread*, pp. 74-75).

William Nielsen in a Harvard thesis (1949) and Charles Magel in a Minnesota thesis (1960) both criticize the translation of these key terms in the Interlude. Mr. Magel in correspondence stated his judgment that *coming into existence* is a clearer and more accurate rendition. The primary objection to employing it, according to Reidar Thomte, is that it makes use of *existence* in an ordinary sense, without the qualitative differentiation implied by "What does it mean to exist?" The English language just does not yield different expressions to equate separately with *vaere, vaere til, bliver, bliver til, Tilblivelse*, and *existere*. Therefore we must use *exist* and *existence* also in the ordinary sense of being in time-space. This Kierkegaard (Johannes Climacus) himself points out in *Postscript* (sv VII, 574): "Sin is the new existence-medium. Aside from this, *to exist* means merely that the individual, by coming into existence, exists and is in the process of becoming; ... aside from this *to exist* is not a more sharply defining predicate but the form of all more sharply defining predicates. . . ." With such authorization and for the sake of clarity and fidelity of meaning in *Fragments* the words *exist* and *existence* are obliged to do daily duty in the ordinary sense, but, after all, it is on this level that all existing particular men must begin in beginning *existence* as individuals.

St. Olaf College, Northfield, Minnesota
May 30, 1961

Translator's Introduction

BY DAVID F. SWENSON

THE little book which here for the first time appears in English dress, presents its own thought with all needed completeness. Nevertheless, it also belongs to a larger whole, a "literature within the literature," the product of Sören Kierkegaard's pen, and the realization of a coherent plan. Within this literature it has its own immediate sequel in the *Unscientific Postscript*, whose intended publication is hinted at in the closing paragraph of the present work. This sequel is described by its author as performing the task of clothing in concrete historical costume the problem here dealt with in terms of imaginative hypothesis and algebraic abstraction. It really does more than this; for it contributes a new and more detailed study of the problem itself, setting it in the widest psychological and philosophical context, the result being a highly original and significant contribution to the philosophy of religion. In the writer's opinion this book is one which future students of that subject will no more be able to neglect, if they are to write significantly, than the present-day logician can afford to ignore the contributions made by Aristotle to the science of logic.

However, both the *Fragments* and the *Postscript* are but single items in a literature of much wider scope, partly religious in purport and spirit, and partly quite consciously and expressly non-religious. Kierkegaard himself divides the writings into two main groups, designated respectively as esthetic and religious. The *Postscript* marks a line of division, for the bulk of the religious writings comes after

that work, just as the bulk of the esthetic writings precedes
it. Nevertheless, there appeared simultaneously with the
earlier esthetic series, all the items of which were pseudonymous, a series of devotional works, eighteen religious
addresses published in Kierkegaard's own name. And
towards the close of the religious series as originally
conceived, not including in the reckoning the more polemic religious writings of his last years, there appeared
one or two purely esthetic essays: a critical study of an
opera singer in a role of Mozart's *Don Juan*; and a psychological orientation in the crisis produced or signalized in
the life of an actress, when after an interval of twenty years
she reenacts the role of Shakespeare's Juliet. The idea
behind this planned duality was to give expression to
Kierkegaard's thought that the esthetic and the religious
are not related as youth and age, or as the presence of
sensibility and the lack of it, which is what most people
consciously or unconsciously assume; but that these factors
are normally co-present in the personality, as controlled
material on the one hand, and as major formative passion
on the other.

Thus the Kierkegaardian literature is a varied one,
striking a multitude of different notes, evaluating life
from a number of different points of view, and even
experimenting with a variety of different styles, exhibiting
in these respects an extraordinary virtuosity. What gives
to all this multitudinousness a peculiar significance is that
Kierkegaard himself views it throughout in the perspective of a single idea, subjecting the varied material to a
conscious dialectical control. In other words, the creative
multiplicity of the poet in him is simultaneously trans-
lucent to the thinker who was his *alter ego*. For Kierke-

gaard was poet and thinker in one; like the poet-philosopher of antiquity, the immortal Plato, his endowment embraced that rarest of all syntheses: an equal proportion of imaginative and dramatic power, with the capacity for abstract conceptual thought in precise and consecutive form.

Taken as a whole, these writings illuminate and bring to a high degree of conscious clarity the subjective life of the human spirit, the life of passion, emotion, aspiration, evaluation, hope, despair, anxiety, dread, confidence, trust, doubt, faith. This is a problem for thought generally neglected by philosophers, or at most merely half-heartedly pursued. They have had much more to say about the environing conditions of life, and about the abstract problems of being and knowledge, than about life itself in its inner core; and they have expended a finer workmanship upon objectivities than they have condescended to bestow upon subjectivities. Kierkegaard's writings form an outstanding exception to this general rule; in his case the entire energy of a great genius of reflection was expended upon the clarification of the realm of the subjective, which is the realm of spirit.[1] There exists at present a school of thinkers whose fundamental principle it is to make a sharp cleavage between what they call "logical" and "emotive" significance, denying to the latter all verifiability, and

[1] The only important modern thinker who resembles Kierkegaard in making the problem of the personality central in his philosophy, is Nietzsche. But Nietzsche has only one string to his bow, where Kierkegaard has many. Both agree, however, in posing as the deepest problem of thought and the future, the question of what kind of a personality it is necessary to develop, instead of with Hegel making society and its institutions central, or with the naturalists focusing attention upon the scientific knowledge of instrumentalities and their control for the enhancement of power.

hence all real truth or error; by this means they hope to exclude from philosophy practically everything that makes it worth pursuing. The Kierkegaardian literature is not so much an argument against this view, which erects into a philosophical principle the vulgar prejudice which identifies the emotional with the structureless and the arbitrary, as it is a demonstration of its falsity through the actual production of a reflectively critical system of evaluations. The criticism is for the most part effected by means of a confrontation with one another of different or opposed valuations, exhibited through the self-expression of representative personalities, endowed as few novelists know how to endow their characters, with a radical consistency of attitude, and a philosophical clarity concerning themselves. Such is not the outstanding trait of what is currently called Theory of Value, which consists for the most part of abstract-logical considerations, a prolegomena for a valuation process that never quite gets started, possibly because the philosopher has exhausted his energies in preliminaries, like boys who take too long a run in order to give them an impetus for the jump.

A brief glance at some of the chief items in the Kierkegaardian literature will serve to give some degree of substance to the above general characterization. Two works of apprenticeship, the one a slight volume containing a critical estimate of the famed author of fairy tales for children young and old, and poet of the sentimental, his contemporary Hans Christian Andersen, viewing him chiefly in the role of a novelist and as the author of a novel depicting a genius who goes to pieces because of an unfavorable environment; and the other a substantial study of irony, with special reference to Socrates as the historic embodiment of this category, comparing the Socratic irony with the irony of the German romantic movement (Tieck, the Schlegels, Solger)—these works of his youth stand outside the "literature," which begins with *Either/Or* (1843), published when Kierkegaard had reached the age of thirty. Each of the two volumes of this last work presents and illustrates a point of view with respect to human life; the two views are divergent, and indeed opposed, since one of them is esthetic and amoral while the other is ethical, whence the title's suggestion of a choice between alternatives. The papers constituting the two sections of the work are supposed to have been accidentally found in a secret drawer of an old secretaire, bought of a dealer in second-hand furniture; they are prepared for publication by the discoverer, Victor Eremita, who also furnishes them with a title and a preface. A study of the two sets of papers shows that the respective authors have been known to each other; *A*, the writer of the first volume, appears as a young man who is a frequent and welcome visitor in the house of *B*, the writer of the second volume; the latter's name is Wilhelm, surname not given, a civil servant, a judge in one of the inferior courts. This acquaintance serves as point of departure for the essays of the second volume, which have the form of lengthy letters addressed to *A*, not with any explicit reference to his writings, of which *B* does not seem cognizant, but rather as to a valued though inexperienced and errant friend.

A consciously non-ethical philosophy of enjoyment inspires the varied contents of the first volume. These consist of a group of lyrical aphorisms (Diapsalmata); a study of the spirit of modern tragedy in its difference from the ancient, together with a poetic sketch of a modernized

Antigone; a psychological analysis of certain heroines of reflective grief (Donna Elvira, Marie Beaumarchais, Margaret in Goethe's *Faust*) with a poetic rendering of their inner self-communion; an oration on the subject of who can be regarded as the unhappiest of mortals; a review and interpretation of Scribe's comedy, *The First Love*, sparkling with wit and buoyed up by an esthetic enthusiasm which puffs its subject up into a masterpiece; a study of the sensuous-erotic in human nature, in so far as it is present in an unconsciously immediate manner, described through an analysis of Mozart's music, particularly in the opera of *Don Juan*; and a parallel study of a reflective seducer, in entire contrast with Mozart's Don Juan, who is not so much a personality with a consciousness, as he is the abstract embodiment of a force of nature. This seducer is presented through a section of his diary, copied surreptitiously, a diary which besides sketching brilliantly minor erotic episodes tells the story of a diabolically clever seduction, so managed that the outward appearances leave it doubtful who is the seducer and who the seduced. In addition, there is in these papers a bit of pure theorizing in the essay called "The Method of Rotations," in which a thoroughly sophisticated enjoyment-philosophy explains by means of what artistry its goal may best be realized, and the devil of boredom be exorcised.

I quote here two of the Diapsalmata in translation, the first and the last, as well as a section from the Seducer's diary, an extract from an essay on Woman.

"What is a poet? A poet is an unhappy creature, whose heart is tortured by deepest suffering, but whose lips are so formed that when his sighs and cries stream out over them, their

sound becomes like the sound of beautiful music. His fate is
that of the unfortunates who were imprisoned in Phalaris'
brazen bull, there to be slowly tortured over a low fire; their
cries could not reach the tyrant's ear to strike terror into his
heart, they came to him transformed into sweet music. And
men flock about the poet, saying: Sing for us soon again; that
is to say, may new sufferings torture your soul, and may your
lips continue to be formed as before; for the cries would only
make us anxious, but the music is lovely. And the critics come
upon the scene; they say: Quite correct, so it ought to be by
the rules of esthetics. To be sure, a critic resembles a poet to
a hair; he lacks only the sufferings in his heart and the music
on his lips. And that is why I would rather be a herder of
swine, and be understood by the swine, than be a poet and be
misunderstood by men."

"Something wonderful has happened to me. I was caught up
into the seventh heaven. There all the gods sat assembled. As a
mark of their especial favor I was granted a wish. Said Mercury:
Will you have youth, or beauty, or power, or a long life, or the
most beautiful maiden, or any other of the many treasures we
have here in the chest? Choose what you will, but remember,
only one thing. For a moment I stood there at a loss, but then
I addressed myself to the gods as follows: Most honored contemporaries, I choose this one thing, always to have the laugh
on my side. Not one of the gods answered by a single word,
but they all began to laugh. From this I concluded that my
prayer was fulfilled, and found that the gods knew how to
express themselves with taste; for it would scarcely have been
fitting for them to have solemnly replied: Your wish is
granted."

"Each woman has her share [of beauty]: the merry smile,
the roguish glance, the wistful eye, the pensive head, the
exuberant spirits, the still sadness, the deep foreboding, the
brooding melancholy, the earthly homesickness, the unbaptized

movements, the beckoning eyebrows, the questioning lips, the mysterious forehead, the ensnaring curls, the drooping lashes, the heavenly pride, the earthly modesty, the angelic purity, the secret blush, the light step, the airy grace, the languishing posture, the dreamy yearning, the unexplained sigh, the slender form, the soft outlines, the luxuriant bosom, the swelling hips, the tiny feet, the dainty hand.—Each woman has her own trait, and the one does not merely repeat the other. Then, when I have seen and again seen, when I have contemplated and again contemplated all this multitudinous variety, when I have smiled, sighed, flattered, threatened, desired, tempted, laughed, wept, hoped, feared, won, lost—then I shut up my fan, and assemble the diverse elements into one, the parts into the whole. Then my soul rejoices, my heart beats, my passion flames. This one woman, the only one in all the world, she must belong to me, she must be mine. Let God keep His heaven if only I may keep her. I know full well what I choose; it is something so great that Heaven itself must be the loser by the division, for what is there left in heaven when I keep her? The believing Moslems will be cheated of their hopes when in their Paradise they embrace pale, weak shadows; for warm hearts they cannot find, since all the warmth is concentrated in her breast; comfortless they will despair when they find only pale lips, lustreless eyes, a lifeless bosom, a limp pressure of the hand; for all the redness of the lips and the fire of the eye and the heaving of the bosom and the promise of the hand and the foreboding of the sigh and the seal of the kiss and the trembling of the touch and the passion of the embrace—all, all is united in her, who lavishes upon me a wealth sufficient for a world, both in time and eternity."

These extracts may suffice to give some impression of the hectic eloquence of *A*'s style, but they can furnish no adequate conception of the wealth of psychological analysis, of philosophic insight, and of easy superiority in the handling of the most difficult abstractions characteristic of this sensationally brilliant production. By way of contrast, and as suits the calm and assured seriousness of its ethical content, the style of the second volume is notably restrained, sober, and even at times pedestrian. Judge Wilhelm has indeed upon occasion a deep and moving eloquence of his own, but he never essays the high flights of audacious abandon characteristic of his young friend. The manner is intimate, casual, and a bit desultory, as befits a letter-writer. In the first of his two long letters he deals with marriage, with romantic love, with objections urged against marriage from various points of view, championing especially its esthetic validity and moral significance over against the love-is-heaven-but-marriage-is-hell school of thought. He writes as a husband of long standing, whose experience has but deepened his enthusiasm and confirmed his faith. When Kierkegaard's pen framed this eulogy of marriage he had about made up his mind that its values were not for him; hence his pathos is here the deep pathos of the unhappy lover. The second letter deals with a broader theme, namely the normal equilibrium that should ideally obtain between the esthetic and the ethical in the full development of the personality. Here there is unfolded an ethic somewhat in the Kantian spirit, except that the rigid separation of duty from inclination is corrected, and that the abstract formalism characteristic of Kant is replaced by a rich concreteness. Judge Wilhelm is not so much the theorist unfolding a doctrine as he is a mature personality attempting to help and influence a friend.

The plan of this work as a whole suggests a comparison with Plato's *Gorgias,* where also an enjoyment philosophy is placed in contrast with an ethical view of life. However, there are some significant differences in the mode of treatment. In the *Gorgias* Socrates is of course the ethical representative, and he readily conquers each of his three antagonists in turn, through his own superior dialectical skill gaining their more or less unwilling consent to his conclusions. Gorgias himself is presented to us as a somewhat naïve and well-meaning gentleman, a rhetorician who is innocently in love with the wonderful power of his weapon, and absolves himself from all responsibility for its possible misuse. When Socrates asks him what the rhetorician would do, if someone who did not understand how rightly to use this great power were to present himself for instruction, Gorgias airily concedes that if such a thing should by exception happen, he would of course feel himself bound to take a few minutes off for preliminary instruction in justice. This concession at once puts him at Socrates' mercy, and he gracefully bows himself out of the picture; or rather, he is elbowed out by the younger and more insolent Polos. The latter repudiates all concern for justice, scorning Socrates for his countrified introduction into polite conversation of so obsolete a conception; you talk like a fundamentalist, he is made to say to Socrates in Paul Shorey's inspired paraphrase. But while Polos insists that it is better and more pleasant in every way to be able with impunity to wreak injustice upon others than to suffer injustice in one's self, he is weak enough to admit that it is nevertheless more disgraceful to do wrong than to suffer it. When Socrates shows him the unexpected dialectical consequences of this admission, he is silenced, and thereafter consents to the Socratic position like a man convinced against his will, breaking through with the old opinion ever and anon. Callicles, the third disputant, is made of sterner stuff, or so it at first seems; he takes up the gage of battle by boldly repudiating all moral evaluations, including the notion of the greater disgrace attached to wrongdoing as compared with suffering wrong; he interprets them as mere human conventions, hypocritical attempts by weaker men to obscure the natural law of the stronger's right to take what he desires, and to restrain the strong by cunning where strength fails. The really strong man is not restrained however, but breaks through and despises all such conventional agreements, unnatural as they are. But though Callicles is bold and intelligent and frank, he is no match for Socrates in dialectic and ultimately meets the same fate as Polos and Gorgias.

In Plato's dialogue the ethical conquers because it is fortunate enough to have incomparably the abler protagonist; it conquers, and the reader can see the victory achieved and the opponents humbled. Not so in *Either/Or*. In the first place, this work does not reach a decision as between the rival views; the debate is unfinished, just as life is unfinished as long as it lasts, and it is significant that the subtitle of the book is: *A Fragment of Life*. The reader is asked a question, not furnished with an answer. In the second place, the ethicist is not decked out with a superior dialectical skill; on the contrary, the estheticist appears to be unquestionably the more brilliant mind. The author of the Method of Rotations is super-sophisticated, and his amoralism is thoroughly consistent, conscious of every consequence and bold enough to commit himself radically; he is not to be caught in the net of such a Socratic dialectic as vanquishes Callicles. Hence it becomes clearer precisely in what the ethicist differs from the estheticist, namely in the quality of his pathos, and in his more calm and secure assurance with respect to the problems of life; a moral and existential superiority is not confused with a merely intellectual giftedness; the choice offered becomes a choice of character, not of brains. This comparison may serve to point the difference so often insisted upon in the Kierkegaardian literature, between ordinary methods of persuasion and that form of communication which Kierkegaard has erected into a category, namely "indirect" communication. In this latter form the reader is indeed helped, because the question at issue is clarified for him. But he is not coddled or tricked or allured, and the responsibility for a choice remains with him, there being no authority to influence his decision by the intrusion of an alien prestige. The category of indirect communication is given a multiform interpretation in Kierkegaard's practice, and he has taken infinite pains to achieve it in all sorts of ways; in the last analysis he so understands it as to express the very heart of Christianity, for is not a God helpless in the hands of his enemies, a God on the cross, the very *non plus ultra* of indirect communication? But indirect communication is an inevitable necessity when the problem is to attract without deception, to attract the higher but to repel the lower in a man.

Judge Wilhelm advises the estheticist that his road to a genuine grasp of life lies through despair; in this despair, if he endures in it, he will find his real and underlying self, just as in the Hegelian philosophy the philosophic truth is immanently found in a universal doubt. In order to give his ethical philosophy a religious expression, the Judge sends his young friend a sermon written by a country parson, an issue of his solitary meditations while walking on the heath, the theme of which is that over against God we human beings are always in the wrong, and that precisely this is the source of our deepest happiness. The finite spirit cries out to God: I cannot understand Thee; but by enduring this misunderstanding to the very end, enthusiasm gains its victory and happiness is achieved. The religiosity of this sermon thus corresponds in all essentials with the ethical spirit of the "Equilibrium" essay in the second volume; both give expression to the principle of immanence, the same principle which in the *Fragments* is identified with the Greek doctrine of Recollection. Personally, Kierkegaard had at this time, as well as throughout, a different view, being committed to the principle of transcendence, the principle of a new point of departure for the human spirit, involving the presence in its consciousness of a radical breach of continuity. But he desired to say what was to be said successively rather than all at once, convinced that one must at least understand what the ethicist in *Either/Or* understands, before one can profitably essay to understand more.

The literature now proceeds to elucidate this something more. As the *Fragments* seek to show, the central psychological category in a radically transcendent interpretation of life is the Christian concept of Faith. This concept now becomes the focus of attention; it is explored with patient and painstaking gradualness, beginning at the periphery and only bit by bit proceeding to the central core. Within a year from the publication of *Either/Or* appeared two shorter works addressing themselves to this problem, each from a different point of view. In *Fear and Trembling*, described on the title-page as a dialectical lyric, the story of Abraham's sacrifice of his son is made the point of departure for poetical delineations and conceptual characterizations of that faith of which Abraham is said to be the father. The book brings out as *problemata* the private relationship to God which the story of Abraham assumes, as well as the implied teleological suspension of ethical principles, both in the attempted sacrifice of his son, and in the refusal to take the environment into his confidence; Abraham speaks only cryptically, and cannot speak otherwise, for he has by his procedure put himself beyond the pale of that universal sphere of reference which is the basis of all understanding between man and man, namely the ethical. The second of the two works here referred to is called *Repetition*. Here an unhappy love experience furnishes the psychological point of departure for the posing of the central problem of human life, the problem which in faith receives its answer, namely the restitution of the consciousness of the individual to its pristine integrity after an experienced breach.

A young man falls deeply in love, becomes engaged, but to his surprise and chagrin discovers almost at once that what the object of his affection has done for him is to awaken in him the poetic afflatus that had hitherto been dormant and undeclared. This so modifies his nature that though he still loves her, he finds his happiness rather in remembering her in her absence than in the actual face-to-face presence; and he becomes convinced against his will that he is quite unfitted for the role of husband, though he would a thousand times rather be this than be a poet. The strain finally becomes so severe that he cannot endure it; he runs away without a word of explanation, for what is there that he can say? His pride has suffered a crushing blow, for he has lost his honor. And yet he is not conscious that he could possibly have acted otherwise; it is existence itself that has conspired against him. While struggling with his reflections he discovers Job, another sufferer who had a similar grievance against existence, and one who dared, moreover, to take his cause away from the tribunal of his friends and his environment directly to the throne of the Almighty. Job thus becomes the young man's solace; "if Job is a fictitious figure, I hereby make myself responsible for his words." What he needs is nothing less than a reintegration of his personality; and it comes to him one day, as he reads in a newspaper that *she* has had the "high-mindedness," so he interprets it, to marry another. This news comes like a thunderstorm to clear the air; the hour of his trial is over, and now he is jubilant. He writes to his acquaintance of the Latin name, Constantin Constantius, the objective-minded psychologist who has taken an interest in the "case," and tells him what the event has done for him.

"I am again myself. This self, which no one else would stoop to pick up if it lay on the highway, I now possess again. The cleft which threatened to divide my nature is again closed; I again experience a unified personality. . . . Is there then not a repetition? Did I not receive everything again twofold? Did I not receive myself again, and precisely in such a manner as to make me feel doubly its significance?

"I am again myself; the machinery has been set going. The snares in which I was entangled have been cut through; broken are the enchantments which had bewitched me, so that I could not come to myself. There is no one now to lift his hand against me, my liberation is sure, I am born to myself; for as long as

Ilithya folds her hands, the travailing woman cannot be delivered.

"It is over, my yawl is afloat, in another minute I am again where my soul yearns to be, where the ideas seethe and foam like the elements in storm, where the thoughts rise up like the nations in the great migration; where at other times there rules a stillness like the silence of the South Seas, a stillness that lets one hear one's self speak even if the movements are all within the soul; where each moment I risk my life, each moment lose it, and again win it.

"Now I belong to the Idea. When it beckons I follow, when it makes an appointment with me I wait a day and a night; no one calls me to dinner, no one waits for me at suppertime. When the Idea calls me I leave all, or rather, I have nothing to leave, I desert no one, I grieve no one by my loyalty to the Idea, my spirit is not grieved by having to grieve another. . . . The cup of intoxication is again offered me, I already breathe its perfume, I already perceive its foaming music—but first a libation for her, who saved a soul that sat in the solitude of despair: all honor to womanly highmindedness!—Long live the flight of thought, long live the venture of one's life in the service of the Idea, long live the danger of the battle, long live the festive joy of victory; long live the dance in the whirl of the infinite, long live the storm-wave that buries me in the depths, long live the storm-wave that hurls me above the stars!"

Constantin Constantius, author of the book and coolheaded psychological analyst, plays with the category of Repetition, which in his hands is made to cover a second journey to Berlin, a landlord who has changed beyond recognition, a vaudeville performance that refuses to repeat its entertainment, and on the other hand also includes the highest interest of the human spirit, thus so mingling jest with earnest that the "heretics will not be able to understand him." However, the essential scope and purport of the concept is sketched in the opening paragraphs of the book; two passages are here reproduced, as offering a commentary of sorts upon the first chapter of the *Fragments*.

"Say what you will, this problem (i.e., whether a repetition is possible) will come to play a very important role in modern philosophy: for Repetition is a decisive expression for what Recollection was among the Greeks. Just as these taught that all knowledge is recollection, so the new philosophy will teach that the whole of life is a repetition. The only modern philosopher who has had a suspicion of this is Leibniz. Repetition and Recollection are the same movement, only in opposite directions; for that which is remembered has been, and is repeated backwards; while the real repetition is remembered forwards. Hence it is that repetition, if it be possible, makes a man happy; while memory makes him unhappy, provided namely he gives himself time to live, and does not at once, in the very hour of his birth, seek opportunity to steal out of life again, on the pretext for example that he has forgotten something. . . . Repetition is the *interest* of metaphysics, and at the same time the interest on which metaphysics suffers shipwreck; it is the solution of every ethical view of life; it is the *sine qua non* for every dogmatic problem."

"Hope is a new garment, starched and stiff and glittering, but it has never yet been worn, and hence one does not know whether it will fit or how it may become one. Memory is an old garment, and quite useless, however beautiful; for it has been outgrown. But repetition is an imperishable garment, fitting intimately and tenderly; it neither flutters too loosely nor presses too close. Hope is a beautiful maiden who slips through your fingers; memory is a handsome old dowager, never quite serving the purpose of the moment; repetition is a beloved wife, of whom one never tires. It is only the new that tires; the old never tires, and when the mind is engrossed with the old it achieves happiness. He only finds a genuine happiness who refuses to delude himself into thinking that repetition ought to yield him something new; of this illusion boredom is the inevitable consequence. Hope is the prerogative of youth, and memory likewise; but it requires courage to will repetition. Whoever rests content with hope is a coward, and whoever falls back on memory is a pleasure-seeker; but whoever has the courage to will repetition is a man, and the more profoundly he has understood how to interpret this category, the deeper and more substantial is his manhood. Whoever fails to understand that life is repetition, and that this is its beauty, has passed judgment upon himself; he deserves no better fate than that which will befall him, namely to be lost. Hope is an alluring fruit which does not satisfy, memory is a miserable pittance that does not satisfy, but repetition is life's daily bread, which satisfies and blesses. When a man has circumnavigated the globe it will appear whether he has the courage to understand that life is repetition, and the enthusiasm to find therein his happiness. Whoever does not circumnavigate the globe before he begins to live, will never begin to live. Whoever starts the journey, but is overcome by weariness on the way, proves thereby that he had a poor constitution. But whoever chooses repetition lives. He does not like a child run hither and thither to catch butterflies, nor does he stand on tiptoe to behold the glories of the world, for he knows them. He does not sit like an old grandam at memory's spinning wheel, but makes his way through life in peace and quietness, happy in repetition. And what indeed would life be if there were no repetition? Who could wish to be a tablet, on which every new moment writes a new inscription? Who could wish to be a mere memorial of the past? Who could wish to be subject to everything that is new and flighty, or wish forever to be the vehicle for an ephemeral pleasure? If God had not willed repetition the world would never have come into being; for he would then either have indulged his fancy in pursuit of the easy plans of hope, or he would have recalled all his plans and kept them only in the memory. But this he did not do, and therefore the world stands, and stands because it is a repetition. In repetition inheres the earnestness and reality of life. Whoever wills repetition proves himself to be in possession of a pathos that is serious and mature."

In these two books two chief aspects of the concept of faith have been dramatically exemplified, poetically interpreted, and dialectically defined. In *Fear and Trembling*, the aspect delineated is the suspension of the ethical consciousness, and the consequent private and individual relationship to God; in *Repetition*, the restoration of the personal consciousness to its normal integrity. But the heart of the matter has not yet been touched; for an essential and fundamental aspect has been omitted. In line with the idea of a step-by-step unfoldment of the thought in hand, nothing has as yet been said of the universally human point of departure, necessary background, and motivating force for the leap of faith: namely the consciousness of Sin. To delineate faith without making this consciousness central, is to perform *Hamlet* with the role of Hamlet left out. This omission is repaired in a new volume, *The Concept of Dread*, issued from the press almost the same day as the *Philosophical Fragments*, and hence marked as a companion volume. This book is a psychological study of the predispositions in the human consciousness out of which the anti-ethical emerges by a leap, and of the consequences of this leap in the life of the individual and of the race. The treatment is exceptional in the Kierkegaardian literature, since it is to a certain degree objectively didactic, and makes use of a systematic schematism for the arrangement

of its material; the pseudonym who writes, Vigilius Haufniensis, cuts almost a professorial figure. Nevertheless, his
psychological insight into the very depths of the human
heart is startling, his style challenging; the book is calculated to give any reader pause who has been nurtured upon
the superficialities of recent and contemporary theology.
Among other things it presents a genuinely dialectical
formulation of the dogma of Original Sin, exhibiting this
idea as the necessary consequence of an organic and non-
atomistic conception of the human race, an ideal point of
view for every individual implicit in the sin-experience of
any one individual. Thus the Kierkegaardian interpretation of this doctrine avoids the twin pitfalls of either so
stressing the ethical content of the concept that it becomes
a self-contradictory idea, or so emasculating its ethical
content that it becomes an entirely different idea. It rejects
the notion of an actual inherited sin as analogous to the
idea of a square circle, and *a fortiori* also excludes the
pseudo-scientific, pseudo-evolutionary, pseudo-ethical and
pseudo-optimistic notion of a human race on its upward
path of a gradual liberation from the burden of a "brute
inheritance of sin," than which no conception could be
more confused. On the other hand it also escapes the iden-
tification of the concept with the abstract metaphysical and
premoral condition in human nature for the existence of
the moral task, namely the fact that the individual is a
synthesis of particularity and sociality, is both himself and
in a sense also the human race, as is done by Josiah Royce
in the *Problem of Christianity*. To call the existence in
human nature of conditions making possible a moral task
by the name of a moral burden from which the individual

needs to be saved, as does Royce, is also to indulge one's self in the luxury of a confusion of the categories.

Between the publication of the *Fragments* (1844) and its sequel the *Postscript* (1846), there was interposed *Stages on the Way of Life* (1845). This is a work in three sections by three different pseudonyms, besides including in the third section a diary by still another, entirely unidentified. The papers have been put through the press by one Hilarius, a bookbinder by profession, in whose shop they had been left by unknown parties; in view of the excellent handwriting, they had for a time been turned over to the son of the house, to be used as copyscript. The contents constitute a fresh resumé and reproduction in new form of the points of view illustrative of the three spheres already described, namely the esthetic, the ethical, and the religious. The esthetic stage is represented by a banquet scene, *In vino veritas*, where each of the participants contributes a speech on Woman and her role in life. The speakers are five in number: The Young Man who vainly tries to think love through before experiencing its power; Victor Eremita, who ironically apprehends gallantry as the investment of woman with an unreal ideality which puts her outside the actual life; Constantin Constantius, who denies that it makes sense to apply ethical categories to women; the Dealer in Feminine Fashions, who satisfies his rage against the sex by prostituting every woman who enters his shop to the service and slavery of the reigning modes; and finally Johannes the Seducer, who from his standpoint eulogizes woman as the most wonderful invention the gods had the wit to find, when they needed to offer men an alluring diversion, lest they succeed in storming the heavens; only the Seducer understands her, and only the

Seducer knows how to enjoy her without being deceived. This speech makes use of a fable in the style of a modern Aristophanes; the thought-content in all the speeches is abundant, and the treatment challenges comparison with Plato's *Symposium*.

The ethical sphere is represented by a new essay on marriage from Judge Wilhelm's pen, stolen from him the morning after the banquet of the preceding section; it by no means merely repeats the thoughts of his essay in *Either/Or*, and the style has become a shade more pungent and epigrammatic. He opposes to the esthetic principle that woman lives for a single climactic moment, the ethical principle that her beauty increases with the years. The third section is entitled, Guilty or Not Guilty: A Story of Suffering. It contains the diary mentioned above, with extended comments by Frater Taciturnus, dialectician and psychologist. The diary makes use of a sort of double-entry bookkeeping, in that it contains each day a morning entry for the current events, and a midnight entry for the events of a year before, both sets describing the same history, an unhappy love affair, a broken engagement. The story forms a parallel, a contrasting counterpart, to the Seducer's diary in *Either/Or*. For an outside observer of the factual occurrences it might seem to be the same story, in the one case furnished with a behind-the-scenes explanation which reveals the truth, in the other with a similar interpretation which is false but plausible. The contrast consists in the fact that the motivating force is in the one case sympathy, in the other, egoism. The material for the story is of course drawn from Kierkegaard's own personal experience, the broken engagement which made him a poet, and a poet of the religious. The pathos is mighty, and reminds the reader of Kierkegaard's boast in the journals, that he had lived more poetry during this year of his life than most poets write in a lifetime. Frater Taciturnus explains that the hero of the diary is a pathological case, involved in a struggle with himself as he faces the transition-problems between two modes of existence; he is about to discover the category of sin, and thereby the sphere of the religious life *sensu strictissimo*; this is what gives him an interest as throwing light on the third of Kierkegaard's stages.

Then came the *Unscientific Postscript*, described on the title-page as a mimic-pathetic-dialectic composition. Here was not merely a new philosophical book, but as Brandes truly says, a new kind of philosophical book. Besides handling with superior ease abstractions and dialectical combinations original to itself, and those arising out of the prevailing Hegelian modes of thought which the book combats, it is thickly intersprinkled with anecdote, humor, satire, irony and pathos in rich abundance; no book previously written on the philosophy of religion had ever commanded more precise categories, or ever presented so rich a background of psychological insight. Though only about sixty copies of the book were sold during Kierkegaard's lifetime, he was bold to predict for it an extraordinary future; the signs are gathering that this prediction will come to pass, and the abandonment by present-day German theologians generally of the traditional reliance upon idealism as a basis for theology, in order to explore the possibilities of the "existential dialectic" of the *Postscript*, together with the influence of these ideas upon such philosophers as Jaspers and Heidegger, not to speak of many others, constitute a beginning of fulfillment for Kierkegaard's expectation.

Though the writings already described deal trenchantly with moral and religious themes, their manner of presentation is such as to appeal chiefly to an esthetic sensibility, as well as to an abstract intellectual interest. It is for this reason that they constitute in Kierkegaard's terminology an esthetic literature, not religiously aiming at the individual's moral reconstruction and disciplinary edification, except in so far as an unexpressed motivation underlies them. However, they certainly constitute an esthetic literature of a very peculiar kind. When Kierkegaard became an author, the religious and the esthetic had received a simultaneous awakening; the esthetic was permitted its expression, but the religious stood by to take over the direction, in consequence of which the esthetic literature had from the beginning a religious teleology. The underlying religious interest was also formally expressed by the parallel publication of devotional addresses in Kierkegaard's own name. These eighteen addresses are not designated as sermons, partly because Kierkegaard lacked authority to preach, but chiefly because they do not make use of the transcendent categories of orthodox Christianity. They explore instead the possibilities of edification within the limits of an immanent religiosity, i.e., they express what we should perhaps call a Unitarian Christianity. This was again purposeful restraint on Kierkegaard's part, an expression for his principle of leaving no unexplored territory behind him as he advanced to new positions.

In an explanatory note attached to the *Postscript*, Kierkegaard takes responsibility for the entire series of preceding pseudonymous works, and explains how these authors stand related to him personally. He is the author of the authors, whose words and prefaces are dramatically their own; they are ideal personalities, expressing themselves with an uncompromising regardlessness in good and evil impossible for any actual person in an actual situation, who must needs respect his own relativity. In the case of the *Fragments* and the *Postscript*, which cannot claim to be merely works of the imagination, but have a content actually significant in the actual world, Kierkegaard's own name was affixed, not as author but as responsible for their publication, as a mark of respect for the requirement that there should be someone to take the consequences, if any. This explanation is given with the air of one closing a chapter in his life (the book is called *"Concluding" Unscientific Postscript to the Philosophical Fragments*), and it was indeed Kierkegaard's original intention to cease at this point his activity as a writer, giving expression to the underlying religious motivation of his literary career by finding a post as clergyman in some rural parish. But external circumstances as well as an unforeseen inner spiritual development altered his determination, and he stayed on in Copenhagen to become a religious author, a preacher without a pulpit.

This devotional literature may be divided into two sections; to the first half belong *Devotional Addresses of Varied Tenor* (1847), *The Works of Love* (1848), and *Christian Discourses* (1848); to the second half belong *The Sickness unto Death* by Anti-Climacus (1849), *Practical Introduction to Christianity* by the same pseudonym (1850), and *For Self-Examination* (1851), of which last title one-half was given posthumous publication. The chief purpose of this Introduction being to place the work translated in its immediate setting in the esthetic literature, no detailed description of the distinctly devotional literature

will here be attempted. It constitutes a presentation of the
Christian ideals in a reflective context, a conceptualization
of Christian teaching about life. The writings are religious,
in that they set before themselves the goal of stimulating
the reader to self-examination, thus seeking his edification.
By "edification" is meant the reconstruction of the reader's
mode of existence, not the stimulation of an imaginative
excursus or the encouragement of an emotional spree.

The second section of the works mentioned above is
marked by the introduction of a new pseudonym. As the
Christian ideals were being delineated with a steadily in-
creasing sharpness of outline, their presentation came to
involve the expression of an increasingly critical attitude
toward the religiosity of Christendom. To make the sever-
ity of judgment thus indicated as indirect and impersonal
as possible, and to avoid seeming to claim a high degree
of Christian ideality for himself, Kierkegaard invented the
pseudonym of Anti-Climacus, whose standpoint was higher
than Kierkegaard's own, just as the standpoint of Climacus
had been lower. Kierkegaard describes himself as a reader
who humbles himself under these ideals, suggesting that
his and the Church's proper standpoint is that of standing
in need of grace, even with respect to the use made of
grace. Later he withdrew this last concession as incompatible with Christianity.

No one can understand Kierkegaard who does not
understand these devotional works, or assimilate their content; they constitute the most adequate expression for his
central thought, the center of gravity for his authorship.
The form of presentation in these works is amplified and
simplified, learning and wit and hectic eloquence are not
paraded or displayed; but the thought-content is weighty,

and the conceptual form precise, for Kierkegaard, like Socrates, "philosophized with equal absoluteness everywhere."

A pause in the steady stream of publications marks the interval between September 1851 and December 1854, which last date saw the beginning of that powerful agitation, through newspaper articles and pamphlets, which continued until his last illness in October 1855, his death coming on the 11th of November, when he was but forty-two and a half years old. The immediate focus of this agitation was the established Church in Denmark and the religious state of the country; but the attack was quickly expanded to include Christendom as a whole, and particularly Protestantism. A single sentence may epigrammatically serve to sum up the scope of this agitation, a sentence from a leaflet: "This must be said, so let it then be said. Whoever you are, my friend, and whatever your life may have been, by refusing any longer (if you have hitherto done so) to participate in the public worship as now conducted, with the pretense of being the Christianity of the New Testament, you will have one less crime upon your conscience, and that a heavy one; for you will no longer take part in making a mockery of God." The points of attack were many, the entire front of modern Christianity was under fire. There are students of Kierkegaard who although otherwise sympathetic, feel that this attack was the expression of something pathological in his nature. Others interpret it as the beginning of a development which would inevitably have taken place, had he lived, in the direction of a modern non-Christian liberalism, perhaps humanism; still others think he would have become a Catholic. To anyone who has read his journals, all these guesses must seem fantastic. Without committing myself to all the details of the indictment which Kierkegaard draws up against Christendom, both in the name of Christianity and in the name of common human honesty—not committing myself because I cannot claim to have thought them through, I am nevertheless convinced that this final polemic in its essential spirit and purport was a necessary element in that delineation of the Christian ideals which Kierkegaard had set himself to realize. For just as it would be impossible truthfully to delineate the ethical concept of "service" without letting a satirical light fall upon the caricature that usurps this name in the business and advertising patter of the day, so it seems to me also impossible truthfully to delineate the Christian ideals without an implied or expressed condemnation of the trivialization and emasculation of these ideals that has long prevailed in Christendom.

Significant of Kierkegaard's personal attitude toward this agitation was the calm peace and happy content which marked his demeanor as he lay at death's door in the hospital. He welcomed his approaching death, thought it necessary for the success of the cause he had had the honor to serve. His friend Emil Boesen visited him, and said that he ought to live longer, so as to retract and soften some of the expressions he had used in the agitation. To him Kierkegaard replied, No, No, you do not understand what you are saying; "you think only about earthly things, and have no sense for that which is from above," reminding him of Christ's reply to Peter. "You must remember," he said in another connection, "that I have seen things from the very heart of Christianity, and from that point of view all this [the religiosity of Christendom] is pure marking of time." And in still another conversation with the same friend he tried to give him a simplified impression of the meaning of the whole: "The clergy are royal officials, and officialdom is incommensurable with Christianity. . . . You see, God is sovereign, but then we also have all these human beings who want to live at ease in comfort, and so they give them all Christianity, and thus support a thousand clergymen; nobody in the country can die happy without belonging [to this vested interest]; the consequence is that they become sovereign, and it is all over with God's sovereignty; but he must be obeyed throughout."

The personal life of the man of genius whose productivity we have thus sketched was the outwardly uneventful life of an unattached student and man of letters, an observer of his fellow men and a critic of his life and theirs. A gifted, strict and melancholy father; a discipline in a Christianity that centered about Christ on the cross, mocked, scorned, derided, spit upon; a classical school; desultory studies at the University continuing for ten years or so; a brief excursion into dissolute ways of life; an engagement of marriage, broken after a year upon his own initiative; a collision with a popular journal of satire, resulting in his being caricatured for the mob; and finally an agitation that shook his own little country to its depths, conducted with weapons of the spirit about the things of the spirit—such were the chief outward facts of his life. He had the capacity, to use Wordsworth's words, "to be excited to significant feeling without the application of gross or violent stimulants," and events which in the lives of most men would have passed without leaving a ripple on the surface, stirred his soul to its depths, his reflection to an unrivalled energy, leaving behind him a wealth of thoughts having universal significance.

His poet has not yet come, and may perhaps never come. But Kierkegaard's self-reflection was such that he may perhaps serve as his own poet. In the posthumous work, *The Point of View for my Authorship*, he indulges himself in prophecy as to what such a poet will say, if and when he comes. "He will assign me a place among those who have suffered for an idea," and among other things, will describe this suffering as "the martyrdom of being a genius in a market town. And yet he found also in this life what he sought: if no one else was an individual, he was himself one, and became one increasingly. The cause he served was Christianity, and his life was from childhood wonderfully adapted to this end. He succeeded in realizing the reflective task of translating Christianity whole and entire into terms of reflection. The purity of his heart was to have had but a single aim. That which while he lived constituted the accusation his contemporaries brought against him, that he would not compromise, that he would not yield, this is precisely the tribute that succeeding ages pay to his memory, namely that he would not compromise, would not yield. . . . The dialectical edifice he erected, whose individual parts are by themselves works of independent significance, he could not dedicate to any man, much less to himself. If any dedication of it were to be made, it would have to be dedicated to Providence, to whom it also was dedicated, day by day, year after year, by the author, who historically speaking died of a mortal disease, but poetically speaking died of longing for eternity, where he desires naught else but uninterruptedly to give thanks to God."

Commentator's Introduction

BY NIELS THULSTRUP

Philosophical Fragments is a small book. It can be read in one evening. But however easily it is written, however unburdensome the reading, its content is nevertheless weighty. Briefly and clearly Sören Kierkegaard raises philosophical and Christian problems one after the other and gives his solutions, which open one's eyes to ever-widening perspectives.

The main theme of the book is the relationship between philosophical Idealism and Christianity. The point of departure is the Platonic understanding of how men come into right relationship to the highest truth. In the form of a thought-experiment, Christianity is set over against this understanding and the consequences are drawn, and it is made clear that the relationship between philosophical Idealism and Christianity is one of thoroughgoing contrast. When the basic relationship has been set forth, Kierkegaard poses the problem which Lessing first raised concerning the relationship between revelation and history and the problem which had been made important by Hegel and the views of his theological disciples, that of the relationship between revelation and reason.

These three problems are not considered by Kierkegaard in this order. The question on the title-page takes the investigation straightway into Lessing's question. In the Preface no doubt is left about the author's position regarding Speculative Idealism. In the first chapter, as a formal point of departure, a very brief formulation of Platonism is presented.

It is natural, then, for purposes of introduction, to begin

at the same point as Kierkegaard, or better, a step farther back, with Leibniz's distinction between the truths of reason and the truths of experience, the distinction which he maintains in his polemical writings on the philosophy of religion. Thereupon follows a brief historical presentation of Kant's, Schleiermacher's, Hegel's, Strauss's, and Feuerbach's views on philosophy of religion, with special reference to their positions on Lessing's problem. By way of Strauss's quotations from Lessing, Kierkegaard became aware of the problem which he here places in a larger context. In the Preface to *Philosophical Fragments* he shapes up his position toward the right-wing Hegelians and then goes back to the sources, Plato as the founder of Idealism and the New Testament as the earliest testimony of Christian faith.

Basic in a more limited sense are Kierkegaard's studies and reflections, usually undertaken with direct reference to the carrying out of his extensive plans for writing. In particular, mention must be made here of his studies in the history of philosophy during 1842-1843.

The next point in the discussion here is his mode of composition and the movement of the thought. Then follows an account of the problem of the pseudonymous authorship and of the relationship in *Philosophical Fragments* to Idealism, and the Introduction closes with mention of the reception of the book, its later significance, translations, texts, and editorial principles.

I

General Historical Introduction

The last of the great philosophical system-builders in the Seventeenth Century, Leibniz, was the first in post-

Cartesian philosophy to draw a clear distinction between the truths of reason and the truths of experience.

He affirmed that every cognition can be expressed in a sentence which has the form of a logical judgment, and in a genuine cognitive judgment the predicate must be a necessary and essential qualification belonging to the very nature of the thing. Universal and necessary cognitive judgments are truths, and these are divided into two categories according to the extensiveness of what is spoken about. If true cognitive judgment has to do with all that is possible or conceivable, then it is a truth of pure reason. If, on the other hand, it has to do with things factually existing in nature, it is a truth of nature or a truth of experience. Consequently all human knowledge consists of the truths of reason and of experience.[1] The truths of reason are based on the principle of possibility, the principle of conceivability; the truths of experience are based on the principle of actuality, the principle of factuality. By the first is meant the condition under which something can be or can be thought. What fulfills this condition is possible; what contradicts it is simply impossible. By the second is meant the condition under which things factually exist. The highest truth of reason declares the predicate of all objects which can be thought; the highest truth of experience declares the predicate of all actual things given in nature and experience. These highest propositions can be called basic propositions or axioms. The rational sciences build upon the first axiom and the empirical

---

[1] "There are two kinds of truths: those of Reasoning and those of Fact. The Truths of Reasoning are necessary, and their opposite is impossible. Those of Fact, however, are contingent, and their opposite is possible. When a truth is necessary, the reason can be found in analysis in resolving it into simple ideas and into simple truths until we reach those which are primary." Leibniz, *Monadology*, 33.

sciences upon the second. Without exception the axioms define the predicates which may be ascribed to all conceivable and all actual things. These universal predicates are the categories which make knowledge and experience possible and therefore they precede both. The categories can be reduced to two fundamental categories. For Spinoza thought and extension are the two attributes of every being; for Leibniz active and passive force (form and matter) are the attributes of every actual substance. By virtue of the active force every being is a unity which is identical with itself and unalterable. By virtue of the passive force it is a limited entity among other likewise limited entities. The active force brings about the agreement of every entity with itself; the passive force brings about its agreement with other beings, so that harmony is preserved. In the agreement of a thing with itself lies its ideal, possible, conceivable existence. In the agreement of an entity with the factors of nature lies its actual, conditioned, factual existence. All ideal, conceivable things are subject to logical conditions; all actual, factual things are subject to physical conditions. As mentioned above, it holds true of all objects of knowledge that they are either possible or actual. There is a predicate which must without exception be declared of all things which are possible. Inasmuch as these two statements hold true of everything which can be known, they make knowledge possible and constitute its highest fundamental propositions. It holds true of all things which are possible that they agree with themselves; here the principle of identity applies. It holds true of all things which are actual that they are in agreement with the conditions of nature and are to be explained thereby; here the principle of causality applies. The principle of identity is the highest truth of reason; the principle of causality is the highest truth of experience; and the two axioms are related to each other as metaphysics to physics. The principle of identity holds without exception for all things; the principle of causality holds without exception only for the facts of actuality. All formal knowledge is based on the principle of identity; all empirical knowledge is based on the principle of causality.[2]

Leibniz's distinction is fundamental for Lessing's thesis. In Lessing's main work (1777) on philosophy of religion and philosophy of history, *Über den Beweis des Geistes und der Kraft*, it reads: *"accidental truths of history can never become proof of necessary truths of reason."*[3] The predicates in Lessing correspond to those in Leibniz, but whereas the distinction for Leibniz is logical and metaphysical, Lessing applies it in philosophy of religion. For Lessing in the debate following his publication of parts of Herman Samuel Reimarus' posthumous *Apologie oder Schutzschrift für die vernünftigen Verehrer Gottes* it was an indisputable presupposition that the truths of reason, whatever their content, are eternally valid and therefore stand higher than the truths of experience, of which all historical truths are a part.

Lessing distinguishes sharply between the generation

[2] Among the chief recent works which treat Leibniz's philosophy as a whole or only his epistemology the following may be mentioned: Bertrand Russell, *A Critical Exposition of the Philosophy of Leibniz* (London: Allen and Unwin, 1900, 2nd ed., 1937); L. Couturat, *La Logique de Leibniz* (1901); Ernst Cassirer, *Leibniz' System in seinen wissenschaftlichen Grundlagen* (1902); Kuno Fischer's exposition in *Geschichte der neuern Philosophie*, III, 5th ed., edited by Willy Kabitz (1920); G. Stammler, *Gesetz und Freiheit* . . . (1948); K. Huber, *Leibniz* (1951).

[3] G. E. Lessing, *Sämmtliche Schriften* (1828), v, 80; G. E. Lessing, *Theological Writings* (Stanford: Stanford University Press, 1957), p. 53.

which is directly contemporaneous with an historical event, that is, a truth of experience (e.g., the generation which in Jesus' time saw promises fulfilled in accordance with tradition and in any case became aware and in some instances with humbled understanding believed that he was the Christ, the Messiah, and believed in his miracles), and on the other hand every later generation, which can have only the historical report—however trustworthy and reliable it may otherwise be in accordance with its nature as a historical source. No later generation can be contemporary with the events. One knows them only by way of reports and cannot believe by virtue of them alone. If a later generation is to believe, it can believe only by way of a resolution, a venture, a leap. Every historical truth is contingent, essentially accidental, and the same holds true of every historical source, consequently of the New Testament also. Neither of the two, the historical event and the historical report, is logically necessary as are the eternal truths of reason.

Yet the historical truths which are presented in the historical reports in the New Testament lay claim to being eternally valid truths which entered history at a particular time. Their truth, however, is not self-evident as is the truth of eternal truths of reason; on the contrary, they are in content contrary to reason. If they are to be accepted, believed, this can take place only through a leap. Here Lessing does not try, like the orthodox, to use reports of miracles as arguments for the validity of Christian truth, nor does he, like the theologians of the Enlightenment, try to make the content of faith plausible, rational.[4] The

---

[4] Lessing's own conviction, which clearly shows a relationship to Spinoza's thought and has a distinctly ethical character, and his evolu-

historical events reported in the New Testament, like all truths of experience, occurred in accordance with the principle of causality and therefore are necessary in their factuality although regarded logically they are accidental, since there would be no contradiction if they had taken place in another way or if they had not occurred at all. This is the only way rightly to understand Leibniz's discussion of contingent historical truths and their relationship to the eternal truths of reason, whose axiom is the principle of identity. The historical truths—in this case the New Testament reports of Jesus' life, words, and acts—have nothing to do with the eternal truths of reason, which are self-evidently valid, contradiction-free, and whose truth can be ascertained by human thought.

Factual events, historical truths, according to Kant's epistemology as developed in *The Critique of Pure Reason*, must be understood within the category of causation on the basis of the principle of causality and consequently must be recognized as necessary. Another question is this:

---

tionary optimism will not be discussed here in this connection. Among the chief newer works special reference may be made to: Lessing, *Theological Writings* (Stanford: Stanford University Press, 1957); Erich Schmidt, *Lessing*, I-II (4th ed., 1923); G. Fittbogen, *Die Religion Lessings* (in *Palaestra*, 141, 1923); H. Leisegang, *Lessings Weltanschauung* (1931); H. Thielecke, *Vernunft und Offenbarung, eine Studie über die Religionsphilosophie Lessings* (3rd ed., 1957); E. Lunding, *Lessing und Kierkegaard* (in *Orbis Litterarum*, II, 1944, pp. 158-87). Concerning Kierkegaard's knowledge of Lessing see Commentary to p. 1. Reimarus and Lessing are discussed in Albert Schweitzer, *The Quest of the historical Jesus* (London: A. and C. Black, 1900, 2nd ed., 1931). The theology of the Enlightenment is amply discussed in K. Aner, *Die Theologie der Lessingzeit* (1929) and in Emanuel Hirsch, *Geschichte der neuern evangelischen Theologie*, IV (1952), and the philosophy of the Enlightenment in Ernst Cassirer, *The Philosophy of the Enlightenment* (Boston: Beacon Press, 1955) and in Paul Hazard, *European Thought in the Eighteenth Century* (New Haven: Yale University Press, 1954). A copious bibliography is available in the original of Hazard's work, *La Pensée européenne au XVIIIe siècle*, I-III (1947).

according to Kant what validity and significance can be attributed to historical truths, more specifically the truths of revelation affirmed in the New Testament? This problem Kant considers in *Religion within the Limits of Pure Reason* (1793), where it is solved by the distinction between the natural truths accessible to reason, which it is asserted Jesus proclaimed, and the cultic, sacramental characteristics which have their place only in the so-called dogmatic forms of religion, not in the ethical religions of reason. Inasmuch as the essential content of divine revelation is held to be purely moral, identical with rational ethical law, and therefore universally sharable and approachable, the historical revelation is considered not as genuine revelation but as an historically particularized communication of moral truths universally accessible in principle. The validity of the historical truths which are found in the New Testament comes to be dependent upon the sanction of practical reason; whereas their historical significance becomes unessential.[5]

In the philosophy of religion which Fichte developed in the latter part of his life, presented in his Berlin lectures in 1806 and published under the title, *Die Anweisung zum seeligen Leben oder auch die Religionslehre* (*The Way towards the blessed Life, or the Doctrine of Religion*;

[5] *Religion within the Limits of Pure Reason* (Chicago: Open Court, 1934) especially pp. 85-138. Of the more recent studies of Kant, mention may be made of F. Paulsen, *Immanuel Kant, his Life and Doctrine* (New York: Scribner's, 1902); E. Cassirer, *Rousseau, Kant, and Goethe* (Princeton: Princeton University Press, 1945); A. E. Teale, *Kantian Ethics* (Oxford: Oxford University Press, 1951), with bibliographical footnotes; A. Schweitzer, *Die Religionsphilosophie Kants* (1899); Kuno Fischer, "Kant" in *Geschichte der neuern Philosophie* iv-v (5th ed., 1909-1910); E. Cassirer, *Kants Leben und Lehre* (1918); B. Jansen, *Die Religionsphilosophie Kants* (1929); and particularly to J. Bohatec, *Die Religionsphilosophie Kants* (1938), which also includes a bibliography.

London: Chapman, 1949), the position is maintained, as by Kant and Lessing, that the historical aspect of Christianity is really insignificant. At most it can be said that Jesus' career can serve as an ideal. There really is, according to Fichte, only the spontaneous divine life in which it is not man but God who acts, and this doctrine is as old as the world itself. But according to Fichte's understanding this has been profoundly expressed in the Gospel of John; in the prologue he finds expressed the view that Jesus' historical appearance was only a temporally localized external form of the eternal truths. The upshot of this view must be that "only the metaphysical, by no means the historical, makes for blessedness; the latter only gives intelligibility."[6]

In Schleiermacher's theology, both from the early and mature periods, there is stated, in a different way and for different reasons than by Lessing, Kant, and Fichte, that the historical revelation, whose factuality is not denied, is of unessential significance. It contributes nothing qualitatively new. As early as in the first edition (1799) of *Über die Religion* (*On Religion, Speeches to Its Cultured Despisers;* New York: Harper, 1958) revelation is actually identified with the individual's religious experience, and the historical revelation cannot therefore be credited with any decisive importance. Revelation and history are really no problem for Schleiermacher, in whose pantheizing general religiosity God is not conceived as in transcendent

---

[6] Johann Gottlieb Fichte, *The Way towards the blessed Life*, p. 111. Of the works on Fichte special reference is made to Xavier Léon, *La philosophie de Fichte* (1902) and *Fichte et son temps*, ii, 1 (1924); Kuno Fischer, "Fichte" in *Geschichte der neuern Philosophie*, vi (4th ed., 1914); H. Heimsoeth, *Fichte* (1923); and Nicolai Hartmann, *Die Philosophie des deutschen Idealismus*, i (2nd ed., 1961), which contains a bibliography.

relationship to the world but is present and grasped in feeling without being mediated by and bound to a particular and unique historical revelation. In Schleiermacher-research a sharp distinction is often made between his early and his later works, but on the decisive point in this connection there are only shades of difference between his early and his later view-points. In *Der christliche Glaube* (second German edition, 1830-1831) he prefers to speak of piety instead of religion as previously, and the subjectivism is thereby accentuated. In the *Speeches* Jesus Christ is considered a mediator among others, and in *The Christian Faith* he is considered as the original pattern who possessed the God-consciousness in an unsurpassed degree; but his appearance in history signifies nothing supernatural, no break with the continuity of nature. The God-consciousness is found in all men, just as the world-consciousness. In Christ the God-consciousness conquered completely, but this indicates a change in quantity, not in quality. It is, then, entirely consistent that Schleiermacher says, "It can never be necessary in the interest of religion [original: *Frömmigkeit*, not *Religion*] so to interpret a fact that its dependence on God absolutely excludes its being conditioned by the system of Nature."[7]

In Hegel everything is apparently different from what is found in the thinkers already mentioned. In his system nothing is accidental or indifferent; everything is con-

---

[7] *The Christian Faith*, ed. H. R. Mackintosh and J. S. Stewart (Edinburgh: T. and T. Clark, 1956), paragraph 47, p. 178. From the literature on Schleiermacher selective reference is made to Richard B. Brandt, *The Philosophy of Schleiermacher* (New York: Harper, 1941); Emil Brunner, *Die Mystik und das Wort* (1924); Hjalmar Lindroth, *Schleiermachers religionsbegrepp*, I (1926), II (1930); and E. Flückiger, *Philosophie und Theologie bei Schleiermacher* (1947).

ceived as being necessary and significant in the self-unfolding of the Idea, in its inner life in logic, in its emergence from its proper element into natural philosophy, and in its striving toward return to itself in philosophy of Mind, of which the philosophy of history is a part. Since the Idea, the Absolute, in principle unfolds itself sovereignly according to its own law, the series of events in the dialectical development can be called free, inasmuch as in principle nothing external can intervene, and with the same justification it can be called necessary, since it occurs in agreement with the basic dialectical law and in principle cannot occur in any other way. The Idea unfolds itself timelessly and spacelessly in logic, which can justifiably be called a theology, a doctrine of the divine (impersonal) life before creation and of its unfolding spatially as described in natural philosophy and temporally in the philosophy of history.

It is axiomatic in Hegel's philosophy that religion in its highest form, Christianity, and philosophy in its highest form, Hegel's own Speculative Idealism, have the same content, only that it appears in different forms, in the lower, imperfect representational form of religion and in the higher, perfect, adequate conceptual form of Speculative Idealism. Since cognition of the highest truth is possible with the help of the dialectical method, in which the law-abiding forward movement of thought and the unfolding of Mind are not only parallel but are essentially identical, something evident at the end of the development, it is self-evident that no revelation, according to Hegel's view, has been able or will be able to bring any truth, anything qualitatively, absolutely new, which is not approachable and attainable by way of speculative thought. This means that for Hegel revelation is superfluous, even though he can maintain that the Christ-revelation has occurred with necessity as a consequence of the self-unfolding of Mind on earth in a particular time and place. This means, further, that Hegel's thought is only a variation of Idealism and of the position of its founder, Plato, that men possess the truth and only need to become conscious of it. Plato held that this evocation of the truth takes place by recollection; Hegel held that it takes place with the help of the dialectical method. For Hegel the relationship between revelation and history is contradiction-free and is not a problem, inasmuch as revelation occurs as a necessary historical event, and not only the particular event itself but the entire sequence of historical events is determined, as well as the conception of it. The relationship between reason and revelation is also no problem for Hegel, since according to his view they have the same content, and, finally, the relationship between Idealism and Christianity is no problem for Hegel, since according to his view they are not only harmonious but identical. The distinction between truths of reason and truths of experience is abrogated by Hegel; he can indeed speak of the truth of revelation, but on the basis of his presupposition it becomes a superfluity.[8]

Left-wing Hegelians David F. Strauss and Ludwig Feuerbach, during the first decade after Hegel's death (1831), drew the radical consequences of Hegel's philosophy for the philosophy of religion.[9] In Strauss' *Leben Jesu* (*The Life of Jesus*; London: Allen, 1913, 6th ed.) the New

---

[8] Quotations from Hegel's works and consideration of his philosophy are given in the Commentary, especially pp. 145ff., 159ff., and 167.

[9] See Commentary, pp. 204 and 221.

Testament reports are explained as myth-making by the early church; in his *Die christliche Glaubenslehre* (*The Christian Faith*; London: 1873) he presents in a similar way the history of dogma, which for him becomes the same as the dissolution of dogma, its destruction. Feuerbach asserts in his *Das Wesen des Christenthums* (*The Essence of Christianity*; New York: Harper, 1951) that all religion is an expression of mankind's wishful dreaming and that in consequence all theology must be psychology.

The right-wing Hegelians protested against this extension of Hegel's thought. They desired, as did Hegel himself, that his system should be interpreted as being in harmony with traditional church orthodoxy. In this connection special mention must be made of the extensive treatise directed against Strauss by Carl Daub, who made Kierkegaard aware of the problem of revelation and history in his student days.[10] Also in Danish theological circles attention was quickly given to Strauss's thought. In the excellent survey *Tidskrift for udenlandsk theologisk Litteratur*, which the two theological professors H. N. Clausen and M. H. Hohlenberg edited from 1833, there appeared as early as 1836, the same year the second and last volume of Strauss's *Life of Jesus* was published in Germany, a translation of the principal parts of the renowned work, together with some of the criticism (of no significance in this particular discussion) against Strauss. The following year the theological faculty even announced an essay-competition on a most timely subject and worded it as follows: "Cum recentiore tempore autoritas librorum N.T. saepius impugnata sit, ut periculum inde fidei et ecclesiae imminere visum sit, instituatur disquisitio philoso-

[10] See Commentary, p. 244, with references.

phica, num et quatenus religio et ecclesia Christiana ab authentia vel axiopistia historica librorum sacrorum N.T. pendeant."[11] In 1837 the *Tidskrift* also published an extract of F. C. Baur's *Das Christliche des Platonismus, oder Socrates und Christus*. Two years earlier, in 1835, there had appeared the great work, *Die christliche Gnosis*, with its critical presentation of the history of Christian philosophy of religion, by this foremost Hegelian historian of theology. Sören Kierkegaard had procured both works and also Baur's *Die christliche Lehre von der Versöhnung*, which came out in 1838.[12] The first work in particular, by its very title first of all, incited Kierkegaard's opposition. It is not accidental that the first thesis in his dissertation for the Magister degree in philosophy, *Begrebet Ironi* (*The Concept of Irony, with Constant Reference to Socrates*) which was defended September 27, 1841, reads thus: "Similitudo Christum inter et Socratem in dissimilitudine praecipue est posita."[13]

Strauss's and Feuerbach's views, advocated in Denmark by A. F. Beck and Hans Bröchner, seem not to have become at that time a serious object for Kierkegaard's consideration. He knew them, and in *Philosophical Fragments* he takes a position toward them, but for an understanding

[11] Quoted from the *University of Copenhagen Yearbook 1837*, p. 91. From the *Yearbook 1838*, pp. 103-104, it must be concluded that there were no entries in this competition, the subject of which may be translated: "Since the authority of the New Testament books has in recent times frequently been attacked so that there appears to be a danger for the Faith and the Church, the philosophical question is posed: whether and to what extent the Christian religion and church are dependent upon the authenticity or historical reliability of the sacred books of the New Testament."

[12] Ktl. 421-23.

[13] sv XIII, 107. "The likeness between Socrates and Christ consists essentially in unlikeness."

of the whole polemical orientation of this work, it must
be pointed out that in his reading of Bröchner's Danish
translation of Strauss's *Die christliche Glaubenslehre*,
Kierkegaard was not engaged by Strauss's own line of
thought but by his quotation of Lessing's most famous
polemical work. The thesis in this work Kierkegaard links
formally to *Philosophical Fragments* by the question on
the title-page; then he proceeds in the Preface to indicate
his position towards Hegelianism, not left-wing Hegelianism but right-wing Hegelianism's foremost representative
in Denmark, his former tutor in Schleiermacher's dogmatics, H. L. Martensen, honored in the forties as professor
of theology, whose aim was to "go further" than the
master, Hegel. After entering the current debate by way
of introduction, Kierkegaard goes back to the fundamental
question and to the sources, to Plato and the New Testament, and again to a central problem: truth and man's
relationship to the highest truth. The main problem, then,
in *Philosophical Fragments* is not the relationship between
revelation and history, between truths of reason and truths
of experience, between reason and revelation, but the relationship between philosophic Idealism (Greek, Platonic,
or German, Hegelian, are the same to him) and New
Testament Christianity, and this relationship becomes,
since the Instant is postulated as a category (the Moment
in which the divine comes to the human, the earthly, in
which the Eternal and the temporal meet), a relationship
of absolute, qualitative contrast.

Since Kierkegaard does not see his task to be that of
direct proclamation of the truths of Christian revelation,
for these are well known, but rather a clarification of its
qualitative difference from philosophical Idealism both in

the Platonic and Hegelian speculative formulation to which it had been joined, distortedly joined, by the right-wing Hegelians, he must speak a language which they understand. Therefore he uses both Platonic and Hegelian language in the work in order to express the truths of revelation, and he also parodies the Hegelian method of letting the various concepts develop out of each other. In this he has in mind a definite effect: the reader, the un-suspecting Hegelian (Kierkegaard always had respect for Hegel himself, in spite of disagreement, and disrespect for his chattering disciples) is not to be disturbed at the outset, but rather he ought to be calmed by meeting something well-known. The well-known are the Platonic (note Kierkegaard's use of the Platonic expression "the God," in Danish, *Guden*), which in the book is always called the Socratic, and the Christian catechism. The new, however, is the absolute difference which Kierkegaard points out actually lies between Idealism (the Socratic) and Chris-tianity, which is presented in the form of a hypothesis, a thought-experiment.[14]

[14] Both theological and philosophical Idealism have been treated so frequently that it is possible to mention here only selected works. Surveys, for example, are found in Hugh Ross Mackintosh, *Types of Modern Theology, Schleiermacher to Barth* (New York: Scribner's, 1939); Karl Barth, *Protestant Thought from Rousseau to Ritschl* (New York: Harper, 1959); Richard Kroner, *Speculation and Revelation in the Age of Christian Philosophy* (Philadelphia: Westminster, 1959); Horst Stephan, *Geschichte der evangelischen Theologie im 19. Jahr-hundert* (2nd ed., revised by Martin Schmidt, 1960); N. H. Söe, *Fra Renaessancen til vore Dage* (3rd ed., 1960); Emanuel Hirsch, *Ge-schichte der neuern evangelischen Theologie*, v (1954). Among the studies in the history of philosophy the still indispensable work by J. E. Erdmann merits special mention: *A History of Philosophy* (New York: Macmillan, 1892-1897). See also J. Royce, *Lectures on Modern Idealism* (New Haven: Yale Press, 1934); H. Höffding, *A History of Modern Philosophy* (New York: Humanities Press, 1950, and Dover, 1955); Richard Kroner, *Von Kant bis Hegel*, I-II (2nd ed., 1961);

II

Historical Introduction
to "Philosophical Fragments"

It has been mentioned that Kierkegaard clearly distinguishes in his dissertation between Christianity and philosophical Idealism (Socrates as representative of the purely human at its highest), but in that work he does not undertake the task of developing the distinction more sharply. If one goes back to his first little book, *From the Papers of One Still Living* (1838), he will find the posing of yet another problem. Generally Kierkegaard poses one main problem in each of his works and in the solution employs the literary procedure which seems best suited, and as far as form is concerned he makes his choice with great care.[15]

In Kierkegaard's *Journals*—much less in his letters, in which he only reluctantly and unwittingly reveals himself—one can trace how his experiences, studies, and reflections crystallized in one problem after the other, and in the works we find the definitive formulations and solutions. This is also the case with *Philosophical Fragments*.

Wilhelm Lütgert, *Die Religion des deutschen Idealismus und ihr Ende*, I-IV (1923-1930); Helmut Groos, *Der deutsche Idealismus und das Christentum* (1927); and the chief work, Karl Löwith's *Von Hegel zu Nietzsche* (2nd ed., 1950). T. Bohlin's *Kierkegaards dogmatiska åskådning* (1925; German translation, 1927, *Kierkegaards dogmatische Anschauung*) contains a full presentation (pp. 354-440) of the problem of revelation and history in Hegel and in Kierkegaard. A systematic and historical treatment of this question is found in Reidar Hauge's *Inkarnasjon og opstandelse* (1941), and the general historical presuppositions of Kierkegaard's solution are presented in Sören Holm's *Sören Kierkegaards Historiefilosofi* (1952).

[15] Reference is made to F. J. Billeskov Jansen's *Studier i Sören Kierkegaards litteraere Kunst* (1951), the basic study of this subject.

Philosophy to him was essentially synonymous with Idealistic philosophy in its Greek or modern German form. Christianity to him was essentially identical with orthodox New Testament Christianity. This he became acquainted with at home; he was first introduced to philosophy in his student days. Especially in the first two volumes of the *Journals* one can observe how one impression after the other and one book after the other literally rolled in over the theological student. His horizon steadily became wider. Ideas, reflections, writing-plans, personal confessions, and provisional solutions of problems which pressed in alternate rapidly with one another in the journal entries.[16] Slowly Kierkegaard achieved clarification. His terminology and his working on the definition of concepts in the *Journals* are clear indications of his struggling with the problems and of his attempt not merely to find tenable points of view but a tenable standpoint, a philosophy of life. He met a rationalistic understanding of Christianity, he became acquainted with Schleiermacher's thought, he received an impression of Grundtvig's theological teaching, and he protested against it all, not only against the various understandings of Christianity but even against Christianity itself. So he began on his own to read the latest German philosophy and theology, the difficult works of the speculative theists and Johannes Georg Hamann's profoundly obscure, mutinous discourses against the absolute power of reason. Toward the end of his student days,

---

[16] The most careful treatments of Sören Kierkegaard's development as philosopher are Valdemar Ammundsen, *Sören Kierkegaards Ungdom* (1912) and Emanuel Hirsch, *Kierkegaard-Studien*, I-II (1931-1933), especially parts 1 and 3. The most recent composite presentation, Sejer Kühle, *Sören Kierkegaards barndom og ungdom* (1950), has some additional material, but an even moderately exhaustive investigation of Kierkegaard's early studies is still needed.

Hegelianism, especially in Heiberg's and Martensen's formulations, came within his range of vision. Immediately he was critically oriented, but most of his time was taken by the already initiated intensive study for comprehensive examinations. Only when his obligatory work was done could he throw himself into the study of sources, the first fruit of which was the doctoral thesis, *The Concept of Irony*. In the course of a few months he went through the major portion of Hegel's works, read the larger share of Plato and the most essential part of the accessible literature on Socrates, and completed his acquaintance with German romantic poets and philosophers.

His settlement with Speculative Idealism begins in his first book, but even in the dissertation, where, with Hegel's views explicitly in mind, he discusses the correct conception and evaluation of Socrates, he is quite clearly under Hegel's influence. In *Either/Or* Kierkegaard is much clearer and more independent as a thinker; in *Repetition* and in *Fear and Trembling*, which appeared simultaneously (October 16, 1843), the main positions in Hegel's philosophy are the polemical points of departure for the posing of the problems, and Kierkegaard's attitude, not only to Hegel but to Speculative Idealism as a whole, is one of rejection. Old Testament figures, Job and Abraham, are purposely chosen as symbols. The line of thought is "pre-Christian" but moves toward the specifically Christian categories. The same holds true of the small collections of edifying discourses, which Kierkegaard published under his own name concurrently with the pseudonymous works.

It is first in the original form of a thought-experiment in

Philosophical Fragments that Kierkegaard gives the outline of his dogmatics.

To the general background of this work, including Plato, Hegel, and the works and studies influenced by Hegel, which are mentioned in the preceding portion of this Introduction and in the Commentary, there are added Kierkegaard's own philosophical presuppositions.

In his *Journals* (IV c) one can observe how Kierkegaard carried on wide-ranging study in the history of philosophy during 1842-1843. With the aid of other works, he carefully went through the first volumes, on ancient philosophy, of W. G. Tennemann's exhaustive history of philosophy and was especially occupied with the pre-Socratic thinkers, Aristotle, and the Sceptics. There are clear traces of these concerns in *Philosophical Fragments*. In this period Kierkegaard also read many of Aristotle's own works, with the aid of German translations, and he was absorbed in Gottsched's translation of Leibniz's *Theodicy*. Descartes and Spinoza also occupied him. Kierkegaard's concern with Schelling and Baader as independent representatives of "Speculation" and Trendelenburg as a carrier of the Aristotelian tradition were of somewhat less importance, however, in connection with *Philosophical Fragments*.

A central purpose for Kierkegaard in these studies in the history of philosophy was the forming of a doctrine of categories in original association with Aristotelianism and in contrast to Hegelianism. The very question, what is to be understood by a category, is raised in the *Journals*, and such basic concepts as possibility, actuality, necessity, freedom, transition, moment, doubt, faith, etc., gradually become clearly marked out.[17] *Philosophical*

---

[17] An important preparatory work to *Philosophical Fragments* to which the reader is referred is the partially autobiographical philosophical account from 1842-1843, *Johannes Climacus eller De Omnibus*

Fragments contains a series of forthright definitions. The concepts of truth, Grecianism, recollection, revelation, paradox, sin, moment, God's love, faith, offence, doubt, existence, being, essence, proof, passion, contemporaneity, the eternal, coming into existence, disciple, the historical, and the past may be mentioned as important examples of concepts whose early history can be traced in Kierkegaard's papers back to their first appearance. He gradually makes a sharp distinction between the philosophical and theological concepts even though they appear together, and with the postulation of the Moment, more accurately the Moment of Christ's revelation in time and in the individual, all the other Christian concepts in the "situation of contemporaneity" gain their significance, their full content.

Thereby Lessing's problem is solved in an original way by Kierkegaard, who speaks neither of the contingent truths of history nor of the eternal truths of reason but of the truths of revelation, which are accessible only when the "condition of faith" is given by God himself. In this way the problem of the relationship between Speculative Idealism and Christianity is solved. If it is granted that Christianity is the truth of revelation given in a particular place at a particular time and in a particular form, the Incarnation, then it follows that Speculative Idealism, which claims to reach the same goal and the same truth with the help of the dialectical method by way of reason, and Christianity are incompatible. Therefore in the Preface

---

Dubitandum Est (*Pap.* IV B 1-17; English translation, *Johannes Climacus, or De Omnibus Dubitandum Est*; London: A. and C. Black, 1958). The sketch from Kierkegaard's student days, *Striden mellem den gamle og nye Saebekielder* (*Pap.* II B 1-21) is, as emphasized especially by Hirsch (*Kierkegaard-Studien*, II, 556ff.), significant for an understanding of the young Kierkegaard's view of Danish Hegelians.

Kierkegaard can polemically turn especially against Martensen and his attempt to "go beyond" Hegel, and he turns against this representative Danish Hegelian by going back to Idealism in its pure Greek form, the Platonic, and to the New Testament—that is, to the sources—whereby he gains the right to say in "The Moral" of the work that his "projected hypothesis indisputably makes an advance upon the Socratic [the Idealistic], which is apparent at every point." The main problem in the book, the relationship between Platonism and Christianity, is thereby solved by pointing out a relationship of thorough-going contrast.

If, apart from the view Kierkegaard had of the relationship between Idealism (Greek or German) and Christianity, which had been misunderstood by the Speculative Idealists, there had been adequate reason for his writing a book about this relationship, the occasion itself must be found in his encounter with Lessing's thoughts in Bröchner's Danish translation of Strauss's *The Christian Faith*."[18]

The general historical background for *Philosophical Fragments* is, then, the problem of the relationship between revelation and history and between revelation and reason as they were formulated with reference to Leibniz's distinctions first by Lessing and by German Idealistic thinkers with essentially the same solution. In his writing Kierkegaard goes into this posing of the problem, but the main purpose in so doing is not to solve this problem, which remains a subordinate issue, although certainly not a matter of indifference to him. The direct historical background is his knowledge of Plato, Aristotle, ancient sceptical philosophy, Descartes, Spinoza, Leibniz, and Hegel,

[18] See Commentary, pp. 149-50.

especially the Danish Hegelians, particularly Martensen, and Kierkegaard's exceptional attempt through historical-philosophical studies to clarify philosophical and Christian categories and concepts in their uniqueness, in their purity. The immediate occasion for the work is to be found in Kierkegaard's encounter with Lessing's thoughts by way of Strauss.

We now turn to two questions: how did he compose this work and what is the thought-structure?

III

The Composition of "Philosophical Fragments" and Its Thought-Structure

Philosophical Fragments is compactly written, and the development of thought is rigorous. The book is like a classical drama in five acts, with an interlude interpolated between the last two acts, comparable to "a symphony or the like" and suggestive of the "passage of time" (p. 89). The two main actors, Socrates and Christ, who is not directly named but is called "the God in time" (see note in Commentary on this expression, which first appears in the Preface and on page 12 of the text), the experimental author of the drama, and the reader are contemporary. The main characters carry the dialogue, which is interrupted at the end of each chapter by the reader's remarks to which the author replies. There is a single place, which may be anywhere and therefore here and now. There is only one unified action, the inquiry into the question of what the highest truth is and how it can be apprehended by the individual human being.

When the main theme of the entire work has been declared, the development of the individual chapters is self-explanatory. The point of departure of the first three chapters is the Socratic, which is identical with philosophical Idealism as formulated in Greece by Plato and in Germany by Hegel. In the last two chapters Socrates, who symbolizes Idealism, moves into the background, as in the later Platonic dialogues, and Christ and the disciple, the single individual human being, are alone. Finally only the author is left, and in response to the reader's continuous complaint that " 'This poem of yours is the most wretched piece of plagiarism ever perpetrated, for it is neither more nor less than what every child knows' " (p. 43) he gladly concedes that what he says in experimental form is nothing other and is supposed to be nothing other than the well-known Christian catechism. Then he closes the work with a Moral.

The form of the work can be compared with a drama, but it can also be likened to a Platonic dialogue, which has as its purpose the internal clarification of concepts and categories and their distinction from others. This is done without laboriousness, with a certain ease, with well-considered little side-remarks, and yet with an incomparable consciousness of purpose and coherence. There is no fumbling for the right word, no loitering over the many difficult problems which appear gradually as the inquiry proceeds. The words seem to come of themselves and the problems are solved without labor by the writer, the experimental author, but at the same time he has a presentiment that it may be difficult for the reader to follow at such a pace and therefore he waits for him. Then a moment later the development picks up speed again and the reader is carried along.

The question is: how is a human being related to the highest truth, whether one possesses it within himself or does not possess it; or, formulated more precisely, in what comprehensive view is it affirmed that man possesses the highest truth and what consequences does this affirmation have, and within what comprehensive view or, more correctly, in what Kerygma is it affirmed that man does not possess the highest truth and what are the consequences of this? Or what is the relationship between philosophic Idealism and Christianity—are they identical, partially different, or entirely different; can they be joined or are they essentially irreconcilable? The answer is that they are entirely different and are not reconcilable. But this answer is not given as a postulate. The whole conceptual development is clothed in the form of an experiment. The point of departure is in the Socratic (the Platonic, the Idealistic), and thereupon—in Platonic, Greek linguistic forms—Christianity is construed.

The Preface contains an explanation of this procedure. Here the author's view of the contemporary situation becomes clear; this is found in his conviction that neither his contemporaries nor any other human being is automatically a Christian or understands what Christianity is in its essential distinction from all human thought, which has been most clearly formulated by Socrates. The contemporary situation for Kierkegaard was that the dominant philosophical movement, Hegelianism, affirmed the identity of its own thought and Christianity and that although the leading theologians perhaps did not affirm their complete identity, they did assert the complete com-

patibility of Idealism and Christianity. Kierkegaard coun-
tered this confusion of ideas, but his mode of procedure
had to be determined by the position and thought-mode
of the opposition and he had to speak their language and
assume their point of departure in order to be able with
assurance to lead them to the point intended, to the understanding that Idealism and Christianity are entirely different.

The movement of thought in the work begins with the
supposed author's (Johannes Climacus) being unwilling
to participate in the period's common preoccupation with
understanding, spreading, and extending the Hegelian
System but rather desiring merely to undertake a little
philosophical experiment on his own. If he can only have
permission to do this in peace, he will readily forfeit both
civic respectability and remuneration. He has disciplined
himself to "be able to execute a sort of nimble dancing in
the service of Thought, so far as possible also to the honor
of the God, and for my own satisfaction" (p. 6), and just
as he desires to gain no personal honor through his work,
just as little does he desire to be asked his opinion, because
his personal opinion is a matter of indifference, since it is
the thoughts themselves which are of significance.

After the Preface the author begins his "Project of
Thought," as he calls it, and poses the question: can the
truth be learned? The presupposition for this question is
that the truth is not present, is not actual, to the learner.
The answer to the question, given by Socrates, who, as
mentioned, is the symbol for all philosophical Idealism,
is that men possess the truth from eternity and that the
problem is at most one of making it actual. This can be
done by the accidental teacher at any accidental time when

the human being exerts himself with sufficient vigor, and what the accidental teacher has accidentally been and has accidentally said can at best have historical interest but can never have decisive significance for the single individual person (pp. 11-16).

If one is to develop a view quite different from the Socratic, he must postulate that the moment in time does not remain something accidental but gains decisive significance. If one postulates this, it follows that man cannot be in possession of the truth but must be untruth, on the way away from the truth, and the teacher's task cannot consist, as in the Socratic view, of showing the learner, mankind, that the truth is in its possession, but rather to show that mankind is untruth. Since men cannot of themselves get clear on this, the teacher must not only bring the truth to the learner but "he must also give him the condition necessary for understanding it" (p. 17). If the teacher were just a human being like the learner, who is in untruth, he naturally could neither give the learner the truth nor the condition for understanding the truth, and therefore the teacher, if the moment in time is to have decisive significance, must be "the God" himself, that is, Christ. Men as created have had the condition necessary for understanding the truth but through their own fault have lost it, that is, men are in sin and cannot free themselves from it. This means that the teacher, the God himself, is Saviour, since he saves the learner out of unfreedom, is Deliverer, since he delivers the learner who has bound himself, is the Atoner who takes away the wrath impending upon that of which the learner has made himself guilty, and is Judge, since in contrast to the Socratic teacher he can in a life to come judge one who at a particular time had received the requisite condition in trust. Just as the teacher has been more definitely characterized, the Moment in time must also have a name, for it has been postulated that it is to have decisive and not accidental significance, and it can be fittingly named with an expression which is just as Biblical as the characteristics of the teacher—the Fullness of Time. The learner, the disciple, the human being, who has received the condition and the truth from God, can now be called a New Creature, and the change from the state of untruth can be called Conversion, just as grief over having remained through his own guilt so long in untruth can be called Repentance and the transition New Birth. Through all these qualifications the Moment in time has gained decisive significance, and the project of thought has thereby in every respect gone beyond the Socratic (pp. 16-22). This line of thought must itself be developed out of the Moment in time in which the human being becomes conscious that he is born, that is, it is developed out of Faith.

The outline of the project of thought, as it is called, is set forth in this way, but now the reader enters into it and insists that the project-maker has not hit upon this himself but presents as new something which everyone knows. The author readily concedes that he is not the inventor; furthermore, what has been presented as a project of thought was invented neither by him nor by the reader nor by any human being at all, because, stated in other words, it is the Gospel—confronted by Idealistic philosophy, which had been taken as a point of departure (pp. 26-27).

In Chapter II begins a more detailed development of the thought. The point of departure is again Socrates, who is depicted as the teacher who appeared at a particular time, without having any new, positive teaching, as an accidental occasion for the learner's understanding himself, just as the learner became the accidental occasion for the teacher, Socrates, to understand himself. The teacher and the learner were equal and neither of them had in the strictest sense anything to give the other. "Circumstances seeming propitious" (p. 28), Socrates emerged as teacher, and he thereby satisfied both the demands of his own being and the demands others might make upon him. Christianly it is all quite different: "the God" does not need the learner in order to understand himself and the external occasion does not become a demand, that is, the Fall does not make the Incarnation and Atonement a necessity. Only God's love can move him to reveal himself in the Moment according a resolve "from eternity," that is, independent of the Fall, and the purpose of the act of revelation is to win the learner. The difficulty in achieving this goal is "the great difference" (p. 31) between God in revelation and the learner so that they cannot understand one another directly and immediately. In order to explain how this difficulty is overcome, Kierkegaard uses an analogy:[19] "Suppose there was a king who loved a humble maiden" (p. 32). Such a king cannot in a direct way and in the categories of immediacy bring about the equality which is the goal; if he were to appear before the beloved, the humble maiden, in his glory and majesty, he would repel her. A solution must be found for this difficulty; the union, the understanding of the beloved, must be brought about.

[19] Kierkegaard's use of poetic analogies to illuminate the thought is examined particularly by F. J. Billeskov Jansen in his *Studier in Sören Kierkegaards litteraere Kunst* (1951). See also his "Essai sur l'art de Kierkegaard" in *Symposion Kierkegaardianum* (1955).

If, then, the king, the God, would elevate the learner up to himself, to his majesty, it could take place only by means of a deception whereby the learner acquires majesty as a garment, as something external. And if the God would appear before the learner in his majesty and receive the learner's adoration, the God, not the learner, would be glorified, and the love would not be a happy love. The union therefore can be achieved not by an elevation, for the goal is that the learner "becomes as nothing and yet is not destroyed" (p. 38), but by a descent, whereby God appears not in his glory but in poverty, "in the form of a servant," which is his true form, not merely an outer garment. God becomes true man, does not merely seem to be a human being. Here Kierkegaard is clearly in opposition to Docetism, which would deny Christ's true humanity. Since God reveals himself in this way, he is not directly recognizable as God; but only in this way is there a possibility of understanding, only in this way can the unity sought after be brought about. But the result is that God, "absolutely like the humblest" (p. 40), must endure all things, must die forsaken, misunderstood by men who instead of loving him hang him on a cross.

Again at the close of this chapter the reader breaks in, saying: " 'This poem of yours is the most wretched piece of plagiarism ever perpetrated' " (p. 43), and again the author concedes that the reader is right, and he makes this admission readily, inasmuch as the poem is not and cannot be a human product. Without mentioning his opponents by name, Kierkegaard here is addressing himself to the left-wing Hegelians, Strauss and Feuerbach. It is emphasized that here we stand before the miraculous, the Miracle.

In Chapter III Kierkegaard begins again with Socrates.

At a particular point in history God has appeared in the form of a humble human being, but this humble human being really is God. How, then, can men grasp this, that here they are in the presence of God? Socrates strove to understand other men and to understand himself, and yet he acknowledged that he really could not make anything of himself. This seems to be a paradox, which is here characterized as "the passion of Reason," the "passion . . . in all thinking" (p. 46), something which reason cannot comprehend and which leads reason to founder in its passion, the passion which wills the collision, which strives to discover that which cannot be thought and cannot be comprehended in the categories of human thought. What thought meets here as the unthinkable, as the miraculous, as the Miracle, is God's revelation in Jesus Christ. The event cannot be substantiated as an historical event, and that it is an event different from any other event cannot be proved, inasmuch as it transcends the possibilities of human reason. With the Socratic as the point of departure we have again "gone beyond," have reached the limit of what can humanly be understood. That something which reason cannot really grasp, reason itself cannot achieve by itself, as Kierkegaard develops in a dialogue carried on with the reader who raises his voice again. The basis for this is man's sin, which constitutes the absolute unlikeness and makes it impossible for the human being in his actual situation to grasp with his own power the Miracle, the Absolute Paradox.

In the Appendix to this chapter (p. 61) it is shown that if the Absolute Paradox and human reason come together in an understanding of their complete unlikeness, the encounter can be called happy, but if the encounter is not in understanding, the person is offended by the Paradox. The happy encounter is Faith; the unhappy is offense. It looks as if the possibility of offense comes from reason; but it actually comes from the Paradox. Therefore offense can be called an "acoustic illusion." Offense is precisely a mark, a negative mark, of the presence of the Paradox. This Kierkegaard shows by reference to Tertullian, Lactantius, Luther, Shakespeare, and Hamann.

In Chapter ɪᴠ there is a discussion of the relationship of the contemporary disciple. If God has made his appearance in the actual form of a humble man, he could well have sent John the Baptizer in advance to make men aware, and also by the "lofty absorption in his mission" (p. 70) he could have attracted the attention of the multitude, but the curious crowd is not "the disciple." Only when the condition is given by God himself can a man become a disciple; only where there is Faith is there the disciple. The person who is immediately contemporary with Jesus Christ certainly has in his direct contemporaneity, in his actual historical contemporaneity, an occasion, but not an immediate occasion unto faith, only an occasion for becoming aware, an occasion which is accidental, just as one who though temporally contemporary but lives in another part of the world would be contemporary only in an improper sense. What the immediate contemporary knows purely historically and what he can communicate "about the teacher" are, like everything historical, accidental and can bring neither him nor any one else to Faith. The object of Faith is not the doctrine but the teacher, not the message detached from the bearer of the message, but the message which the bearer is. Faith is neither knowledge, since no knowledge can have the Paradox, the God-man Jesus

Christ, as its content, nor an act of will, since such is possible only if the condition is already present, if the will is capable of realizing what it aims at, consequently only if the condition is already present. Since the condition (as discussed earlier) must be given by God, Faith is not an act of will. The condition is given in the Moment, the wondrous moment of the paradox, which means that the condition, Faith, is just as miraculous as its object. God cannot be known directly; therefore immediate contemporaneity in itself is only an occasion for the immediate contemporary to gain purely historical knowledge, or it can be an occasion for the contemporary to achieve deeper self-knowledge in a Socratic sense, or it can ultimately be an occasion for the contemporary, who is in the condition of untruth, to receive the condition, Faith, from God, and thereby see both his own situation in untruth and God as God.

It is clear that the immediately contemporary disciple has no advantage over the later disciple because of his immediate contemporaneity, but now the line of thought is seemingly interrupted by an "Interlude."

The purpose of this Interlude is simply to emphasize that God acts freely, revealing himself when and where he wills, and what the consequences of this are. In a direct polemic against Hegel, Kierkegaard brings together the principal philosophic observations on historical phenomena and human conceptions of them, drawing freely from Aristotle, ancient sceptical philosophy, and from Leibniz. Inasmuch as Kierkegaard concentrates in this section the yield of a long period of philosophical study and reflection and is often satisfied with parenthetical allusions, the Interlude is quite difficult to read.

Just as in the first three chapters, Kierkegaard here takes his formal point of departure not in Christianity but in Platonic Idealism, and the argument is in part by way of Aristotelian objections. Kierkegaard poses the question (part 1 of the Interlude): what happens when something comes into existence, what change is involved? Before it comes into existence, it must be assumed to have been in another form of being, in the form of a plan, in the form of possibility. Inasmuch as it comes into existence, it acquires the form of actuality. But the question, what happens in the process, can be raised only with the presupposition that it is the same plan both before and after coming into existence. The answer is that everything comes into existence by an act of freedom, and this answer can be given only with the presupposition that "Every cause terminates in a freely effecting cause" (p. 93). This presupposition is Kierkegaard's postulate and as a presupposition cannot be proved, since it is the presupposition for the entire line of argument. The freely operating cause is God.

Since every cause terminates in a freely effecting cause, only in the distraction of preoccupation with intermediate causes can one answer the question thus: the change of coming into existence occurs with necessity. "Necessity" is reserved here as a purely logical, not historical or metaphysical, category, and possibility and actuality designate two forms of being, the potential and the actual.

Since something has come into existence by a free act, it is thereby historical and belongs to empirical, factual actuality, but it is past. The necessary, however, is timeless, is neither past nor future but continuously present; it is eternal. Since something has happened, has become an historical actuality, it cannot be changed later, and the question now arises whether this unchangeableness falls within the category of necessity. Kierkegaard's answer, in harmony with the postulate, is that it does not. From this it follows that one can no more prophesy the future than he can justifiably interpret prior events as having occurred with necessity. All past, present, and future events move possibility's form of being to that of actuality by free acts. If the postulate is tenable, then Hegel is not right in his attempt to unite logical, metaphysical, and historical categories in his system, with the result that he understands historical events as having occurred with necessity. This is developed in parts 2 and 3.

In conclusion there is raised in part 4 the question of the "apprehension of the past." A distinction is drawn between natural phenomena, which fall in the category of space, and historical phenomena, which are in the category of time. They have been present, but as historical they are now past. Since the historical phenomena have gone from being in possibility to the existence of actuality by free acts, they have their character which wavers between certainty and uncertainty. If they did not occur with necessity, the apprehension of them must not be such that they are given the appearance of falling within the category of necessity, because the conception of them would then be a misunderstanding. If the historical had not in fact come into existence, the apprehension of the past would not have the difficulties with its object which it now has. Coming into existence cannot be sensed immediately; only that which is present can be sensed immediately. Therefore the apprehension of the historical contains an element of uncertainty, and for this reason Kierkegaard uses in the sphere of human cognition, by way of analogy, the word *belief* [Danish *Tro: faith* or *belief*] as the designation of the organ for the historical; over against the doubt which the intellect can raise up against the historical phenomenon, which is the object of knowledge, belief in this sense asserts itself as an act of will. Inasmuch as belief in this connection is not characterized as Christian Faith, there is no contradiction in Kierkegaard's characterization of belief (as a sense for the historical) as an act of will. Just as the word *truth* in Scriptures has two meanings, so does the word *Tro* [*faith* or *belief*] also. With reference to the historical as having come into existence, it holds true both for immediate experience and for what is later used to establish the historical event that the historical character of having come into existence can be apprehended only in belief, defined as a sense for coming into existence.

If this holds true of ordinary historical events, the Interlude continues, the next question is: What does this mean for the historical fact of the Christ-revelation, the character of which is the object of investigation? As an historical fact in the ordinary sense, it is an object of belief or faith in the ordinary sense. But, as previously indicated, since it is an historical fact which is based on the self-contradiction that the Eternal, which falls in the category of necessity, has become historical, has come into existence, and thereby must be apprehended in the category of freedom, it must be the object of Faith, not in the ordinary sense of belief but in a special sense. Ordinary historical events fall in the categories of reason and are apprehended by belief (faith in the ordinary sense); the unique historical event falls as the historical in the categories of reason but also into the category of the Eternal, and this means that it is humanly conceivable only as self-contradictory, paradoxical, and it can be apprehended only by faith in the unique sense, the Faith which is just as paradoxical as its object.

The conclusion, which follows in Chapter v, is in agreement with the premises presented earlier, all of which rest upon postulates.

Since the unique historical event under discussion has taken place centuries ago (the number is qualitatively unimportant), it seems that a question can be raised about the equality of or distinction between the contemporary and the later disciple. Kierkegaard lets the "reader" pose the problem, and thereafter shows that there is no significant difference if the foregoing thought is tenable.

If one considers "the first generation of secondary disciples," they will certainly be closer to the event in time and they can acquire complete reports, and they will be more easily aroused by "the shock produced by the impact of our fact" (p. 116), and the advantage of this is that the crucial nature of the decision is more clearly evident, not that it is in any way easier. But in relationship to the historical event, which is not some ordinary historical event but is God's revelation in Jesus Christ, it holds first of all that as an historical event it can be apprehended only by belief (faith in the ordinary sense) and, second, that as the unique historical event it can be apprehended only by faith in the unique sense.

If one next considers "the last generation" (p. 117), they are temporally removed from the shock of the event, but in compensation they have the consequences to lean upon. If the Christ-event is a paradox paradoxically become historical, the consequences—just as historical events are free actions since they are grounded upon a primary, freely effecting cause—must have the same character and must be paradoxical. Therefore it is pointless to say that Christianity has become naturalized. No human being is born with Faith, but every human being can receive it and Faith can become his second nature. No generation is born with Faith; Faith is found only where the individual stands in a happy relationship to "this fact." Therefore the later generation of disciples has no advantage over the first.

Because there is no basis for distinguishing between the first and the last generations of secondary disciples, they are equal. But is there no basis for distinguishing between the primary and secondary disciples? If the Christ-revelation were a simple historical fact, there would be an advantage in being immediately contemporary with it; and if it were an eternal fact, it would be equally close to every period. But if, as developed, it is an absolute fact which is also historical, and if this is the object of Faith, and if Christian Faith, as described also, is the condition which God freely gives, then the distinction of eventual secondary disciples is untenable. There is no contradiction, however, in the thought-development, which is consistent with its presuppositions. If a disciple can become a disciple only by receiving the condition from God, there can be no talk of any secondary disciple, that is, a disciple of a disciple, because this would mean that the first disciple becomes God for the later disciple and he again for the next, which would be unreasonable and untenable. The only unanswered question remaining is: what can a contemporary do for someone later? He can only tell someone later that he has believed and that for one later this can become only an occasion, and he can relate the content of the fact, which exists only for Faith. The trustworthiness of the contemporary can, therefore, have only accidental significance for one in Faith, inasmuch as the trustworthy report of a contemporary has significance only as an occasion and no one believes by virtue of it, only by virtue of God's gift. All disciples are therefore essentially equal (p. 131).

Once again for the last time Kierkegaard lets the reader have a voice in the development of the thought; once again the author gives a reply which very clearly indicates that he has drawn the latter portion from the New Testament, and without reservation he acknowledges that there can really be no question of a "disciple at second-hand" (p. 131), because no human being can give himself or another person the condition. The author is right in characterizing his project as a "godly one" which has its formal point of departure in the Socratic and which is Socratic in the sense that it allows the reader to discover little by little that he knew very well in advance what is presented, since it is the Christian catechism.

It is now evident that the questions on the title-page have been answered: there can be an historical point of departure for an eternal consciousness and this can have more than a merely historical interest if it is the unique historical fact, the Christ-revelation, the Moment in time when the eternal miraculously breaks into the temporal; but one cannot base an eternal happiness upon merely historical knowledge, for it can be based only upon Faith.

It has also been shown that Christianity is in every respect different from philosophical Idealism, whatever form it takes. The position of Christianity is that human beings do not possess saving truth; this is revealed in Jesus Christ. The position of Idealism is that human beings possess the truth and only need to be reminded of it. This is the position of Idealism from Plato to Hegel, that men in themselves are in immediate relationship to the divine. It is the position of Christianity that only God can establish the relationship which is broken by sin.

Finally, it has been shown—and here is the particular polemical aim of the work—that the Hegelian theologians, Martensen in particular, speak without justification of making "an advance" upon Hegel and that their attempt to create a contradiction-free synthesis of Idealism and Christianity makes for confusion. If one is really to make "an advance" upon philosophical Idealism, one must first go back from German to Greek Idealism and then go back from a speculative entanglement of dogmatics to the New Testament itself. Then it becomes evident that philosophical Idealism is one thing and Christianity is something else, but this analytical work does not say anything concerning the truth of either.

Kierkegaard does not say that the question of which is the truth, Idealism or Christianity, can be decided by way of a thought-analysis in the form of an hypothesis. By pointing out that every human being through encounter with the absolute paradox must answer by the passionate risk of choice in Faith or in offense, he has given his answer—which is in agreement with the New Testament.

IV

The Problem of Pseudonymity and the Relationship to Idealism in "Philosophical Fragments"

Having sketched briefly the general and more particular historical contexts, the occasion, the composition, and the development of the thought in *Philosophical Fragments*, we have two remaining problems which have bearing on the work as a whole (questions concerning particular portions are considered in the Commentary). They are the problem of pseudonymity and the problem of the relationship to philosophical Idealism.

THE PROBLEM OF PSEUDONYMITY

On the title-page of *Philosophical Fragments* Kierkegaard himself appears as editor and Johannes Climacus as author. The question is: what relationship exists between Kierkegaard and his pseudonym, whether the work is genuinely pseudonymous (has content which Kierkegaard would not vouch for, would not adhere to) or whether it is a mock pseudonym (actually representing Kierkegaard's own views, his own position). The answer to this question must be: the work is both thought and written in Kierkegaard's own name and therefore cannot be considered a truly pseudonymous work.[20] If one compares the thought both with the entries in Kierkegaard's *Journals* of the same period, the first half of the year 1844, and with the *Edifying Discourses* from the same time, extensions and sharpening of the thought can certainly be found, and one can also find much that is new in *Philosophical Fragments*; but one will find hardly any inconsistency between this work and the other private and published thought and writing. *Philosophical Fragments* undoubtedly represents Kierkegaard's own view at the time it was written and published. To say this, however, is not to affirm that the work provides a full picture of Kierkegaard's views. The concurrent work, *The Concept of Dread*, is testimony to

[20] See Commentary on the title-page, pp. 146ff.

this. In *Philosophical Fragments* consideration is given only to one theme, the relationship between Idealism and Christianity, together with those questions which arise in an inquiry into this relationship.

If this is correct, we have a second question: why, then, in the last minute, did Kierkegaard decide to publish *Philosophical Fragments* pseudonymously? If one notes the changes made in the Preface to the book, it is evident that the purpose of pseudonymity is to permit the problems to appear by themselves, to make them problems of universal validity, and to remove as far as possible the author's personality. The problems are not merely Kierkegaard's own private problems, and they ought to be presented in such a way as can make this evident. This is clearly seen in another pseudonymous work, *The Concept of Dread*, by Vigilius Haufniensis, where he says he could just as well assume the name Christian Madsen [in Lowrie's English translation, John Brown], meaning that the author is a matter of indifference, the substance everything.

Although this explanation is adequate for *Philosophical Fragments*, the choice of the pseudonym itself is neither indifferent nor accidental. The experimental author depicts what Christianity is in its distinction from philosophical Idealism. He readily concedes that basically neither he nor any other human being has invented the project he presents, and he concedes that he himself is not a Christian, although he knows what is involved in Christianity and can draw the consequences of this understanding. Inasmuch as the point of departure is taken in the Idealistic view of man's relationship to the highest truth and the thought moves on to the Christian view so that one can properly speak of an ascent, an accentuation of the Christian categories in their qualitative distinction from the philosophical, the pseudonym must symbolize the character of the work, and therefore the name Johannes Climacus is chosen.[21]

THE RELATIONSHIP TO IDEALISM

From the information and quotations in the Commentary, especially from Plato's works and Hegel's *Lectures on the History of Philosophy*, I-III (New York: Humanities Press, 1955), it is clear that Kierkegaard's conception of "the Socratic," or more accurately, the Platonic, or even more particularly, the Idealistic, view of man's relationship to the highest truth, is not original, nor, as already pointed out, is his interpretation of Christianity. Furthermore, he does not assert that he has an original conception of Idealism and Christianity; on the contrary, he willingly admits that what he presents is well-known. The originality does not consist in the comparison of Platonism and Christianity, although this was and is exceptionally well done; it rather consists in pointing out the deep essential difference between Platonism and Christianity because of the fact of the Incarnation.

Since the problem in *Philosophical Fragments* is not set forth in "historical costume" (p. 137) but is presented systematically, "algebraically," it is self-evident that Socrates is of interest as a principle, not as a person. This is consistent with the Idealistic view that the teacher is acci-

[21] See Commentary, pp. 148-49, for the origin of the pseudonym. The problem of pseudonymity, which is closely related to Kierkegaard's concept of indirect communication, is treated best if one considers each pseudonym and each work separately. The most careful study is found in Hirsch, *Kierkegaard-Studien*, II, 672ff., 747ff. and throughout.

dental; an historical delineation of the actual historical Socrates would be a distraction. What there is in *Philosophical Fragments* of information and suggestions about the historical Socrates is intended to serve as an illustration of "the Socratic." In accordance with this principle, there seems to be little point here, or in the Commentary, in making comparisons or in giving references to other more recent presentations of Socrates.

Because in this work Socrates is the prototype of "both an older and more recent speculation" (p. 12), that is, for all philosophical Idealism, Kierkegaard does not regard it necessary to give more than brief, particularized references to thinkers he has in mind. Partly because he writes systematically and not historically and partly because he clearly regards these allusions as sufficient for the readers of the book, he does not consider it appropriate to say more, just as now one should not have to say Bultmann every time he mentions "demythologizing" or Jaspers every time he mentions "communication."

Yet in our day one cannot in every instance assume more than a fragmentary acquaintance with the many Idealists whom Kierkegaard actually refers to, and therefore in the Commentary information, quotations, and references are given. With their help it will be possible for the reader to grasp Kierkegaard's relationship (usually polemical) to many now almost forgotten or more or less unknown thinkers.

Although it is one task to set forth Kierkegaard's conception of Idealism in its various forms, it is still another problem whether or not Kierkegaard's interpretation of Christianity in *Philosophical Fragments* is qualified by Idealism.

In Kierkegaard-research it has been asserted in various ways that Kierkegaard's understanding of Christianity is qualified by the Idealistic philosophy which he opposed. Here there can be only a summary sketch of the most important contributions on behalf of this theory, the works of A. B. Drachmann, Torsten Bohlin, Emanuel Hirsch, and Sören Holm.

A. B. Drachmann maintains[22] that "the decisive Christian category is developed [in *Philosophical Fragments*] not out of Christianity itself . . . , but only out of Christianity in relationship to the Socratic; and it is Christianity which must there conform to the Socratic and not the reverse." Torsten Bohlin asserts in his entire copious authorship[23] on Kierkegaard that what is called the theme of paradox in Kierkegaard's thought, dominant in *Philosophical Fragments*, is an extension of what Bohlin himself considers to be false Athanasian (orthodox) Christology. Like Drachmann, Bohlin holds the view of the historical development of dogma for which Adolph Harnack, the leading figure in liberal Idealistic theology at the turn of the century, had made himself the spokesman. According to this view the formation of dogma in the early church was not a development out of the given of the New Testament but "a work of the Greek spirit on the basis of the Gospel." If Kierkegaard holds to the orthodox theology, it means, according to this view, that his understanding of Christianity is determined by "the Greek spirit," that is, by Platonism and not by the New Testament, and that it thereby can be rejected as false. Emanuel

[22] *Hedenskab og Christendom hos Sören Kierkegaard* in *Udvalgte Afhandlinger* (1911), pp. 134-40. Quotation is from p. 132.

[23] Most explicit in *Kierkegaards dogmatiska åskådning* (1925), pp 432ff. and throughout.

Hirsch maintains[24] with an entirely different sort of argument than Drachmann's and Bohlin's that as a thinker Kierkegaard belongs in the tradition of Schleiermacher and speculative theism and that Kierkegaard teaches that there is an unbroken line from the purely human to the Christian, and also that in almost every decisive point there are parallel concepts in the human and in the Christian spheres. To a large degree, therefore, according to Hirsch, Kierkegaard's thought must be understood as an extension of tendencies in German Idealism rather than as a radical break with either German Idealism or with Greek Idealism. Sören Holm takes the position[25] that "Kierkegaard's philosophy of history and his subsequent characterization of Christianity were determined by his polemic against Hegel's philosophy," and that in his doctrine of God, his theology, he was a Platonist and in his Christology a fictionalist. Whereas Drachmann and Bohlin expressly criticize Kierkegaard, Hirsch and Holm only document and explain, but the conclusion they all come to is that Kierkegaard maintains an understanding of Christianity qualified in one way or another by Idealistic philosophy, which understanding is then implicitly or explicitly objected to as false in favor of the author's own equally Idealistic view of Christianity, essentially of the Kant-Schleiermacher type. It is asserted that Kierkegaard, with the help of Idealistic philosophy, interprets Christianity as an irrational, unreasonable, absurd doctrine, but in every case it is asserted that Kierkegaard is essentially dependent upon philosophical Idealism, whose complete difference

---

[24] *Kierkegaard-Studien*, especially Volume II, 499ff., and in *Geschichte der neuern evangelischen Theologie*, v (1954), 433-91.

[25] *Sören Kierkegaards Historiefilosofi*, p. 6 and throughout; cf. also Sören Holm's *Philosophy of Religion* (Copenhagen: 1955) throughout.

from the Christian Gospel he wants to point out in *Philosophical Fragments.*

It is correct that in *Philosophical Fragments* Kierkegaard takes his point of departure in "the Socratic" and that in proceeding he makes extensive use of the expressions and language of Idealism. But this mode of procedure is based on the purpose and the setting of the work. It was written and published in a situation in which the influential thinkers were convinced, if not of the identity of Christianity and Idealism in every instance, at least of the harmonious relationship between them. It had to be written in a well-known language, and that meant the language of Idealism, in order to serve its purpose: to make the readers understand that the relationship between Idealistic philosophy and Christianity is not one of harmony. Kierkegaard therefore translated as much of the language of the Gospel into contemporary philosophical terms as he regarded necessary to set forth the difference between contemporary philosophy and Christianity.

It cannot, however, be regarded as correct to say that Kierkegaard is a philosophical Idealist in his characterization of the content of Christianity or that he was influenced by Idealism. Plato and Hegel teach, each in his own way, that there is an identity between the knowing subject and the object known, an identity which is not automatically obvious to everyone but which becomes apparent through their philosophical methods. Kierkegaard maintains, in agreement with the New Testament, that there is no identity of the object of knowledge, which is not the doctrine but the teacher, as Kierkegaard says, and the believer, but rather maintains that there is a distinction, a distance, which becomes more clear the more inward the Faith is.

Kierkegaard affirms that rational apprehension of the object of Faith is not possible, either by self-deepening or by any other procedure. In other words, Plato and Hegel, the greatest representatives of Idealism, teach that the human being possesses the highest truth in himself; Kierkegaard affirms, in agreement with the New Testament, that the highest truth, saving truth, comes to human beings from the outside. Subjectivity as truth, according to Kierkegaard, means appropriation in the inwardness of Faith, not immanental possession of the truth or the immanental condition for acquiring the truth.

If this is the case, there is agreement between the New Testament and what Kierkegaard says in *Philosophical Fragments*, since all that can be mentioned otherwise is only a conscious choice of the expressions of Idealism.

The interpreters and critics mentioned apparently do not understand in exactly the same way as does Kierkegaard the Gospel and Christianity as a proclamation coming from without, the truth incarnate as a particular person who in the Moment, in the contemporary situation, meets the individual human being in his actual situation unto offense or unto Faith. Instead, they tend to understand Christianity as a viewpoint, a doctrine, a system of independent, timeless truths which can be appropriated by every man without decisive difficulties. If this doctrine of the critics is formulated in a consistent system which is in harmony with human thought, thought which for the critics is Idealistically oriented, Kierkegaard's presentation of the truth of Christianity in the language employed in *Philosophical Fragments* will naturally be opposed to the liberal theological views of the critics, but there is nothing in this opposition to prevent Kierkegaard's presentation from being fundamentally in agreement with the New Testament.

In reply particularly to Bohlin it must be noted that the formation of dogma by the early church and Kierkegaard's mode of procedure in *Philosophical Fragments* may very well be regarded as two parallel phenomena—an attempt by use of current philosophical language to express what is characteristic in Christianity and its opposition to the generally accepted philosophy. To Sören Holm's interpretation mention may be made that Kierkegaard's understanding of Christianity, including its presentation in *Philosophical Fragments*, must be regarded as primary and his philosophy of history secondary, that his philosophy of history is certainly directed polemically against Hegel, but that for him Hegel is only a variant of Platonic Idealism and that Hegel must therefore be seen as the occasional object of the polemic, and that one can call Kierkegaard a Platonist in his conception of God if one thereby only means one who affirms the reality of something beyond-the-human, trans-subjective, and that one can term Kierkegaard's Christology fictional only if one sees the "matter from the viewpoint of history alone,"[26] which Kierkegaard certainly did not do. For Kierkegaard Christianity's revelation is a fact beyond discussion; in a miraculous way it has come into the world and defies all understanding whether historical or rational, inasmuch as it transcends the categories of human understanding. To Hirsch's interpretation it can be objected that Kierkegaard briefly but unambiguously makes an accounting not only with Hegel and the Hegelian thinkers but also with the

[26] *Sören Kierkegaards Historiefilosofi*, p. 117.

other German Idealists, with whose works he had occupied himself for a time. If one centers his attention not upon the external, more or less accidental, likenesses in language but looks to the intention, the purpose, of the speculative theists' efforts, the fundamental difference between them and Kierkegaard becomes so clear that all talk about spiritual-intellectual relationship (which does not preclude acquaintance) is silenced from within.

V

Reception of the Work, Its Later Significance, Translations, the Text, and Editorial Principles

There is point in mentioning only two reviews of *Philosophical Fragments*. The first appeared in *Neues Repertorium für die theologische Literatur und kirchliche Statistik* in April 1845, and the second, written by a Martensen disciple, J. F. Hagen, appeared in C. T. Engelstoft's *Theologisk Tidsskrift* in May 1846. Both reviews exhibit their writers' incompetence more adequately than a treatment of Kierkegaard's book and are important evidence of the meager understanding Kierkegaard found even in those very quarters where with some good reason a basis for understanding could have been expected.

The book was printed in an edition of 525 copies, distributed on consignment by University book-seller C. A. Reitzel,[27] and sold slowly. By July 1847, only 229 copies had been sold, and not until 1865 did Kierkegaard's brother, P. C. Kierkegaard, publish a second edition, almost worthless from the standpoint of the text.

[27] Frithjof Brandt and Else Rammel, *Sören Kierkegaard og Pengene* (1935), pp. 12ff.

The role *Philosophical Fragments* came to play in Kierkegaard's time is hardly worth mentioning. When Martensen's *Den christelige Dogmatik* was published in July 1849, with ridiculously arrogant remarks in the preface, obviously directed against Kierkegaard, Rasmus Nielsen attempted, as is known, to attack Martensen's Christian speculations[28] on the basis of a supposedly Kierkegaardian position but neither with Kierkegaard's approval nor to his satisfaction. During the time of liberal theology and theology-of-experience up until World War I, when in philosophy positivism had almost a monopoly, *Philosophical Fragments* could hardly be expected to engage much interest either among theologians or philosophers. By way of the usually popularly oriented surveys of Kierkegaard's life and thought, the psychological analyses which gradually began to appear, and the critical studies such as H. Höffding's well-known work on Kierkegaard as a philosopher, *Philosophical Fragments* became rather well known but was hardly taken seriously. In the last generation it has been quite different. Emil Brunner's *Kristologi Der Mittler* (*The Mediator*; Philadelphia: Westminster, 1947) can be read as a modern edition of *Philosophical Fragments*, and Reidar Hauge's learned work, *Inkarnasjon og opstandelse, til spörsmalet om den historiske åpenbaring* (1941) can be read rewardingly in connection with *Philosophical Fragments*. Anders Nygren's motif-research, *Eros och agape*, I (*Agape and Eros*; London: S.P.C.K., 1957), and the more extensive book by Johannes Hessen, *Plato-*

---

[28] Skat Arildsen, *H. L. Martensen*, I (1932), 245ff.; *Breve og Aktstykker vedr. Sören Kierkegaard*, I (1953), no. 212ff. with references also in the Commentary. Hal Koch, "Tiden 1800-1848," in *Den Danske Kirkes Historie*, VI (1954), especially pp. 285-323, gives the ecclesiastical-theological situation in Kierkegaard's time.

nismus und Prophetismus (2nd ed., 1955) both achieve through an historical-systematic approach an understanding of the relationship between Platonism and Christianity which on decisive points is in agreement with Kierkegaard's view.[29]

A German translation of *Philosophical Fragments* appeared in 1910 in Volume VI of *Kierkegaards Gesammelte Werke*, edited by H. Gottsched and Christian Schrempf. A second edition of this translation appeared in 1925. A new German translation by Emanuel Hirsch came out in 1952 and another by B. Diderichsen with notes by N. Thulstrup in 1959. The English translation, by David Swenson, came out in 1936 and has been reprinted six times and with some important changes is the text of the present edition. Knud Ferlov and J. J. Gateau made a

[29] No reference is made either in the Introduction or in the Commentary to the many general works on Kierkegaard's thought which have appeared in recent years. The beginning reader might turn first to F. J. Billeskov Jansen, *Hvordan skal vi studere Sören Kierkegaard?* and N. H. Söe, *Subjektiviteten er Sandheden*, then to Gregor Malantschuk's brief, substantial *Indförelse i Sören Kierkegaards Forfatterskab* (all three in the series, Sören Kierkegaard Society's *Populaere Skrifter*, nos. 1 and 2, 2 ed.; Copenhagen: Munksgaard, 1952, and no. 4, 1953). Instructive to the understanding of Kierkegaard's relationship to Hegel is Eduard Geismar, *Sören Kierkegaard, hans Livsudvikling og Forfattervirksomhed*, III, *Livsfilosofi* (Copenhagen: G. E. C. Gad, 1927).

In English the best introduction, through the authorship itself, is the reading of Kierkegaard's *Purity of Heart* (Harper, paperback, 1938), *For Self-Examination* (Augsburg, paperback, 1940; or Princeton, together with *Judge For Yourself*, 1941), and *The Works of Love* (Princeton, 1946; or Harper, 1962). Secondary works of greatest introductory value are Eduard Geismar, *Lectures on the Religious Thought of Sören Kierkegaard* (Augsburg, 1937), David Swenson, *Something about Kierkegaard* (Augsburg, 1941), Reidar Thomte, *Kierkegaard's Philosophy of Religion* (Princeton, 1948), James Collins, *The Mind of Kierkegaard* (Regnery, 1953), Perry LeFevre, translator's Introduction, *The Prayers of Kierkegaard* (Chicago University Press, 1956), Martin Heinecken, *The Moment before God* (Muhlenberg Press, 1956) and Libuse Lukas Miller, *In Search of the Self* (Muhlenberg, 1962).

French translation in 1937 and another French translation was done by Paul Petit in 1947. In 1954 there was published a Japanese translation from the Danish by Masaru Otani. Translations of parts of the work are found in various Kierkegaard anthologies.

Both Kierkegaard's draft and original manuscript are preserved, and the parts which have special interest of one kind or another are printed in *Papirer* (Kierkegaard's *Journals*) v b 1-41, to which reference is made. The most important changes from the manuscript are pointed out in the Commentary at the end of the present edition. The first edition of *Philosophical Fragments* contains a few, usually unimportant, departures from the proof-sheets, concerning which reference is made to A. B. Drachmann's textual apparatus. In 1865 P. C. Kierkegaard undertook, as mentioned, a second edition of the work, but this is full of typographical errors and minor changes in spelling and punctuation and has no value as a text. It was A. B. Drachmann's edition in *Sören Kierkegaards Samlede Vaerker*, iv (Copenhagen: 1902), which restored order. The same text is used essentially in Drachmann's second edition in *Samlede Vaerker*, iv, 2nd ed. (Copenhagen: 1923) and later reprintings. The second edition is followed here. In the centenary edition of Kierkegaard's works (*Philosophiske Smuler* og *Afsluttende uvidenskabelig Efterskrift* in one volume (Copenhagen: Hagerup, 1946) the original published edition is regarded as definitive, although obvious errors are corrected.[30]

---

[30] The ordinary textual problems which may arise in the publication of a work by Kierkegaard are treated by A. B. Drachmann in *Textkritik, anvendt paa S. Kierkegaards Skrifter* (Copenhagen: 1903), reprinted in *Udvalgte Afhandlinger* (Copenhagen: 1911), pp. 154-75. Problems concerning Kierkegaard's texts are also considered in P. V. Rubow, *Den kritiske Kunst* (Copenhagen: 1938), pp. 25-30.

Philosophical Fragments

or

A Fragment of Philosophy

MOTTO

"Better well hung

than ill wed."

—Shakespeare

Preface

THE present offering is merely a piece, *proprio Marte, propriis auspiciis, proprio stipendio*. It does not make the slightest pretension to share in the philosophical movement of the day, or to fill any of the various roles customarily assigned in this connection: transitional, intermediary, final, preparatory, participating, collaborating, volunteer follower, hero, or at any rate relative hero, or at the very least absolute trumpeter. The offering is a piece and such it will remain, even if like Holberg's *magister* I were *volente Deo* to write a sequel in seventeen pieces, just as half-hour literature is half-hour literature even in folio quantities. Such as it is, however, the offering is commensurate with my talents, since I cannot excuse my failure to serve the System after the manner of the noble Roman, *merito magis quam ignavia*; I am an idler from love of ease, *ex animi sententia*, and for good and sufficient reasons. Nevertheless, I am unwilling to incur the reproach of ἀπραγμοσύνη, at all times an offense against the State, and especially so in a period of ferment; in ancient times it was made punishable by death. But suppose my intervention served merely to increase the prevailing confusion, thus making me guilty of a still greater crime, would it not have been better had I kept to my own concerns? It is not given to everyone to have his private tasks of meditation and reflection so happily coincident with the public interest that it becomes difficult to judge how far he serves merely himself and how far the public good. Consider the example of Archimedes, who sat unperturbed in the contemplation of his circles while Syracuse was being taken, and the beautiful words he spoke to the Roman soldier who slew him: *nolite perturbare circulos meos.* Let him who is not so fortunate look about him for another example. When Philip threatened to lay siege to the city of Corinth, and all its inhabitants hastily bestirred themselves in defense, some polishing weapons, some gathering stones, some repairing the walls, Diogenes seeing all this hurriedly folded his mantle about him and began to roll his tub zealously back and forth through the streets. When he was asked why he did this he replied that he wished to be busy like all the rest, and rolled his tub lest he should be the only idler among so many industrious citizens. Such conduct is at any rate not sophistical, if Aristotle be right in describing sophistry as the art of making money. It is certainly not open to misunderstanding; it is quite inconceivable that Diogenes should have been hailed as the saviour and benefactor of the city. And it seems equally impossible that anyone could hit upon the idea of ascribing to a piece like the present any sort of epoch-making significance, in my eyes the greatest calamity that could possibly befall it. Nor is it likely that anyone will hail its author as the systematic Salomon Goldkalb so long and eagerly awaited in our dear royal residential city of Copenhagen. This could happen only if the guilty person were by nature endowed with extraordinary stupidity, and presumably by shouting in antistrophic and antiphonal song every time someone persuaded him that now was the beginning of a new era and a new epoch, had howled his head so empty of its original *quantum satis* of common sense as to have attained a state of ineffable bliss in what might be called the howling madness of the higher lunacy, recognizable by such symptoms as convulsive shouting; a constant reiteration of the words "era," "epoch," "era and epoch," "epoch and era," "the System"; an irrational exaltation of the spirits as if each day were not merely a quadrennial leap-year day, but one of those extraordinary days that come only once in a thousand years; the concept all the while like an acrobatic clown in the current circus season, every moment performing these everlasting dog-tricks of flopping over and over, until it flops over the man himself. May a kind Heaven preserve me and my piece from such a fate! And may no noise-making busybody interfere to snatch me out of my carefree content as the author of a little piece, or prevent a kind and benevolent reader from examining it at his leisure, to see if it contains anything that he can use. May I escape the tragicomic predicament of being forced to laugh at my own misfortune, as must have been the case with the good people of Fredericia, when they awoke one morning to read in the newspaper an account of a fire in their town, in which it was described how "the drums beat the alarm, the fire-engines rushed through the streets"—although the town of Fredericia boasts of only one fire-engine and not much more than one street; leaving it to be inferred that this one engine, instead of making for the scene of the fire, took time to execute important maneuvers and flanking movements up and down the street. However, my little piece is not very apt to suggest the beating of a drum, and its author is perhaps the last man in the world to sound the alarm.

But what is my personal opinion of the matters herein discussed? . . . I could wish that no one would ask me this question; for next to knowing whether I have any

opinion or not, nothing could very well be of less importance to another than the knowledge of what that opinion
might be. To have an opinion is both too much and too
little for my uses. To have an opinion presupposes a sense
of ease and security in life, such as is implied in having a
wife and children; it is a privilege not to be enjoyed by
one who must keep himself in readiness night and day,
or is without assured means of support. Such is my situation in the realm of the spirit. I have disciplined myself
and keep myself under discipline, in order that I may be
able to execute a sort of nimble dancing in the service of
Thought, so far as possible also to the honor of the God,
and for my own satisfaction. For this reason I have had to
resign the domestic happiness, the civic respectability, the
glad fellowship, the *communio bonorum*, which is implied
in the possession of an opinion.—Do I enjoy any reward?
Have I permission, like the priest at the altar, to eat of the
sacrifices? . . . That must remain my own affair. My
master is good for it, as the bankers say, and good in quite
a different sense from theirs. But if anyone were to be so
polite as to assume that I have an opinion, and if he were
to carry his gallantry to the extreme of adopting this
opinion because he believed it to be mine, I should have
to be sorry for his politeness, in that it was bestowed upon
so unworthy an object, and for his opinion, if he has no
other opinion than mine. I stand ready to risk my own
life, to play the game of thought with it in all earnest;
but another's life I cannot jeopardize. This service is perhaps the only one I can render to Philosophy, I who have
no learning to offer her, "scarcely enough for the course
at one drachma, to say nothing of the great course at fifty

drachmas" (*Cratylus*). I have only my life, and the instant a difficulty offers I put it in play. Then the dance goes merrily, for my partner is the thought of Death, and is indeed a nimble dancer; every human being, on the other hand, is too heavy for me. Therefore I pray, *per deos obsecro*: Let no one invite me, for I will not dance.

J. C.

PROPOSITIO

The question is asked in ignorance,
by one who does not even know
what can have led him to ask it.

CHAPTER I

A Project of Thought

A

How far does the Truth admit of being learned? With this question let us begin. It was a Socratic question, or became such in consequence of the parallel Socratic question with respect to virtue, since virtue was again determined as insight. (*Protagoras, Gorgias, Meno, Euthydemus.*) In so far as the Truth is conceived as something to be learned, its non-existence is evidently presupposed, so that in proposing to learn it one makes it the object of an inquiry. Here we are confronted with the difficulty to which Socrates calls attention in the *Meno* (80, near the end), and there characterizes as a "pugnacious proposition"; one cannot seek for what he knows, and it seems equally impossible for him to seek for what he does not know. For what a man knows he cannot seek, since he knows it; and what he does not know he cannot seek, since he does not even know for what to seek. Socrates thinks the difficulty through in the doctrine of Recollection, by which all learning and inquiry is interpreted as a kind of remembering; one who is ignorant needs only a reminder to help him come to himself in the consciousness of what he knows. Thus the Truth is not introduced into the individual from without, but was within him. This thought receives further development at the hands of Socrates, and it ultimately becomes the point of concentration for the pathos of the Greek consciousness, since it serves as a proof for the immortality of the soul; but with a backward reference, it is important to note, and hence as proof for the soul's preëxistence.[1]

In the light of this idea it becomes apparent with what wonderful consistency Socrates remained true to himself, through his manner of life giving artistic expression to what he had understood. He entered into the role of midwife and sustained it throughout; not because his thought "had no positive content,"[2] but because he perceived that this relation is the highest that one human being can sustain to another. And in this surely Socrates was everlastingly right; for even if a divine point of departure is ever given, between man and man this is the true relationship,

[1] Taking the thought in its naked absoluteness, not reflecting upon possible variations in the soul's preëxistent state, we find this Greek conception recurring in both an older and more recent speculation: an eternal creation; an eternal procession from the Father; an eternal coming into being of the Deity; an eternal self-sacrifice; a past resurrection; a past judgment. All these thoughts are essentially the Greek doctrine of Recollection, only that this is not always perceived, since they have been arrived at by way of an advance. If we split the thought up into a reckoning of the different states ascribed to the soul in its preëxistence, the everlasting *prae*'s of such an approximating mode of thought are like the everlasting *post*'s of the corresponding forward approximations. The contradictions of existence are explained by positing a *prae* as needed (because of an earlier state the individual has come into his present otherwise inexplicable situation); or by positing a *post* as needed (on another planet the individual is to be placed in a more favorable situation, in view of which his present state is not inexplicable).

[2] Such is the criticism commonly passed upon Socrates in our age, which boasts of its positivity much as if a polytheist were to speak with scorn of the negativity of a monotheist; for the polytheist has many gods, the monotheist only one. So our philosophers have many thoughts, all valid to a certain extent; Socrates had only one, which was absolute.

provided we reflect upon the absolute and refuse to dally with the accidental, from the heart renouncing the understanding of the half-truths which seem the delight of men and the secret of the System. Socrates was a midwife subjected to examination by the God; his work was in fulfilment of a divine mission (Plato's *Apology*), though he seemed to men in general a most singular creature (ἀτοπώτατος, *Theaetetus*, 149); it was in accordance with a divine principle, as Socrates also understood it, that he was by the God forbidden to beget (μαίνεσθαί με ὁ Θεὸς ἀναγκάζει, γεννᾶν δὲ ἀπεκώλυσεν, *Theaetetus*, 150); for between man and man the maieutic relationship is the highest, and begetting belongs to the God alone.

From the standpoint of the Socratic thought every point of departure in time is *eo ipso* accidental, an occasion, a vanishing moment. The teacher himself is no more than this; and if he offers himself and his instruction on any other basis, he does not give but takes away, and is not even the other's friend, much less his teacher. Herein lies the profundity of the Socratic thought, and the noble humanity he so thoroughly expressed, which refused to enter into a false and vain fellowship with clever heads, but felt an equal kinship with a tanner; whence he soon "came to the conclusion that the study of Physics was not man's proper business, and therefore began to philosophize about moral matters in the workshops and in the market-place" (Diogenes Laertius, II, v, 21), but philosophized with equal absoluteness everywhere. With slipshod thoughts, with higgling and haggling, maintaining a little here and conceding a little there, as if the individual might to a certain extent owe something to another, but then again to a certain extent not; with loose words that explain everything except what this "to a certain extent" means—with such makeshifts it is not possible to advance beyond Socrates, nor will one reach the concept of a Revelation, but merely remain within the sphere of idle chatter. In the Socratic view each individual is his own center, and the entire world centers in him, because his self-knowledge is a knowledge of God. It was thus Socrates understood himself, and thus he thought that everyone must understand himself, in the light of this understanding interpreting his relationship to each individual, with equal humility and with equal pride. He had the courage and self-possession to be sufficient unto himself, but also in his relations to his fellowmen to be merely an occasion, even when dealing with the meanest capacity. How rare is such magnanimity! How rare in a time like ours, when the parson is something more than the clerk, when almost every second person is an authority, while all these distinctions and all these many authorities are mediated in a common madness, a *commune naufragium*. For while no human being was ever truly an authority for another, or ever helped anyone by posing as such, or was ever able to take his client with him in truth, there is another sort of success that may by such methods be won; for it has never yet been known to fail that one fool, when he goes astray, takes several others with him.

With this understanding of what it means to learn the Truth, the fact that I have been instructed by Socrates or by Prodicus or by a servant-girl, can concern me only historically; or in so far as I am a Plato in sentimental enthusiasm, it may concern me poetically. But this enthusiasm, beautiful as it is, and such that I could wish both for myself and all others a share of this εὐκαταφορία εἰς πάθος, which

only a Stoic could frown upon; and though I may be
lacking in the Socratic magnanimity and the Socratic self-
denial to think its nothingness—this enthusiasm, so Socrates would say, is only an illusion, a want of clarity in a
mind where earthly inequalities seethe almost voluptu-
ously. Nor can it interest me otherwise than historically
that Socrates' or Prodicus' doctrine was this or that; for
the Truth in which I rest was within me, and came to
light through myself, and not even Socrates could have
given it to me, as little as the driver can pull the load for
the horses, though he may help them by applying the
lash.[3] My relation to Socrates or Prodicus cannot concern
me with respect to my eternal happiness, for this is given
me retrogressively through my possession of the Truth,
which I had from the beginning without knowing it. If I
imagine myself meeting Socrates or Prodicus or the servant-
girl in another life, then here again neither of them could
be more to me than an occasion, which Socrates fearlessly
expressed by saying that even in the lower world he
proposed merely to ask questions; for the underlying
principle of all questioning is that the one who is asked
must have the Truth in himself, and be able to acquire it
by himself. The temporal point of departure is nothing;
for as soon as I discover that I have known the Truth from
eternity without being aware of it, the same instant this

---

[3] There is a passage in the *Clitophon*, which I cite only as the
testimony of a third party, since this dialogue is not believed to be
genuine. Clitophon complains that the discourses of Socrates about
virtue are merely inspirational ($\pi\rho\text{o}\tau\rho\epsilon\pi\tau\iota\kappa\acute{o}\varsigma$), and that as soon as
he has sufficiently recommended virtue in general he leaves each
one to himself. Clitophon thinks that this must find its explanation
either in the fact that Socrates does not know more, or else that
he is unwilling to communicate more.

moment of occasion is hidden in the Eternal, and so incorporated with it that I cannot even find it so to speak, even if I sought it; because in my eternal consciousness there is neither here nor there, but only an *ubique et nusquam.*

B

Now if things are to be otherwise, the Moment in time must have a decisive significance, so that I will never be able to forget it either in time or eternity; because the Eternal, which hitherto did not exist, came into existence in this moment. Under this presupposition let us now proceed to consider the consequences for the problem of how far it is possible to acquire a knowledge of the Truth.

A. THE ANTECEDENT STATE

We begin with the Socratic difficulty about seeking the Truth, which seems equally impossible whether we have it or do not have it. The Socratic thought really abolishes this disjunction, since it appears that at bottom every human being is in possession of the Truth. This was Socrates' explanation; we have seen what follows from it with respect to the moment. Now if the latter is to have decisive significance, the seeker must be destitute of the Truth up to the very moment of his learning it; he cannot even have possessed it in the form of ignorance, for in that case the moment becomes merely occasional. What is more, he cannot even be described as a seeker; for such is the expression we must give to the difficulty if we do not wish to explain it Socratically. He must therefore be characterized as beyond the pale of the Truth, not approaching it like a proselyte, but departing from it; or as being in

Error. He is then in a state of Error. But how is he now to be reminded, or what will it profit him to be reminded of what he has not known, and consequently cannot recall?

B. THE TEACHER

If the Teacher serves as an occasion by means of which the learner is reminded, he cannot help the learner to recall that he really knows the Truth; for the learner is in a state of Error. What the Teacher can give him occasion to remember is, that he is in Error. But in this consciousness the learner is excluded from the Truth even more decisively than before, when he lived in ignorance of his Error. In this manner the Teacher thrusts the learner away from him, precisely by serving as a reminder; only that the learner, in thus being thrust back upon himself, does not discover that he knew the Truth already, but discovers his Error; with respect to which act of consciousness the Socratic principle holds, that the Teacher is merely an occasion whoever he may be, even if he is a God. For my own Error is something I can discover only by myself, since it is only when I have discovered it that it is discovered, even if the whole world knew of it before. (Under the presupposition we have adopted concerning the moment, this remains the only analogy to the Socratic order of things.)

Now if the learner is to acquire the Truth, the Teacher must bring it to him; and not only so, but he must also give him the condition necessary for understanding it. For if the learner were in his own person the condition for understanding the Truth, he need only recall it. The condition for understanding the Truth is like the capacity to inquire for it: the condition contains the conditioned, and the question implies the answer. (Unless this is so, the moment must be understood in the Socratic sense.)

But one who gives the learner not only the Truth, but also the condition for understanding it, is more than teacher. All instruction depends upon the presence, in the last analysis, of the requisite condition; if this is lacking, no teacher can do anything. For otherwise he would find it necessary not only to transform the learner, but to re-create him before beginning to teach him. But this is something that no human being can do; if it is to be done, it must be done by the God himself.

In so far as the learner exists he is already created, and hence God must have endowed him with the condition for understanding the Truth. For otherwise his earlier existence must have been merely brutish, and the Teacher who gave him the Truth and with it the condition was the original creator of his human nature. But in so far as the moment is to have decisive significance (and unless we assume this we remain at the Socratic standpoint) the learner is destitute of this condition, and must therefore have been deprived of it. This deprivation cannot have been due to an act of the God (which would be a contradiction), nor to an accident (for it would be a contradiction to assume that the lower could overcome the higher); it must therefore be due to himself. If he could have lost the condition in such a way that the loss was not due to himself, and if he could remain in the state of deprivation without his own responsibility, it would follow that his earlier possession of the condition was accidental merely. But this is a contradiction, since the condition for understanding the Truth is an essential condition. Error is then not only outside the Truth, but polemic in its attitude toward it; which is expressed by saying that the learner has himself forfeited the condition, and is engaged in forfeiting it.

The Teacher is then the God himself, who in acting as an occasion prompts the learner to recall that he is in Error, and that by reason of his own guilt. But this state, the being in Error by reason of one's own guilt, what shall we call it? Let us call it *Sin*.

The Teacher, then, is the God, and he gives the learner the requisite condition and the Truth. What shall we call such a Teacher?—for we are surely agreed that we have already far transcended the ordinary functions of a teacher. In so far as the learner is in Error, but in consequence of his own act (and in no other way can he possibly be in this state, as we have shown above), he might seem to be free; for to be what one is by one's own act is freedom. And yet he is in reality unfree and bound and exiled; for to be free from the Truth is to be exiled from the Truth, and to be exiled by one's own self is to be bound. But since he is bound by himself, may he not loose his bonds and set himself free? For whatever binds me, the same should be able to set me free when it wills; and since this power is here his own self, he should be able to liberate himself. But first at any rate he must will it. Suppose him now to be so profoundly impressed by what the Teacher gave him occasion to remember (and this must not be omitted from the reckoning); suppose that he wills his freedom. In that case, i.e., if by willing to be free he could by himself become free, the fact that he had been bound would become

a state of the past, tracelessly vanishing in the moment of
liberation; the moment would not be charged with decisive
significance. He was not aware that he had bound himself,
and now he had freed himself.[4] Thus interpreted the

[4] Let us take plenty of time to consider the point, since there is
no pressing need for haste. By proceeding slowly one may sometimes fail to reach the goal, but by indulging in undue haste one
may sometimes be carried past it. Let us talk about this a little in
the Greek manner. Suppose a child had been presented with a
little sum of money and could buy with it either a good book, for
example, or a toy, both at the same price. If he buys the toy, can
he then buy the book for the same money? Surely not, since the
money is already spent. But perhaps he may go to the bookseller
and ask him to make an exchange, letting him have the book in
return for the toy. Will not the bookseller say: My dear child,
your toy is not worth anything; it is true that when you still had
the money you could have bought the book instead of the toy, but
a toy is a peculiar kind of thing, for once it is bought it loses all
value. Would not the child think that this was very strange? And
so there was also a time when man could have bought either freedom or bondage at the same price, this price being the soul's free
choice and commitment in the choice. He chose bondage; but if
he now comes forward with a proposal for an exchange, would
not the God reply: Undoubtedly there was a time when you could
have bought whichever you pleased, but bondage is a very strange
sort of thing; when it is bought it has absolutely no value, although
the price paid for it was originally the same. Would not such an
individual think this very strange? Again, suppose two opposing
armies drawn up in the field, and that a knight arrives whom both
armies invite to fight on their side; he makes his choice, is vanquished and taken prisoner. As prisoner he is brought before the
victor, to whom he foolishly presumes to offer his services on the
same terms as were extended to him before the battle. Would not
the victor say to him: My friend, you are now my prisoner; there
was indeed a time when you could have chosen differently, but now
everything is changed. Was this not strange enough? Yet if it
were not so, if the moment had no decisive significance, the child
must at bottom have bought the book, merely imagining in his
ignorance and misunderstanding that he had bought the toy; the

moment receives no decisive significance, and yet this was the hypothesis we proposed to ourselves in the beginning. By the terms of our hypothesis, therefore, he will not be able to set himself free.—And so it is in very truth; for he forges the chains of his bondage with the strength of his freedom, since he exists in it without compulsion; and thus his bonds grow strong, and all his powers unite to make him the slave of sin.—What now shall we call such a Teacher, one who restores the lost condition and gives the learner the Truth? Let us call him *Saviour*, for he saves the learner from his bondage and from himself; let us call him *Redeemer*, for he redeems the learner from the captivity into which he had plunged himself, and no captivity is so terrible and so impossible to break, as that in which the individual keeps himself. And still we have not said all that is necessary; for by his self-imposed bondage the learner has brought upon himself a burden of guilt, and when the Teacher gives him the condition and the Truth he constitutes himself an *Atonement*, taking away the wrath impending upon that of which the learner has made himself guilty.

Such a Teacher the learner will never be able to forget. For the moment he forgets him he sinks back again into

captive knight must really have fought on the other side, the facts having been obscured by the fog, so that at bottom he had fought on the side of the leader whose prisoner he now imagined himself to be.—"The vicious and the virtuous have not indeed power over their moral actions; but at first they had the power to become either the one or the other, just as one who throws a stone has power over it until he has thrown it, but not afterwards" (Aristotle). Otherwise throwing would be an illusion; the thrower would keep the stone in his hand in spite of all his throwing; it would be like the "flying arrow" of the sceptics, which did not fly.

himself, just as one who while in original possession of the condition forgot that God exists, and thereby sank into bondage. If they should happen to meet in another life, the Teacher would again be able to give the condition to anyone who had not yet received it; but to one who had once received the condition he would stand in a different relation. The condition was a trust, for which the recipient would always be required to render an account. But what shall we call such a Teacher? A teacher may determine whether the pupil makes progress or not, but he cannot judge him; for he ought to have Socratic insight enough to perceive that he cannot give him what is essential. This Teacher is thus not so much teacher as *Judge*. Even when the learner has most completely appropriated the condition, and most profoundly apprehended the Truth, he cannot forget this Teacher, or let him vanish Socratically, although this is far more profound than illusory sentimentality or untimely pettiness of spirit. It is indeed the highest, unless that other be the Truth.

And now the moment. Such a moment has a peculiar character. It is brief and temporal indeed, like every moment; it is transient as all moments are; it is past, like every moment in the next moment. And yet it is decisive, and filled with the Eternal. Such a moment ought to have a distinctive name; let us call it the *Fullness of Time*.

C. THE DISCIPLE

When the disciple is in a state of Error (and otherwise we return to Socrates) but is none the less a human being, and now receives the condition and the Truth, he does not become a human being for the first time, since he was a man already. But he becomes another man; not in the frivolous sense of becoming another individual of the same quality as before, but in the sense of becoming a man of a different quality, or as we may call him: *a new creature.*

In so far as he was in Error he was constantly in the act of departing from the Truth. In consequence of receiving the condition in the moment the course of his life has been given an opposite direction, so that he is now turned about. Let us call this change *Conversion*, even though this word be one not hitherto used; but that is precisely a reason for choosing it, in order namely to avoid confusion, for it is as if expressly coined for the change we have in mind.

In so far as the learner was in Error by reason of his own guilt, this conversion cannot take place without being taken up in his consciousness, or without his becoming aware that his former state was a consequence of his guilt. With this consciousness he will then take leave of his former state. But what leave-taking is without a sense of sadness? The sadness in this case, however, is on account of his having so long remained in his former state. Let us call such grief *Repentance*; for what is repentance but a kind of leave-taking, looking backward indeed, but yet in such a way as precisely to quicken the steps toward that which lies before?

In so far as the learner was in Error, and now receives the Truth and with it the condition for understanding it, a change takes place within him like the change from non-being to being. But this transition from non-being to being is the transition we call birth. Now one who exists cannot be born; nevertheless, the disciple is born. Let us call this transition the *New Birth*, in consequence of which the disciple enters the world quite as at the first birth, an individual human being knowing nothing as yet about the world into which he is born, whether it is inhabited, whether there are other human beings in it besides himself; for while it is indeed possible to be baptized *en masse*, it is not possible to be born anew *en masse*. Just as one who has begotten himself by the aid of the Socratic midwifery now forgets everything else in the world, and in a deeper sense owes no man anything, so the disciple who is born anew owes nothing to any man, but everything to his divine Teacher. And just as the former forgets the world in his discovery of himself, so the latter forgets himself in the discovery of his Teacher.

Hence if the *Moment* is to have decisive significance—and if not we speak Socratically whatever we may say, even if through not even understanding ourselves we imagine that we have advanced far beyond that simple man of wisdom who divided judgment incorruptibly between the God and man and himself, a judge more just than Minos, Aeacus and Rhadamanthus—if the Moment has decisive significance the breach is made, and man cannot return. He will take no pleasure in remembering what Recollection brings to his mind; still less will he be able in his own strength to bring the God anew over to his side.

———

But is the hypothesis here expounded thinkable? Let us not be in haste to reply; for not only one whose deliberation is unduly prolonged may fail to produce an answer, but also one who while he exhibits a marvelous promptitude in replying, does not show the desirable degree of slowness in considering the difficulty before explaining it. Before we reply, let us ask ourselves from whom we may expect an answer to our question. The being born, is this fact thinkable? Certainly, why not? But for whom is it thinkable, for one who is born, or for one who is not born? This latter supposition is an absurdity which could never have entered anyone's head; for one who is born could scarcely have conceived the notion. When one who has experienced birth thinks of himself as born, he conceives this transition from non-being to being. The same principle must also hold in the case of the new birth. Or is the difficulty increased by the fact that the non-being which precedes the new birth contains more being than the non-being which preceded the first birth? But who then may be expected to think the new birth? Surely the man who has himself been born anew, since it would of course be absurd to imagine that one not so born should think it. Would it not be the height of the ridiculous for such an individual to entertain this notion?

If a human being is originally in possession of the condition for understanding the Truth, he thinks that God exists in and with his own existence. But if he is in Error he must comprehend this fact in his thinking, and Recollection will not be able to help him further than to think just this. Whether he is to advance beyond this point the *Moment* must decide (although it was already active in giving him an insight into his Error). If he does not understand this, we must refer him to Socrates, though through being obsessed with the idea that he has advanced far beyond this wise man he may cause him many a vexation, like those who were so incensed with Socrates for taking away from them one or another stupid notion (ἐπειδάν τινα λῆρον αὐτῶν ἀφαιρῶμαι) that they actually wanted to bite him (*Theaetetus*, 151). In the *Moment* man becomes conscious that he is born; for his antecedent state, to which he may not cling, was one of non-being. In the *Moment* man also becomes conscious of the new birth, for his antecedent state was one of non-being. Had his preceding state in either instance been one of being, the moment would not have received decisive significance for him, as has been shown above. While then the pathos of the Greek consciousness concentrates itself upon Recollection, the pathos of our project is concentrated upon the Moment. And what wonder, for is it not a most pathetic thing to come into existence from non-being?

*   *

There you have my project. But I think I hear someone say: "This is the most ridiculous of all projects; or rather, you are of all projectors of hypotheses the most ridiculous. For even when a man propounds something nonsensical, it may still remain true that it is he who has propounded it; but you behave like a lazzarone who takes money for exhibiting premises open to everybody's inspection; you are like the man who collected a fee for exhibiting a ram in the afternoon, which in the forenoon could be seen gratis, grazing in the open field."—"Perhaps it is so; I hide my head in shame. But assuming that I am as ridiculous as you say, let me try to make amends by proposing a new hypothesis. Everybody knows that gunpowder was invented centuries ago, and in so far it would be ridiculous of me to pretend to be the inventor; but would it be equally ridiculous of me to assume that somebody was the inventor? Now I am going to be so polite as to assume that you are the author of my project; greater politeness than this you can scarcely ask. Or if you deny this, will you also deny that someone is the author, that is to say, some human being? In that case I am as near to being the author as any other human being. So that your anger is not vented upon me because I appropriated something that belongs to another human being, but because I appropriated something of which no human being is the rightful owner; and hence your anger is by no means appeased when I deceitfully ascribe the authorship to you. Is it not strange that there should be something such in existence, in relation to which everyone who knows it knows also that he has not invented it, and that this "pass-me-by" neither stops nor can be stopped even if we ask all men in turn? This strange fact deeply impresses me, and casts over me a spell; for it constitutes a test of the hypothesis and proves its truth. It would certainly be absurd to expect of a man that he should of his own accord discover that he did not exist. But this is precisely the transition of the new birth, from non-being to being. That he may come to understand it afterwards can make no difference; for because a man knows how to use gunpowder and can resolve it into its constituent elements, it does not follow that he has invented it. Be then angry with me and with whoever else pretends to the authorship of this thought; but that is no reason why you should be angry with the thought itself."

CHAPTER II

The God as Teacher and Saviour: An Essay of the Imagination

LET us briefly consider Socrates, who was himself a teacher. He was born under such and such circumstances; he came under the formative influences of the people to which he belonged; and when upon reaching maturity he felt an inner impulse and call to this end, he began in his own way to teach others. Thus after having lived for some time as Socrates, circumstances seeming propitious, he emerged in the role of Socrates the teacher. He was himself influenced by circumstances, and reacted upon them in turn. In realizing his task he satisfied at one and the same time the demands of his own nature, and those that others might make upon him. So understood, and this was indeed the Socratic understanding, the teacher stands in a reciprocal relation, in that life and its circumstances constitute an occasion for him to become a teacher, while he in turn gives occasion for others to learn something. He thus embodies in his attitude an equal proportion of the autopathic and the sympathetic. Such also was the Socratic understanding, and hence he would accept neither praise nor honors nor money for his instruction, but passed judgment with the incorruptibility of a departed spirit. Rare contentment! Rare especially in a time like ours, when no purse seems large enough nor crown of glory sufficiently glittering to match the splendor of the instruction; but when also the world's gold and the world's glory are the precisely adequate compensation, the one being worth as much as the other. To be sure, our age is positive and understands what is positive; Socrates on the other hand was negative. It might be well to consider whether this lack of positiveness does not perhaps explain the narrowness of his principles, which were doubtless rooted in a zeal for what is universally human, and in a discipline of self marked by the same divine jealousy as his discipline of others, a zeal and discipline through which he loved the divine. As between man and man no higher relationship is possible; the disciple gives occasion for the teacher to understand himself, and the teacher gives occasion for the disciple to understand himself. When the teacher dies he leaves behind him no claim upon the soul of the disciple, just as the disciple can assert no claim that the teacher owes him anything. And if I were a Plato in sentimental enthusiasm, and if my heart beat as violently as Alcibiades' or more violently than that of the Corybantic mystic while listening to the words of Socrates; if the passion of my admiration knew no rest until I had clasped the wondrous master in my arms— Socrates would but smile at me and say: "My friend, how deceitful a lover you are! You wish to idolize me on account of my wisdom, and then to take your place as the friend who best understands me, from whose admiring embrace I shall never be able to tear myself free—is it not true that you are a seducer?" And if I still refused to understand him, he would no doubt bring me to despair by the coldness of his irony, as he unfolded to me that he owed me as much as I owed him. Rare integrity, deceiving no one, not even one who would deem it his highest happiness to be deceived! How rare in our age, when all have transcended Socrates—in self-appreciation, in estimate of benefits conferred upon their pupils, in sentimentality of intercourse, in voluptuous enjoyment of admiration's warm embrace! Rare faithfulness, seducing no one, not even him who exercises all the arts of seduction in order to be seduced!

But the God needs no disciple to help him understand himself, nor can he be so determined by any occasion that there is as much significance in the occasion as in the resolve. What then could move him to make his appearance? He must indeed move himself, and continue to exemplify what Aristotle says of him: ἀκίνητος πάντα κινεῖ. But if he moves himself it follows that he is not moved by some need, as if he could not endure the strain of silence, but had to break out in speech. But if he moves himself, and is not moved by need, what else can move him but love? For love finds its satisfaction within and not without. His resolve, which stands in no equal reciprocal relation to the occasion, must be from eternity, though when realized in time it constitutes precisely the *Moment*; for when the occasion and the occasioned correspond, and are as commensurable as the answer of the desert with the cry that evokes it, the Moment does not appear, but is lost in the eternity of Recollection. The Moment makes its appearance when an eternal resolve comes into relation with an incommensurable occasion. Unless this is realized we shall be thrown back on Socrates, and shall then have neither the God as Teacher, nor an Eternal Purpose, nor the Moment.

Moved by love, the God is thus eternally resolved to reveal himself. But as love is the motive so love must also be the end; for it would be a contradiction for the God to have a motive and an end which did not correspond. His love is a love of the learner, and his aim is to win him.

For it is only in love that the unequal can be made equal, and it is only in equality or unity that an understanding can be effected, and without a perfect understanding the Teacher is not the God, unless the obstacle comes wholly from the side of the learner, in his refusing to realize that which had been made possible for him.

But this love is through and through unhappy, for how great is the difference between them! It may seem a small matter for the God to make himself understood, but this is not so easy of accomplishment if he is to refrain from annihilating the unlikeness that exists between them.

Let us not jump too quickly to a conclusion at this point; if it seems to some that we waste our time while we might be coming to a decision, we take comfort in the thought that it does not follow that we shall have only our trouble for our pains. Much is heard in the world about unhappy love, and we all know what this means: the lovers are prevented from realizing their union, the causes being many and various. There is another kind of unhappy love, the theme of our present discourse, for which there is no perfect earthly parallel, though by dint of speaking foolishly a little while we may make shift to conceive it through an earthly figure. The unhappiness of this love does not come from the inability of the lovers to realize their union, but from their inability to understand one another. This grief is infinitely more profound than that of which men commonly speak, since it strikes at the very heart of love, and wounds for an eternity; not like that other misfortune which touches only the temporal and the external, and which for the magnanimous is as a sort of jest over the inability of the lovers to realize their union here in time. This infinitely deeper grief is essentially the prerogative of the superior, since only he likewise understands the misunderstanding; in reality it belongs to the God alone, and no human relationship can afford a valid analogy. Nevertheless, we shall here suggest such an analogy, in order to quicken the mind to an apprehension of the divine.

Suppose there was a king who loved a humble maiden. But the reader has perhaps already lost his patience, seeing that our beginning sounds like a fairy tale, and is not in the least systematic. So the very learned Polos found it tiresome that Socrates always talked about meat and drink and doctors, and similar unworthy trifles, which Polos deemed beneath him (*Gorgias*). But did not the Socratic manner of speech have at least one advantage, in that he himself and all others were from childhood equipped with the necessary prerequisites for understanding it? And would it not be desirable if I could confine the terms of my argument to meat and drink, and did not need to bring in kings, whose thoughts are not always like those of other men, if they are indeed kingly. But perhaps I may be pardoned the extravagance, seeing that I am only a poet, proceeding now to unfold the carpet of my discourse (recalling the beautiful saying of Themistocles), lest its workmanship be concealed by the compactness of its folding.

Suppose then a king who loved a humble maiden. The heart of the king was not polluted by the wisdom that is loudly enough proclaimed; he knew nothing of the difficulties that the understanding discovers in order to ensnare the heart, which keep the poets so busy, and make their magic formulas necessary. It was easy to realize his purpose. Every statesman feared his wrath and dared not breathe a word of displeasure; every foreign state trembled before his power and dared not omit sending ambassadors with congratulations for the nuptials; no courtier grovelling in the dust dared wound him, lest his own head be crushed. Then let the harp be tuned, let the songs of the poets begin to sound, and let all be festive while love celebrates its triumph. For love is exultant when it unites equals, but it is triumphant when it makes that which was unequal equal in love.—Then there awoke in the heart of the king an anxious thought; who but a king who thinks kingly thoughts would have dreamed of it! He spoke to no one about his anxiety; for if he had, each courtier would doubtless have said: "Your majesty is about to confer a favor upon the maiden, for which she can never be sufficiently grateful her whole life long." This speech would have moved the king to wrath, so that he would have commanded the execution of the courtier for high treason against the beloved, and thus he would in still another way have found his grief increased. So he wrestled with his troubled thoughts alone. Would she be happy in the life at his side? Would she be able to summon confidence enough never to remember what the king wished only to forget, that he was king and she had been a humble maiden? For if this memory were to waken in her soul, and like a favored lover sometimes steal her thoughts away from the king, luring her reflections into the seclusion of a secret grief; or if this memory sometimes passed through her soul like the shadow of death over the grave: where would then be the glory of their love? Then she would have been happier had she remained in her obscurity, loved by an equal, content in her humble cottage; but confident in her love, and cheerful early and late. What a rich abundance of grief is here laid bare, like ripened grain bent under the weight of its fruitfulness, merely waiting the time of the harvest, when the thought of the king will thresh out all its seed of sorrow! For even if the maiden would be content to become as nothing, this could not satisfy the king, precisely because he loved her, and because it was harder for him to be her benefactor than to lose her. And suppose she could not even understand him? For while we are thus speaking foolishly of human relationships, we may suppose a difference of mind between them such as to render an understanding impossible. What a depth of grief slumbers not in this unhappy love, who dares to rouse it! However, no human being is destined to suffer such grief; him we may refer to Socrates, or to that which in a still more beautiful sense can make the unequal equal.

But if the *Moment* is to have decisive significance (and if not we return to Socrates even if we think to advance beyond him), the learner is in Error, and that by reason of his own guilt. And yet he is the object of the God's love, and the God desires to teach him, and is concerned to bring him to equality with himself. If this equality cannot be established, the God's love becomes unhappy and his teaching meaningless, since they cannot understand one another. Men sometimes think that this might be a matter of indifference to the God, since he does not stand in need of the learner. But in this we forget—or rather alas! we prove how far we are from understanding him; we forget that the God loves the learner. And just as that kingly grief of which we have spoken can be found only in a kingly soul, and is not even named in the language of the multitude of men, so the entire human language is so selfish that it refuses even to suspect the existence of such a grief. But for that reason the God has reserved it to himself, this unfathomable grief: to know that he may repel the learner, that he does not need him, that the learner has brought destruction upon himself by his own guilt, that he can leave the learner to his fate; to know also how well-nigh impossible it is to keep the learner's courage and confidence alive, without which the purposed under-standing and equality will fail, and the love become un-happy. The man who cannot feel at least some faint intima-tion of this grief is a paltry soul of base coinage, bearing neither the image of Caesar nor the image of God.

Our problem is now before us, and we invite the poet, unless he is already engaged elsewhere, or belongs to the number of those who must be driven out from the house of mourning, together with the flute-players and the other noise-makers, before gladness can enter in. The poet's task will be to find a solution, some point of union, where love's understanding may be realized in truth, the God's anxiety be set at rest, his sorrow banished. For the divine love is that unfathomable love which cannot rest content with that which the beloved might in his folly prize as happiness.

A

The union might be brought about by an elevation of the learner. The God would then take him up unto him-self, transfigure him, fill his cup with millennial joys (for a thousand years are as one day in his sight), and let the learner forget the misunderstanding in tumultuous joy. Alas, the learner might perhaps be greatly inclined to prize such happiness as this. How wonderful suddenly to find his fortune made, like the humble maiden, because the eye of the God happened to rest upon him! And how wonderful also to be his helper in taking all this in vain, deceived by his own heart! Even the noble king could perceive the difficulty of such a method, for he was not without insight into the human heart, and understood that the maiden was at bottom deceived; and no one is so terribly deceived as he who does not himself suspect it, but is as if enchanted by a change in the outward habiliments of his existence.

The union might be brought about by the God's showing himself to the learner and receiving his worship, causing him to forget himself over the divine apparition. Thus the king might have shown himself to the humble maiden in all the pomp of his power, causing the sun of his presence to rise over her cottage, shedding a glory over the scene, and making her forget herself in worshipful admiration. Alas, and this might have satisfied the maiden, but it could not satisfy the king, who desired not his own glorification but hers. It was this that made his grief so hard to bear, his grief that she could not understand him; but it would have been still harder for him to deceive her. And merely to give his love for her an imperfect expression was in his eyes a deception, even though no one understood him and reproaches sought to mortify his soul.

Not in this manner then can their love be made happy, except perhaps in appearance, namely the learner's and the maiden's, but not the Teacher's and the king's, whom no delusion can satisfy. Thus the God takes pleasure in arraying the lily in a garb more glorious than that of Solomon; but if there could be any thought of an understanding here, would it not be a sorry delusion of the lily's, if when it looked upon its fine raiment it thought that it was on account of the raiment that the God loved it? Instead of standing dauntless in the field, sporting with the wind, carefree as the gust that blows, would it not under the influence of such a thought languish and droop, not daring to lift up its head? It was the God's solicitude to prevent this, for the lily's shoot is tender and easily broken. But if the Moment is to have decisive significance, how unspeakable will be the God's anxiety! There once lived a people who had a profound understanding of the divine; this people thought that no man could see the God and live.—Who grasps this contradiction of sorrow: not to reveal oneself is the death of love, to reveal oneself is the death of the beloved! The minds of men so often yearn for might and power, and their thoughts are constantly being drawn to such things, as if by their attainment all mysteries would be resolved. Hence they do not even dream that there is sorrow in heaven as well as joy, the deep grief of having to deny the learner what he yearns for with all his heart, of having to deny him precisely because he is the beloved.

B

The union must therefore be brought about in some other way. Let us here again recall Socrates, for what was the Socratic ignorance if not an expression for his love of the learner, and for his sense of equality with him? But this equality was also the truth, as we have already seen. But if the *Moment* is to have decisive significance (—), this is not the truth, for the learner will owe everything to the Teacher. In the Socratic conception the teacher's love would be merely that of a deceiver if he permitted the disciple to rest in the belief that he really owed him anything, instead of fulfilling the function of the teacher to help the learner become sufficient to himself. But when the God becomes a Teacher, his love cannot be merely seconding and assisting, but is creative, giving a new being to the learner, or as we have called him, the man born anew; by which designation we signify the transition from non-being to being. The truth then is that the learner owes the Teacher everything. But this is what makes it so difficult to effect an understanding: that the learner becomes as nothing and yet is not destroyed; that he comes to owe everything to the Teacher and yet retains his confidence; that he understands the Truth and yet that the Truth makes him free; that he apprehends the guilt of his Error and yet that his confidence rises victorious in the Truth. Between man and man the Socratic midwifery is the highest relation, and begetting is reserved for the God, whose love is *creative*, but not merely in the sense which Socrates so beautifully expounds on a certain festal occasion. This latter kind of begetting does not signify the relation between a teacher and his disciple, but that between an autodidact and the beautiful. In turning away from the scattered beauties of particular things to contemplate beauty in and for itself, the autodidact begets many beautiful and glorious discourses and thoughts, πόλλους καὶ καλοὺς λόγους καὶ μεγαλοπρεπεῖς τίκτει διανοήματα ἐν φιλοσοφίᾳ ἀφθόνῳ (*Symposium*, 210 D). In so doing he begets and brings forth that which he has long borne within him in the seed (209 E). He has the requisite condition in himself, and the bringing forth or birth is merely a manifestation of what was already present; whence here again, in this begetting, the moment vanishes instantly in the eternal consciousness of Recollection. And he who is begotten by a progressive dying away from self, of him it becomes increasingly clear that he can less and less be said to be begotten, since he only becomes more and more clearly reminded of his existence. And when in turn he begets expressions of the beautiful, he does not so much beget them, as he allows the beautiful within him to beget these expressions from itself.

Since we found that the union could not be brought about by an elevation it must be attempted by a descent. Let the learner be x. In this x we must include the lowliest; for if even Socrates refused to establish a false fellowship with the clever, how can we suppose that the God would make a distinction! In order that the union may be brought about, the God must therefore become the equal of such a one, and so he will appear in the likeness of the humblest. But the humblest is one who must serve others, and the God will therefore appear in the form of a *servant*. But this servant-form is no mere outer garment, like the king's beggar-cloak, which therefore flutters loosely about him and betrays the king; it is not like the filmy summer-cloak of Socrates, which though woven of nothing yet both conceals and reveals. It is his true form and figure. For this is the unfathomable nature of love, that it desires equality with the beloved, not in jest merely, but in earnest and truth. And it is the omnipotence of the love which is so resolved that it is able to accomplish its purpose, which neither Socrates nor the king could do, whence their assumed figures constituted after all a kind of deceit.

Behold where he stands—the God! Where? There; do you not see him? He is the God; and yet he has not a resting-place for his head, and he dares not lean on any man lest he cause him to be offended. He is the God; and yet he picks his steps more carefully than if angels guided them, not to prevent his foot from stumbling against a stone, but lest he trample human beings in the dust, in that they are offended in him. He is the God; and yet his eye rests upon mankind with deep concern, for the tender shoots of an individual life may be crushed as easily as a blade of grass. How wonderful a life, all sorrow and all love: to yearn to express the equality of love, and yet to be misunderstood; to apprehend the danger that all men may be destroyed, and yet only so to be able really to save a single soul; his own life filled with sorrow, while each hour of the day is taken up with the troubles of the learner who confides in him! This is the God as he stands upon the earth, like unto the humblest by the power of his omnipotent love. He knows that the learner is in Error— what if he should misunderstand, and droop, and lose his confidence! To sustain the heavens and the earth by the fiat of his omnipotent word, so that if this word were withdrawn for the fraction of a second the universe would be plunged into chaos—how light a task compared with bearing the burden that mankind may take offense, when one has been constrained by love to become its saviour!

But the servant-form is no mere outer garment, and therefore the God must suffer all things, endure all things, make experience of all things. He must suffer hunger in the desert, he must thirst in the time of his agony, he must be forsaken in death, absolutely like the humblest—behold the man! His suffering is not that of his death, but this entire life is a story of suffering; and it is love that suffers, the love which gives all is itself in want. What wonderful self-denial! for though the learner be one of the lowliest, he nevertheless asks him anxiously: Do you now really love me? For he knows where the danger threatens, and yet he also knows that every easier way would involve a deception, even though the learner might not understand it.

Every other form of revelation would be a deception in the eyes of love; for either the learner would first have to be changed, and the fact concealed from him that this was necessary (but love does not alter the beloved, it alters itself); or there would be permitted to prevail a frivolous ignorance of the fact that the entire relationship was a delusion. (This was the error of paganism.) Every other form of revelation would be a deception from the standpoint of the divine love. And if my eyes were more filled with tears than those of a repentant woman, and if each tear were more precious than a pardoned woman's many tears; if I could find a place more humble than the place at his feet, and if I could sit there more humbly than a woman whose heart's sole choice was this one thing needful; if I loved him more sincerely than the most loyal of his servants, eager to shed the last drop of his life-blood in his service; if I had found greater favor in his eyes than the purest among women—nevertheless, if I asked him to alter his purpose, to reveal himself differently, to be more lenient with himself, he would doubtless look at me and say: Man, what have I to do with thee? Get thee hence, for thou art Satan, though thou knowest it not! Or if he once or twice stretched forth his hand in command, and it happened, and I then meant to understand him better or love him more, I would doubtless see him weep also over me, and hear him say: To think that you could prove so faithless, and so wound my love! Is it then only the omnipotent wonder-worker that you love, and not him who humbled himself to become your equal?

But the servant-form is no mere outer garment; hence he must yield his spirit in death and again leave the earth. And if my grief were deeper than the sorrow of a mother when her heart is pierced by the sword, and if my danger were more terrible than the danger of a believer when his faith fails him, and if my misery were more pitiful than his who crucifies his hope and has nothing left but the cross—nevertheless, if I begged him to save his life and stay upon the earth, it would only be to see him sorrowful unto death, and stricken with grief also for my sake, because this suffering was for my profit, and now I had added to his sorrow the burden that I could not understand him. O bitter cup! More bitter than wormwood is the bitterness of death for a mortal, how bitter then for an immortal! O bitter refreshment, more bitter than aloes, to be refreshed by the misunderstanding of the beloved! O solace in affliction to suffer as one who is guilty, what solace then to suffer as one who is innocent!

Such will be our poet's picture. For how could it enter his mind that the God would reveal himself in this way in order to bring men to the most crucial and terrible decision; how could he find it in his heart to play frivolously with the God's sorrow, falsely poetizing his love away to poetize his wrath in!

And now the learner, has he no lot or part in this story of suffering, even though his lot cannot be that of the Teacher? Aye, it cannot be otherwise. And the cause of all this suffering is love, precisely because the God is not jealous for himself, but desires in love to be the equal of the humblest. When the seed of the oak is planted in earthen vessels, they break asunder; when new wine is poured in old leathern bottles, they burst; what must happen when the God implants himself in human weakness, unless man becomes a new vessel and a new creature! But this becoming, what labors will attend the change, how convulsed with birth-pangs! And the understanding— how precarious, and how close each moment to misunderstanding, when the anguish of guilt seeks to disturb the peace of love! And how rapt in fear; for it is indeed less terrible to fall to the ground when the mountains tremble at the voice of the God, than to sit at table with him as an equal; and yet it is the God's concern precisely to have it so.

* *

Now if someone were to say: "This poem of yours is the most wretched piece of plagiarism ever perpetrated, for it is neither more nor less than what every child knows," I suppose I must blush with shame to hear myself called a liar. But why the most wretched? Every poet who steals, steals from some other poet, and in so far we are all equally wretched; indeed, my own theft is perhaps less harmful, since it is more readily discovered. If I were to be so polite as to ascribe the authorship to you who now condemn me, you would perhaps again be angry. Is there then no poet, although there is a poem? This would surely be strange, as strange as flute-playing without a flute-player. Or is this poem perhaps like a proverb, for which no author can be assigned, because it is as if it owed its existence to humanity at large; was this perhaps the reason you called my theft the most wretched, because I did not steal from any individual man but robbed the human race, and arrogantly, although I am only an individual man, aye, even a wretched thief, pretended to be mankind? If this then is the case, and I went about to all men in turn, and all knew the poem, but each one also knew that he was not the author of it, can I then conclude: mankind must be the author? Would not this be a strange conclusion? For if mankind were the author of this poem, this would have to be expressed by considering every individual equally close to the authorship. Does it not seem to you that this is a difficult case in which we have become involved, though the whole matter appeared to be so easily disposed of in the beginning, by your short and angry word about its being the most wretched plagiarism, and my shame in having to hear it? So then perhaps it is no poem, or at any rate not one for which any human being is responsible, nor yet mankind; ah, now I understand you, it was for this reason you called my procedure the most wretched act of plagiarism, because I did not steal from any individual, nor from the race, but from the God or, as it were, stole the God away, and though I am only an individual man, aye, even a wretched thief, blasphemously pretended to be the God. Now I understand you fully, dear friend, and recognize the justice of your resentment. But then my soul is filled with new wonder, even more, with the spirit of worship; for it would surely have been strange had this poem been a human production. It is not impossible that it might occur to man to imagine himself the equal of the God, or to imagine the God the equal of man, but not to imagine that the God would make himself into the likeness of man; for if the God gave no sign, how could it enter into the mind of man that the blessed God should need him? This would be a most stupid thought, or rather, so stupid a thought could never have entered into his mind; though when the God has seen fit to entrust him with it he exclaims in worship: This thought did not arise in my own heart! and finds it a most miraculously beautiful thought. And is it not altogether miraculous, and does not this word come as a happy omen to my lips; for as I have just said, and as you yourself involuntarily exclaim, we stand here before the *Miracle*. And as we both now stand before this miracle, whose solemn silence cannot be perturbed by human wrangling over mine and thine, whose awe-inspiring speech infinitely subdues all human strife about mine and thine, forgive me, I pray, the strange delusion that I was the author of this poem. It was a delusion, and the poem is so different from every human poem as not to be a poem at all, but the *Miracle*.

CHAPTER III

The Absolute Paradox: A Metaphysical Crotchet

In spite of the fact that Socrates studied with all diligence to acquire a knowledge of human nature and to understand himself, and in spite of the fame accorded him through the centuries as one who beyond all other men had an insight into the human heart, he has himself admitted that the reason for his shrinking from reflection upon the nature of such beings as Pegasus and the Gorgons was that he, the life-long student of human nature, had not yet been able to make up his mind whether he was a stranger monster than Typhon, or a creature of a gentler and simpler sort, partaking of something divine (*Phaedrus*, 229 E). This seems to be a paradox. However, one should not think slightingly of the paradoxical; for the paradox is the source of the thinker's passion, and the thinker without a paradox is like a lover without feeling: a paltry mediocrity. But the highest pitch of every passion is always to will its own downfall; and so it is also the supreme passion of the Reason to seek a collision, though this collision must in one way or another prove its undoing. The supreme paradox of all thought is the attempt to discover something that thought cannot think. This passion is at bottom present in all thinking, even in the thinking of the individual, in so far as in thinking he participates in something transcending himself. But habit dulls our sensibilities, and prevents us from perceiving it. So for example the scientists tell us that our walking is a constant falling. But a sedate and proper gentleman who walks to his office in the morning and back again at noon, probably thinks this to be an exaggeration, for his progress is clearly a case of mediation; how should it occur to him that he is constantly falling when he religiously follows his nose!

But in order to make a beginning, let us now assume a daring proposition; let us assume that we know what man is.[1] Here we have that criterion of the Truth, which in the whole course of Greek philosophy was either *sought*, or *doubted*, or *postulated*, or *made fruitful*. Is it not remarkable that the Greeks should have borne us this testimony? And is it not an epitome, as it were, of the significance of Greek culture, an epigram of its own writing, with which it is also better served than with the frequently voluminous disquisitions sometimes devoted to it? Thus the proposition is well worth positing, and also for another reason, since we have already explained it in the two preceding chapters; while anyone who attempts to explain Socrates differently may well beware lest he fall into the snare of the earlier or later Greek scepticism. For unless we hold fast to the Socratic doctrine of Recollection, and to his principle that every individual man is Man,

[1] It may seem ridiculous to give this proposition a doubtful form by "assuming" it, for in this theocentric age such matters are of course known to all. Aye, if it were only so well with us! Democritus also knew what man is, for he defines man as follows: "Man is what we all know," and then goes on to say: "for we all know what a dog, a horse, a plant is, and so forth; but none of these is a man." We do not aspire to the malice of Sextus Empiricus, nor have we his wit; for he concludes as we know, from the above definition, and quite correctly, that man is a dog; for man is what we all know, and we all know what a dog is, *ergo*—but let us not be so malicious. Nevertheless, has this question been so thoroughly cleared up in our own time that no one need feel a little uneasy about himself when he is reminded of poor Socrates and his predicament?

Sextus Empiricus stands ready to make the transition involved in "teaching" not only difficult but impossible; and Protagoras will begin where Sextus Empiricus leaves off, maintaining that man is the measure of all things, in the sense that the individual man is the measure for others, but by no means in the Socratic sense that each man is his own measure, neither more nor less.

So then we know what man is, and this wisdom, which I shall be the last to hold in light esteem, may progressively become richer and more significant, and with it also the Truth. But now the Reason stands still, just as Socrates did; for the paradoxical passion of the Reason is aroused and seeks a collision; without rightly understanding itself, it is bent upon its own downfall. This is like what happens in connection with the paradox of love. Man lives undisturbed a self-centered life, until there awakens within him the paradox of self-love, in the form of love for another, the object of his longing. (Self-love lies as the ground of all love or is the ground in which all love perishes; therefore if we conceive a religion of love, this religion need make but one assumption, as epigrammatic as true, and take its actuality for granted, namely, the condition that man loves himself, in order to command him to love his neighbor as himself.) The lover is so completely transformed by the paradox of love that he scarcely recognizes himself; so say the poets, who are the spokesmen of love, and so say also the lovers themselves, since they permit the poets merely to take the words from their lips, but not the passion from their hearts. In like manner the paradoxical passion of the Reason, while as yet a mere presentiment, retroactively affects man and his self-knowledge, so that he who thought to know himself is no longer certain whether he is a more strangely composite animal than Typhon, or if perchance his nature contains a gentler and diviner part. (σκοπῶ οὐ ταῦτα, ἀλλὰ ἐμαυτόν, εἴτε τι θηρίον ὢν τυγκάνω πολυπλοκώτερον καὶ μᾶλλον ἐπιτεθυμμένον εἴτε ἡμερώτερόν τε καὶ ἁπλούστερον ζῷον, θείας τινὸς καὶ ἀτύφου μοίρας φύσει μετέχον. *Phaedrus*, 230 A).

But what is this unknown something with which the Reason collides when inspired by its paradoxical passion, with the result of unsettling even man's knowledge of himself? It is the Unknown. It is not a human being, in so far as we know what man is; nor is it any other known thing. So let us call this unknown something: *the God*. It is nothing more than a name we assign to it. The idea of demonstrating that this unknown something (the God) exists, could scarcely suggest itself to the Reason. For if the God does not exist it would of course be impossible to prove it; and if he does exist it would be folly to attempt it. For at the very outset, in beginning my proof, I would have presupposed it, not as doubtful but as certain (a presupposition is never doubtful, for the very reason that it is a presupposition), since otherwise I would not begin, readily understanding that the whole would be impossible if he did not exist. But if when I speak of proving the God's existence I mean that I propose to prove that the Unknown, which exists, is the God, then I express myself unfortunately. For in that case I do not prove anything, least of all an existence, but merely develop the content of a conception. Generally speaking, it is a difficult matter to prove that anything exists; and what is still worse for the intrepid souls who undertake the venture, the difficulty is such that fame scarcely awaits those who concern themselves with it. The entire demonstration

always turns into something very different and becomes
an additional development of the consequences that flow
from my having assumed that the object in question exists.
Thus I always reason from existence, not toward existence,
whether I move in the sphere of palpable sensible fact or
in the realm of thought. I do not, for example, prove that
a stone exists, but that some existing thing is a stone. The
procedure in a court of justice does not prove that a
criminal exists, but that the accused, whose existence is
given, is a criminal. Whether we call existence an *accessorium* or the eternal *prius*, it is never subject to demonstration. Let us take ample time for consideration. We
have no such reason for haste as have those who from concern for themselves or for the God or for some other thing,
must make haste to get existence demonstrated. Under
such circumstances there may indeed be need for haste,
especially if the prover sincerely seeks to appreciate the
danger that he himself, or the thing in question, may be
non-existent unless the proof is finished and does not
surreptitiously entertain the thought that it exists whether
he succeeds in proving it or not.

If it were proposed to prove Napoleon's existence from
Napoleon's deeds, would it not be a most curious proceeding? His existence does indeed explain his deeds, but the
deeds do not prove *his* existence, unless I have already
understood the word "his" so as thereby to have assumed
his existence. But Napoleon is only an individual, and in
so far there exists no absolute relationship between him
and his deeds; some other person might have performed
the same deeds. Perhaps this is the reason why I cannot
pass from the deeds to existence. If I call these deeds the
deeds of Napoleon the proof becomes superfluous, since I

have already named him; if I ignore this, I can never prove from the deeds that they are Napoleon's, but only in a purely ideal manner that such deeds are the deeds of a great general, and so forth. But between the God and his works there is an absolute relationship; the God is not a name but a concept. Is this perhaps the reason that his *essentia involvit existentiam*?[2] The works of God

[2] So Spinoza, who probes the depths of the God-idea in order to bring being out of it by way of thought, but not, it should be noted, as if being were an accidental characteristic, but rather as if it constituted an essential determination of content. Here lies Spinoza's profundity, but let us examine his reasoning. In *principia philosophiae Cartesianae, pars I, propositio VII, lemma I*, he says: "*quo res sua natura perfectior est, eo majorem existentiam et magis necessariam involvit; et contra, quo magis necessariam existentiam res sua natura involvit, eo perfectior.*" The more perfect therefore a thing is, the more being it has; the more being it has, the more perfect it is. This is however a tautology, which becomes still more evident in a note, *nota II: "quod hic non loquimur de pulchritudine et aliis perfectionibus, quas homines ex superstitione et ignorantia perfectiones vocare voluerunt. Sed per perfectionem intelligo tantum realitatem sive esse.*" He explains *perfectio* by *realitas, esse*; so that the more perfect a thing is, the more it is; but its perfection consists in having more *esse* in itself; that is to say, the more a thing is, the more it is. So much for the tautology, but now further. What is lacking here is a distinction between factual being and ideal being. The terminology which permits us to speak of more or less of being, and consequently of degrees of reality or being, is in itself lacking in clearness, and becomes still more confusing when the above distinction is neglected—in other words, when Spinoza does indeed speak profoundly but fails first to consider the difficulty. In the case of factual being it is meaningless to speak of more or less of being. A fly, when it is, has as much being as the God; with respect to factual being the stupid remark I here set down has as much being as Spinoza's profundity, for factual being is subject to the dialectic of Hamlet: to be or not to be. Factual being is wholly indifferent to any and all variations in essence, and everything that exists participates without petty jealousy in being,

are such that only the God can perform them. Just so, but where then are the works of the God? The works from which I would deduce his existence are not directly and immediately given. The wisdom in nature, the goodness, the wisdom in the governance of the world—are all these manifest, perhaps, upon the very face of things? Are we not here confronted with the most terrible temptations to doubt, and is it not impossible finally to dispose of all these doubts? But from such an order of things I will surely not attempt to prove God's existence; and even if I began I would never finish, and would in addition have to live constantly in suspense, lest something so terrible should suddenly happen that my bit of proof would be demolished. From what works then do I propose to derive the proof? From the works as apprehended through an ideal interpretation, i.e., such as they do not immediately reveal themselves. But in that case it is not from the works that I make the proof; I merely develop the ideality I have presupposed, and because of my confidence in *this* I make so bold as to defy all objections, even those that have not yet been made. In beginning my proof I presuppose the

---

and participates in the same degree. Ideally, to be sure, the case is quite different. *But the moment I speak of being in the ideal sense I no longer speak of being, but of essence.* Highest ideality has this necessity and therefore it is. But this its being is identical with its essence; such being does not involve it dialectically in the determinations of factual being, since it is; nor can it be said to have more or less of being in relation to other things. In the old days this used to be expressed, if somewhat imperfectly, by saying that if God is possible, he is *eo ipso* necessary (Leibniz). Spinoza's principle is thus quite correct and his tautology in order; but it is also certain that he altogether evades the difficulty. For the difficulty is to lay hold of God's factual being and to introduce God's ideal essence dialectically into the sphere of factual being.

ideal interpretation, and also that I will be successful in carrying it through; but what else is this but to presuppose that the God exists, so that I really begin by virtue of confidence in him?

And how does the God's existence emerge from the proof? Does it follow straightway, without any breach of continuity? Or have we not here an analogy to the behaviour of the little Cartesian dolls? As soon as I let go of the doll it stands on its head. As soon as I let it go—I must therefore let it go. So also with the proof. As long as I keep my hold on the proof, i.e., continue to demonstrate, the existence does not come out, if for no other reason than that I am engaged in proving it; but when I let the proof go, the existence is there. But this act of letting go is surely also something; it is indeed a contribution of mine. Must not this also be taken into the account, this little moment, brief as it may be—it need not be long, for it is a *leap*. However brief this moment, if only an instantaneous now, this "now" must be included in the reckoning. If anyone wishes to have it ignored, I will use it to tell a little anecdote, in order to show that it nevertheless does exist. Chrysippus was experimenting with a sorites to see if he could not bring about a break in its quality, either progressively or retrogressively. But Carneades could not get it in his head when the new quality actually emerged. Then Chrysippus told him to try making a little pause in the reckoning, and so—so it would be easier to understand. Carneades replied: With the greatest pleasure, please do not hesitate on my account; you may not only pause, but even lie down to sleep, and it will help you just as little; for when you awake we will begin again where you left off. Just so; it boots as little to try to get rid of something by sleeping as to try to come into the possession of something in the same manner.

Whoever therefore attempts to demonstrate the existence of God (except in the sense of clarifying the concept, and without the *reservatio finalis* noted above, that the existence emerges from the demonstration by a leap) proves in lieu thereof something else, something which at times perhaps does not need a proof, and in any case needs none better; for the fool says in his heart that there is no God, but whoever says in his heart or to men: Wait just a little and I will prove it—what a rare man of wisdom is he![3] If in the moment of beginning his proof it is not absolutely undetermined whether the God exists or not, he does not prove it; and if it is thus undetermined in the beginning he will never come to begin, partly from fear of failure, since the God perhaps does not exist, and partly because he has nothing with which to begin.—A project of this kind would scarcely have been undertaken by the ancients. Socrates at least, who is credited with having put forth the physico-teleological proof for God's existence, did not go about it in any such manner. He always presupposes the God's existence, and under this presupposition seeks to interpenetrate nature with the idea of purpose. Had he been asked why he pursued this method, he would doubtless have explained that he lacked the courage to venture out upon so perilous a voyage of discovery without having made sure of the God's existence behind him. At the word of the God he casts his net as if to catch the idea of purpose; for nature herself finds many means of frightening the inquirer, and distracts him by many a digression.

[3] What an excellent subject for a comedy of the higher lunacy!

The paradoxical passion of the Reason thus comes repeatedly into collision with this Unknown, which does indeed exist, but is unknown, and in so far does not exist. The Reason cannot advance beyond this point, and yet it cannot refrain in its paradoxicalness from arriving at this limit and occupying itself therewith. It will not serve to dismiss its relation to it simply by asserting that the Unknown does not exist, since this itself involves a relationship. But what then is the Unknown, since the designation of it as the God merely signifies for us that it is unknown? To say that it is the Unknown because it cannot be known, and even if it were capable of being known, it could not be expressed, does not satisfy the demands of passion, though it correctly interprets the Unknown as a limit; but a limit is precisely a torment for passion, though it also serves as an incitement. And yet the Reason can come no further, whether it risks an issue *via negationis* or *via eminentia*.

What then is the Unknown? It is the limit to which the Reason repeatedly comes, and in so far, substituting a static form of conception for the dynamic, it is the different, the absolutely different. But because it is absolutely different, there is no mark by which it could be distinguished. When qualified as absolutely different it seems on the verge of disclosure, but this is not the case; for the Reason cannot even conceive an absolute unlikeness. The Reason cannot negate itself absolutely, but uses itself for the purpose, and thus conceives only such an unlikeness within itself as it can conceive by means of itself; it cannot absolutely transcend itself, and hence conceives only such a superiority over itself as it can conceive by means of itself. Unless the Unknown (the God) remains a mere limiting conception, the single idea of difference will be thrown into a state of confusion, and become many ideas of many differences. The Unknown is then in a condition of dispersion (διασπορά), and the Reason may choose at pleasure from what is at hand and the imagination may suggest (the monstrous, the ludicrous, etc.).

But it is impossible to hold fast to a difference of this nature. Every time this is done it is essentially an arbitrary act, and deepest down in the heart of piety lurks the mad caprice which knows that it has itself produced the God. If no specific determination of difference can be held fast, because there is no distinguishing mark, like and unlike finally become identified with one another, thus sharing the fate of all such dialectical opposites. The unlikeness clings to the Reason and confounds it, so that the Reason no longer knows itself and quite consistently confuses itself with the unlikeness. On this point paganism has been sufficiently prolific in fantastic inventions. As for the last named supposition, the self-irony of the Reason, I shall attempt to delineate it merely by a stroke or two, without raising any question of its being historical. There exists an individual whose appearance is precisely like that of other men; he grows up to manhood like others, he marries, he has an occupation by which he earns his livelihood, and he makes provision for the future as befits a man. For though it may be beautiful to live like the birds of the air, it is not lawful, and may lead to the sorriest of consequences: either starvation if one has enough persistence, or dependence on the bounty of others. This man is also the God. How do I know? I cannot know it, for in order to know it I would have to know the God, and the nature of the difference between the God and man; and this I cannot know, because the Reason has reduced it to likeness with that from which it was unlike. Thus the God becomes the most terrible of deceivers, because the Reason has deceived itself. The Reason has brought the God as near as possible, and yet he is as far away as ever.

* *

Now perhaps someone will say: "You are certainly a crotcheteer, as I know very well. But you surely do not believe that I would pay any attention to such a crotchet, so strange or so ridiculous that it has doubtless never occurred to anyone, and above all so absurd that I must exclude from my consciousness everything that I have in it in order to hit upon it."—And so indeed you must. But do you think yourself warranted in retaining all the presuppositions you have in your consciousness, while pretending to think about your consciousness without presuppositions? Will you deny the consistency of our exposition: that the Reason, in attempting to determine the Unknown as the unlike, at last goes astray, and confounds the unlike with the like? From this there would seem to follow the further consequence, that if man is to receive any true knowledge about the Unknown (the God) he must be made to know that it is unlike him, absolutely unlike him. This knowledge the Reason cannot possibly obtain of itself; we have already seen that this would be a self-contradiction. It will therefore have to obtain this knowledge from the God. But even if it obtains such knowledge it cannot understand it, and thus is quite unable to possess such knowledge. For how should the Reason be able to understand what is absolutely different from itself? If this is not immediately evident, it will become clearer in the

light of the consequences; for if the God is absolutely
unlike man, then man is absolutely unlike the God; but
how could the Reason be expected to understand this?
Here we seem to be confronted with a paradox. Merely to
obtain the knowledge that the God is unlike him, man
needs the help of the God; and now he learns that the God
is absolutely different from himself. But if the God and
man are absolutely different, this cannot be accounted for
on the basis of what man derives from the God, for in
so far they are akin. Their unlikeness must therefore be
explained by what man derives from himself, or by what
he has brought upon his own head. But what can this
unlikeness be? Aye, what can it be but sin; since the unlikeness, the absolute unlikeness, is something that man has
brought upon himself. We have expressed this in the
preceding by saying that man was in Error, and had
brought this upon his head by his own guilt; and we came
to the conclusion, partly in jest and yet also in earnest,
that it was too much to expect of man that he should find
this out for himself. Now we have again arrived at the
same conclusion. The connoisseur in self-knowledge was
perplexed over himself to the point of bewilderment when
he came to grapple in thought with the unlike; he scarcely
knew any longer whether he was a stranger monster than
Typhon, or if his nature partook of something divine.
What then did he lack? The consciousness of sin, which
he indeed could no more teach to another than another
could teach it to him, but only the God—if the God consents to become a Teacher. But this was his purpose, as
we have imagined it. In order to be man's Teacher, the
God proposed to make himself like the individual man,

so that he might understand him fully. Thus our paradox is rendered still more appalling, or the same paradox has the double aspect which proclaims it as the Absolute Paradox; negatively by revealing the absolute unlikeness of sin, positively by proposing to do away with the absolute unlikeness in absolute likeness.

But can such a paradox be conceived? Let us not be over-hasty in replying; and since we strive merely to find the answer to a question, and not as those who run a race, it may be well to remember that success is to the accurate rather than to the swift. The Reason will doubtless find it impossible to conceive it, could not of itself have discovered it, and when it hears it announced will not be able to understand it, sensing merely that its downfall is threatened. In so far the Reason will have much to urge against it; and yet we have on the other hand seen that the Reason, in its paradoxical passion, precisely desires its own downfall. But this is what the Paradox also desires, and thus they are at bottom linked in understanding; but this understanding is present only in the moment of passion. Consider the analogy presented by love, though it is not a perfect one. Self-love lies as the ground of love; but the paradoxical passion of self-love when at its highest pitch wills precisely its own downfall. This is also what love desires, so that these two are linked in mutual understanding in the passion of the moment, and this passion is love. Why should not the lover find this conceivable? But he who in self-love shrinks from the touch of love can neither understand it nor summon the courage to venture it, since it means his downfall. Such is then the passion of love; self-love is indeed submerged but not annihilated; it is taken captive and become love's *spolia opima*, but may again come to life, and this is love's temptation. So also with the Paradox in its relation to the Reason, only that the passion in this case has another name; or rather, we must seek to find a name for it.

APPENDIX

The Paradox and the Offended Consciousness

(AN ACOUSTIC ILLUSION)

If the Paradox and the Reason come together in a mutual understanding of their unlikeness their encounter will be happy, like love's understanding, happy in the passion to which we have not yet assigned a name, and will postpone naming until later. If the encounter is not in understanding the relationship becomes unhappy, and this unhappy love of the Reason if I may so call it (which it should be noted is analogous only to that particular form of unhappy love which has its root in misunderstood self-love; no further stretching of the analogy is possible, since accident can play no role in this realm), may be characterized more specifically as *Offense*.

All offense is in its deepest root passive.[4] In this respect it is like that form of unhappy love to which we have just alluded. Even when such a self-love (and does it not already seem contradictory that love of self should be passive?) announces itself in deeds of audacious daring, in astounding achievements, it is passive and wounded. It is the pain of its wound which gives it this illusory strength, expressing itself in what looks like self-activity and may easily deceive, since self-love is especially bent on concealing its passivity. Even when it tramples on the object of

---

[4] The Danish language correctly calls emotion (Dan. *"Affekten"*) 'Sinds*lidelse*' [compare Ger. *"Leiden*schaft"]. When we use the word *"Affekt"* we are likely to think more immediately of the convulsive daring which astounds us, and makes us forget that it is a form of passivity. So for example: pride, defiance, etc.

affection, even when it painfully schools itself to a hardened indifference and tortures itself to show this indifference, even then, even when it abandons itself to a frivolous triumph over its success (this form is the most deceptive of all), even then it is passive. Such is also the case with the offended consciousness. Whatever be its mode of expression, even when it exultantly celebrates the triumph of its unspirituality, it is always passive. Whether the offended individual sits broken-hearted, staring almost like a beggar at the Paradox, paralyzed by his suffering, or he sheathes himself in the armor of derision, pointing the arrows of his wit as if from a distance—he is still passive and near at hand. Whether offense came and robbed the offended individual of his last bit of comfort and joy, or made him strong—the offended consciousness is nevertheless passive. It has wrestled with the stronger, and its show of strength is like the peculiar agility induced in the bodily sphere by a broken back.

However, it is quite possible to distinguish between an active and a passive form of the offended consciousness, if we take care to remember that the passive form is so far active as not to permit itself wholly to be annihilated (for offense is always an act, never an event); and that the active form is always so weak that it cannot free itself from the cross to which it is nailed, or tear the arrow from out its wound.[5]

[5] The idiom of the language also supports the view that all offense is passive. We say: "to be offended," which primarily expresses only the state or condition; but we also say, as identical in meaning with the foregoing: "to take offense," which expresses a synthesis of active and passive. The Greek word is σκανδαλίζεσθαι. This word comes from σκάνδαλον (offense or stumbling-block),

But precisely because offense is thus passive, the discovery, if it be allowable to speak thus, does not derive from the Reason, but from the Paradox; for as the Truth is *index sui et falsi*, the Paradox is this also, and the offended consciousness does not understand itself[6] but is understood by the Paradox. While therefore the expressions in which offense proclaims itself, of whatever kind they may be, sound as if they came from elsewhere, even from the opposite direction, they are nevertheless echoings of the Paradox. This is what is called an acoustic illusion. But if the Paradox is *index* and *judex sui et falsi*, the offended consciousness can be taken as an indirect proof of the validity of the Paradox; offense is the mistaken reckoning, the invalid consequence, with which the Paradox repels and thrusts aside. The offended individual does not speak from his own resources, but borrows those of the Paradox; just as one who mimics or parodies another does not invent, but merely copies perversely. The more profound the passion with which the offended consciousness (active or passive) expresses itself, the more apparent it is how much it owes to the Paradox. Offense was not discovered by the Reason, far from it, for then the Reason must also have been able to discover the Paradox. No,

---

and hence means to take offense, or to collide with something. Here the movement of thought is clearly indicated; it is not that offense provokes the collision, but that it meets with a collision, and hence passively, although so far actively as itself to take offense. Hence the Reason is not the discoverer of offense; for the paradoxical collision which the Reason develops in isolation discovers neither the Paradox nor the reaction of offense.

[6] In this sense the Socratic principle that sin is ignorance finds justification. Sin does not understand itself in the Truth, but it does not follow that it may not will itself in Error.

offense comes into existence with the Paradox; it *comes into existence*. Here again we have the Moment, on which everything depends. Let us recapitulate. If we do not posit the Moment we return to Socrates; but it was precisely from him that we departed, in order to discover something. If we posit the Moment the Paradox is there; for the Moment is the Paradox in its most abbreviated form. Because of the Moment the learner is in Error; and man, who had before possessed self-knowledge, now becomes bewildered with respect to himself; instead of self-knowledge he receives the consciousness of sin, and so forth; for as soon as we posit the Moment everything follows of itself.

From the psychological point of view the offended consciousness will display a great variety of nuances within the more active and the more passive forms. To enter into a detailed description of these would not further our present purpose; but it is important to bear fixedly in mind that all offense is in its essence a misunderstanding of the Moment, since it is directed against the Paradox, which again is the Moment.

The dialectic of the Moment is not difficult. From the Socratic point of view the Moment is invisible and indistinguishable; it is not, it has not been, it will not come. Hence the learner is himself the Truth, and the moment of occasion is but a jest, like a bastard title that does not essentially belong to the book. From this point of view the Moment of decision becomes *folly*; for if a decision in time is postulated, then (by the preceding) the learner is in Error, which is precisely what makes a beginning in the Moment necessary. The reaction of the offended consciousness is to assert that the Moment is folly, and that the Paradox is folly, which is the contention of the Paradox that the Reason is absurd now reflected back as in an echo from the offended consciousness. Or the Moment is regarded as constantly about to come; it is so regarded, and the Reason holds it as *worthy of regard*; but since the Paradox has made the Reason absurd, the regard of the Reason is no reliable criterion.

The offended consciousness holds aloof from the Paradox, and the reason is: *quia absurdum*. But it was not the Reason that made this discovery; on the contrary it was the Paradox that made the discovery, and now receives this testimony from the offended consciousness. The Reason says that the Paradox is absurd, but this is mere mimicry, since the Paradox is the Paradox, *quia absurdum*. The offended consciousness holds aloof from the Paradox and keeps to the probable, since the Paradox is the most improbable of things. Again it is not the Reason that made this discovery; it merely snatches the words from the mouth of the Paradox, strange as this may seem; for the Paradox itself says: Comedies and romances and lies must needs be probable, but why should I be probable? The offended consciousness holds aloof from the Paradox, and what wonder, since the Paradox is the Miracle! This discovery was not made by the Reason; it was the Paradox that placed the Reason on the stool of wonderment and now replies: But why are you so astonished? It is precisely as you say, and the only wonder is that you regard it as an objection; but the truth in the mouth of a hypocrite is dearer to me than if it came from the lips of an angel or an apostle. When the Reason boasts of its splendors in comparison with the Paradox, which is most wretched and despised, the discovery was not made by the Reason but by the Paradox itself; it is content to leave to the Reason all its splendors, even the splendid sins (*vitia splendida*). When the Reason takes pity on the Paradox, and wishes to help it to an explanation, the Paradox does not indeed acquiesce, but nevertheless finds it quite natural that the Reason should do this; for why do we have our philosophers, if not to make supernatural things trivial and commonplace? When the Reason says that it cannot get the Paradox into its head, it was not the Reason that made the discovery but the Paradox, which is so paradoxical as to declare the Reason a blockhead and a dunce, capable at the most of saying yes and no to the same thing, which is not good divinity. And so always. All that the offended consciousness has to say about the Paradox it has learned from the Paradox, though it would like to pose as the discoverer, making use of an acoustic illusion.

*   *

But I think I hear someone say: "It is really becoming tiresome the way you go on, for now we have the same story over again; not one of the expressions you have put into the mouth of the Paradox belongs to you."—"Why should they belong to me, when they belong to the Paradox?"—"You can spare us your sophistry, you know very well what I mean. These expressions are not yours, nor by you put into the mouth of the Paradox, but are familiar quotations, and everybody knows who the authors are."— "My friend, your accusation does not grieve me, as you perhaps believe; what you say rather makes me exceedingly glad. For I must admit that I could not repress a shudder when I wrote them down; I scarcely recognized myself, that I who am usually so timid and apprehensive dared say such things. But if the expressions are not by me, perhaps you will explain to whom they belong?"—"Nothing is easier. The first is by Tertullian, the second by Hamann, the third by Hamann, the fourth is by Lactantius and is frequently quoted; the fifth is by Shakespeare, in a comedy called *All's Well that Ends Well*, Act II, Scene iii; the sixth is by Luther, and the seventh is a remark by King Lear. You see that I am well informed, and that I have caught you with the goods."—"Indeed I do perceive it; but will you now tell me whether all these men have not spoken of the relation between some paradox and an offended consciousness, and will you now note that the individuals who spoke thus were not themselves offended, but precisely persons who held to the paradox; and yet they speak as if they were offended, and offense cannot find a more characteristic expression for itself. Is it not strange that the Paradox should thus, as it were, take the bread from the mouth of the offended consciousness, reducing it to the practice of an idle and unprofitable art? It seems as curious as if an opponent at a disputation, instead of attacking the author's thesis, defended him in his distraction. Does it not seem so to you? However, one merit unquestionably belongs to the offended consciousness in that it brings out the unlikeness more clearly; for in that happy passion which we have not yet given a name, the Unlike is on good terms with the Reason. There must be a difference if there is to be a synthesis in some third entity. But here the difference consisted in the fact that the Reason yielded itself while the Paradox bestowed itself (*halb zog sie ihn, halb sank er hin*), and the understanding is consummated in that happy passion which will doubtless soon find a name; and this is the smallest part of the matter, for even if my happiness does not have a name —when I am but happy, I ask for no more."

CHAPTER IV

The Case of the Contemporary Disciple

THE God has thus made his appearance as Teacher (for we now resume our story), and has assumed the form of a servant. To send another in his place, one high in his confidence, could not satisfy him; just as it could not satisfy the noble king to send in his stead even the most trusted man in his kingdom. But the God had also another reason; for between man and man the Socratic relationship is the highest and truest. If the God had not come himself, all the relations would have remained on the Socratic level; we would not have had the Moment, and we would have lost the Paradox. The God's servant-form however is not a mere disguise, but is actual; it is not a parastatic body but an actual body; and from the hour that in the omnipotent purpose of his omnipotent love the God become a servant, he has so to speak imprisoned himself in his resolve, and is now bound to go on (to speak foolishly) whether it pleases him or no. He cannot then betray himself. There exists for him no such possibility as that which is open to the noble king, suddenly to show that he is after all the king—which is no perfection in the king (that he has this possibility), but merely discloses his impotence, and the impotence of his resolve, that he cannot really become what he desires to be. But while the God will not be able to send anyone in his place, he can indeed send someone before him, to arouse the learner's attention. This forerunner can of course know nothing of what the God will teach. For the God's presence is not accidental in relation to his teaching, but essential. The God's presence in human form, aye in the humble form of a servant, is itself the teaching, and the God must give the condition along with it (Chapter I) or the learner will understand nothing. Such a forerunner may then serve to arouse the learner's attention, but nothing more.

But the God did not assume the form of a servant to make a mockery of men; hence it cannot be his intention to pass through the world in such manner that no single human being becomes aware of his presence. He will therefore doubtless give some sort of sign, though every understanding resting upon an accommodation is essentially without value for one who does not receive the condition; for which reason he yields to the necessity only unwillingly. Such a sign when given is as capable of repelling the learner as of drawing him nearer. He humbled himself and took upon him the form of a servant, but he did not come to spend his life as a servant in some private employment, attending to his tasks without in any manner making himself known, either to his master or to his fellow servants—such a measure of wrath we dare not ascribe to the God. That he was a servant means then only that he was a common man, humble and lowly, not to be distinguished from the multitude of men either by soft raiment or other earthly advantages, nor yet by the innumerable legions of angels he left behind him when he humbled himself. But though in these ways resembling common men, his thoughts and cares are not like those which fill the minds of men in general. He goes his way indifferent to the distribution and division of earthly goods, as one who has no possessions and desires none; he is not concerned for his daily bread, like the birds of the air; he does not trouble himself about house and home, as one who neither has nor seeks a shelter or a resting-place; he is not concerned to follow the dead to the grave; he does not turn his head to look at the things that usually claim the attention of men; he is not bound to any woman, so as to be charmed by her and desirous of pleasing her. He seeks one thing only, the love of the disciple. All this seems indeed beautiful, but is it also appropriate? Does he not by this manner of life lift himself above the plane of what is valid for a human life? Is it right for a man to be as care-free as a bird, and even to surpass these creatures in unconcern, since they fly hither and thither in search of food? Ought he not rather to take thought for the morrow? True, we cannot imagine the God otherwise, but what does the imagination prove? Is it permissible thus to become a foot-loose wanderer, stopping wherever evening overtakes him? The question is whether a human being may venture to express the same idea; for otherwise the God has not realized the essential elements of a human life. We answer in the affirmative; a man may so venture if he has the needed strength. If he can so lose himself in the service of the spirit that it never occurs to him to take care for meat and drink; if he is certain that want will not distract him, and that distress will not confound for him the structure of his life, and teach him to rue that he did not first master the simple things before he presumed to understand more—then he may indeed venture, and his greatness will be more glorious than the serene security of the lilies of the field.

This lofty absorption in his mission will of itself suffice to attract the attention of the multitude, among whom the learner will doubtless be found. The latter will in all probability come from the humbler walks of life; for the wise and the learned will presumably wish first to propose captious questions to the Teacher, invite him to *colloquia*, or subject him to an examination, upon which they will assure him a permanent position and a secure livelihood.

Let us now picture the God going about in the city of his appearance (which city this is, is indifferent). To make his teaching known is the sole necessity of his life; it is his meat and drink. Teaching is his labor, and caring for the learner is his rest from labor. He has no friends nor kindred, but the learner is his brother and sister. It may readily be understood that a web of rumor will soon be woven, catching the curious multitude in its snare. Wherever the Teacher appears the crowd gathers, curious to see, curious to hear, and eager to tell others that they have seen and heard him. Is this curious multitude the learner? By no means. Or if some one of the authorized teachers of that city sought him out secretly, in order to try his strength with him in argument—is he the learner? By no means. If this teacher or that multitude *learn* anything, the God serves merely as an occasion in the strict Socratic sense.

The God's appearance has now become the news of the day, in the market-place, in the homes of the people, in the council chamber, in the ruler's palace. It gives occasion for much foolish and idle talk, perhaps also for some earnest reflection. But for the learner the news of the day is not an occasion for something else, not even an occasion for the acquirement in Socratic sincerity of a deeper and fuller self-knowledge; for the learner it is the Eternal, the beginning of eternity. The news of the day the beginning of eternity! If the God had permitted himself to be born in an inn, wrapped in swaddling-clothes and laid in a manger, could the contradiction have been greater than

that the news of the day should be the swaddling-clothes
of the Eternal, aye, as in the supposed instance its actual
form, so that the *Moment* is really decisive for eternity!
Unless the God grants the condition which makes it possible to understand this, how is it to be supposed that the
learner will be able to discover it! But that the God himself
gives this condition has been shown above to be a consequence of the *Moment*, and it has also been shown that the
Moment is the Paradox, and that without it we are unable
to advance, but return to Socrates.

Here at the outset let us take care to make it clear that
the question of an historical point of departure arises even
for a contemporary disciple; for if we are not careful here,
we shall meet with an insuperable difficulty later (in
Chapter V), when we come to deal with the case of the
disciple whom we call the disciple at second hand. The
contemporary disciple gets an historical point of departure
for his eternal consciousness as well as any later disciple;
for he is contemporary with precisely that historical phenomenon which refuses to be reduced to a moment of
merely occasional significance, but proposes to interest
him in another sense than the merely historical, presenting
itself to him as a condition for his eternal happiness. If
this is not so, then (deducing the consequences conversely)
the Teacher is not the God but only a Socrates, and if he
does not conduct himself like a Socrates, he is not even
a Socrates.

But how does the learner come to realize an understanding with this Paradox? We do not ask that he understand
the Paradox but only understand that this is the Paradox.
How this takes place we have already shown. It comes to
pass when the Reason and the Paradox encounter one

another happily in the Moment, when the Reason sets itself aside and the Paradox bestows itself. The third entity in which this union is realized (for it is not realized in the Reason, since it is set aside: nor in the Paradox, which bestows itself—hence it is realized *in* something) is that happy passion to which we will now assign a name, though it is not the name that so much matters. We shall call this passion: *Faith*. This then must be the condition of which we have spoken, which the Paradox contributes. Let us not forget that if the Paradox does not grant this condition the learner must be in possession of it. But if the learner is in possession of the condition he is *eo ipso* himself the Truth, and the moment is merely the moment of occasion (Chapter I).

The contemporary learner finds it easy enough to acquire adequate historical information. But let us not forget that with respect to the Teacher's birth he will be in the same position as the disciple at second hand; if we wish to urge absolute historical precision there will be only one human being who is fully informed, namely the woman of whom he permitted himself to be born. But though a contemporary learner readily becomes an historical eye-witness, the difficulty is that the knowledge of some historical circumstance, or indeed a knowledge of all the circumstances with the reliability of an eye-witness, does not make such an eye-witness a disciple; which is apparent from the fact that this knowledge has merely historical significance for him. We see at once that the historical in the more concrete sense is a matter of indifference; we may suppose a degree of ignorance with respect to it, and permit this ignorance as if to annihilate one detail after the other, historically annihilating the historical; if only the Moment remains, as point of departure for the Eternal, the Paradox will be there. Suppose a contemporary who had reduced his hours of sleep to a minimum in order that he might follow this Teacher about, attending him more closely than the pilot-fish the shark; suppose him to keep a hundred spies in his service to watch over the Teacher everywhere, conferring with them each evening in order to obtain a description of the Teacher's movements exact to the minutest detail, accounting for what he had said and where he had been each hour of the day, because his zeal led him to attach importance even to the least trifle—would such a contemporary be the disciple? By no means. If he is accused of historical inaccuracy he can wash his hands of the accusation, but that is all. Suppose another contemporary who concerned himself solely with the doctrine which this Teacher was wont upon occasion to expound. If every word of instruction that fell from his lips seemed more important to him than his daily bread; if he kept a hundred assistants watching for every syllable, so that nothing should be lost; if he conferred with them carefully each evening, in order to obtain a presentation of the doctrine that should have the highest possible reliability—would he on this account be the disciple? By no means, no more than Plato was a disciple of Socrates. Suppose that a contemporary who had been living abroad returned at a time when the Teacher had only a day or two to live. If engagements had prevented him from going to see the Teacher, so that he was brought into touch with him only at the last moment, when he was about to yield his spirit—would this historical ignorance prevent him from becoming the disciple, provided the Moment became for him decisive for eternity? For the first contemporary, the life of the Teacher was merely an historical event; for the second, the Teacher served as an occasion by which he came to an understanding of himself, and he will be able to forget the Teacher (Chapter I). As over against an eternal understanding of oneself, any knowledge about the Teacher is accidental and historical only, a mere matter of memory. As long as the Eternal and the historical are external to one another, the historical is merely an occasion. If then such a zealous learner, though not carrying things so far as to become a disciple, were to discourse loudly and volubly of how much he owed the Teacher, so that his eulogy was almost endless and its gilding priceless; if he were to resent our explanation that the Teacher had been merely an occasion, neither his eulogy nor his resentment could further our inquiry, since both had the same ground, namely, that though lacking in the courage to understand he had nevertheless not lacked the audacity to go beyond. By romancing and trumpeting in his manner one only deceives oneself and others, in so far as one persuades oneself and others that one really has thoughts— since one owes them to another. Though politeness is ordinarily not supposed to cost anything, such politeness as his is dearly purchased. The enthusiastic outpouring of gratitude, perhaps itself not devoid of tears nor without a moving effect upon others, is a misunderstanding; for the thoughts that such a man has he certainly does not owe to another, and the nonsense he talks is all his own. Ah, how often has it not happened that someone has politely insisted upon owing Socrates a great debt, although he owed Socrates absolutely nothing! Whoever understands Socrates best understands precisely that he owes him nothing, which is as Socrates would have it, and which it is beautiful to have been able to will; whoever believes that he owes Socrates so great a debt may be tolerably certain that Socrates stands ready to acquit him of it without payment, since it will doubtless cause him regret to learn that he has unwittingly furnished anyone with capital for such usurious speculations. But if the entire situation is non-Socratic, as we have assumed, the disciple will owe *all* to the Teacher; which is quite impossible in relation to Socrates, since as he himself says, he was unable to *beget*. This relationship of owing all to the Teacher cannot be expressed in terms of romancing and trumpeting, but only in that happy passion we call Faith, whose object is the Paradox. But the Paradox unites the contradictories, and is the historical made eternal, and the Eternal made historical. Everyone who understands the Paradox differently may keep the honor of having explained it, which honor he won by not being content to understand it.

It is easy to see, though it scarcely needs to be pointed out, since it is involved in the fact that the Reason is set aside, that Faith is not a form of knowledge; for all knowledge is either a knowledge of the Eternal, excluding the temporal and historical as indifferent, or it is pure historical knowledge. No knowledge can have for its object the absurdity that the Eternal is the historical. If I know Spinoza's doctrine, then I am in so far not concerned with Spinoza but with his doctrine; at some other time I may be concerned historically with Spinoza himself. But the disciple is in Faith so related to his Teacher as to be eternally concerned with his historical existence.

Now if we assume that it is as we have supposed (and without this assumption we return to the Socratic order of things), that the Teacher himself contributes the condition to the learner, it will follow that the object of Faith is not the *teaching* but the *Teacher*. The Socratic principle is, that the learner being himself the Truth and in possession of the condition can thrust the teacher aside; the Socratic art and the Socratic heroism consisted precisely in helping men to do this. But Faith must steadily hold fast to the Teacher. In order that he may have the power to give the condition the Teacher must be the God; in order that he may be able to put the learner in possession of it he must be Man. This contradiction is again the object of Faith, and is the Paradox, the Moment. That the God has once for all given man the requisite condition is the eternal Socratic presupposition, which comes into no hostile collision with time, but is incommensurable with the temporal and its determinations. The contradiction of our hypothesis is that man receives the condition in the Moment, the same condition which, since it is requisite for the understanding of the eternal Truth, is *eo ipso* an eternal condition. If the case is otherwise we stand at the Socratic principle of Recollection.

It is easy to see, though it scarcely needs to be pointed out, since it is involved in the fact that the Reason is set aside, that Faith is not an act of will; for all human volition has its capacity within the scope of an underlying condition. Thus if I have the courage to will the understanding, I am able to understand the Socratic principle, i.e., to understand myself, because from the Socratic point of view I have the condition, and so have the power to will this understanding. But if I do not have the condition (and this is our assumption, in order not to be forced back on the Socratic order of things) all my willing is of no avail;

although as soon as the condition is given, the Socratic principle will again apply.

The contemporary learner enjoys one advantage, which the learner of a later generation alas! will doubtless greatly envy him, if only for the sake of doing something. A contemporary may go where he can see the Teacher—and may he then believe his eyes? Why not? But may he also believe that this makes him a disciple? By no means. If he believes his eyes, he is deceived, for the God is not immediately knowable. But then perhaps he may shut his eyes. Just so; but if he does, what profit does he have from his contemporaneity? And when he shuts his eyes he will presumably try to form some conception of the God. But if he is able to do this by himself, he is evidently in possession of the condition. What he conceives, moreover, will be a figure revealing itself to the inner eye of the soul; if he now beholds this, the figure of the servant will confuse him when he again opens his eyes. Let us go on. We have assumed that the Teacher dies; now that he is dead, what will the learner who had been his contemporary do? Perhaps he has sketched some portraits of him; he may even have in his possession an entire series of such portraits, depicting and accurately reflecting every change that by reason of age or state of mind may have taken place in the outward appearance of the Teacher. When he examines these portraits and assures himself that such and such was his appearance, may he then believe his eyes? Why not? But is he on that account a disciple? By no means. But then he may proceed to form some conception of the God. But the God cannot be conceived; it was for this very reason that he appeared in the form of a servant. And yet the servant-form is no deception; for if such were the case, this moment would not be the Moment, but an accidental circumstance, a mere appearance, which as an occasion infinitely vanishes in comparison with the Eternal. And if the learner had the power to form a conception of the God by himself, he must himself have had the condition. Thus he needed only a reminder to be enabled to form this conception, in a manner well within his capacity; though of this he may not previously have been aware. But if this is the case, the reminder will vanish instantly like a tiny atom in the eternal potentiality which was present in his soul, and which now becomes a reality, but again as reality eternally presupposes itself.

How does the learner then become a believer or disciple? When the Reason is set aside and he receives the condition. When does he receive the condition? In the Moment. What does this condition condition? The understanding of the Eternal. But such a condition must be an eternal condition.—He receives accordingly the eternal condition in the Moment, and is aware that he has so received it; for otherwise he merely comes to himself in the consciousness that he had it from eternity. It is in the Moment that he receives it, and from the Teacher himself. All romancing and trumpeting abroad about one's cleverness in penetrating the God's incognito, though without receiving the condition from the Teacher; that one took notice of him by the impression he made, such a strange feeling coming over one in his presence; that there was a something in his voice and mien, etc., etc.—all this is but silly twaddle, by which one does not become a disciple but only makes a mockery of the God.[1] The servant-figure was no incognito.

---

[1] Every determination of his nature which makes the God immediately knowable is indeed a milestone on the way of approxima-

And when in the strength of his omnipotent resolve, which is like his love, the God makes himself the equal of the humblest, let no innkeeper or professor of philosophy imagine that he is a shrewd enough fellow to detect anything, unless the God gives the condition. And when the God in the form of a servant stretches forth the hand of omnipotence, let no astonished and open-mouthed beholder imagine that he is a disciple because he is astonished, and because he can gather others about him who in their turn are astonished over his story. If there is no necessity for the God to give the condition, the learner knew from the beginning how it is with the God, even if he did not know that he knew it; the other is not even the Socratic thought, but infinitely lower.

But the outward figure (we do not mean its detail) is not a matter of indifference to the disciple. It is what he has seen and his hands have handled. However, the outward figure is not important in the sense that he would cease to be a believer if he happened to meet the Teacher some day on the street and did not at once recognize him or even walked some distance with him on the way without realizing that it was he. The God gave to the disciple the condition that enables him to see him, opening for him the eyes of Faith. But it was a terrible thing to see this

---

tion, but one which marks an increase instead of a decrease in the distance; it does not measure toward the Paradox but away from it, back past Socrates and the Socratic ignorance. This needs to be carefully noted, lest one experience in the world of the spirit what befell the traveller who asked if the road on which he was journeying went to London, and was told by the Englishman that it did; in spite of which he failed to reach London, because the Englishman had omitted to mention that he needed to turn about, since he was proceeding in the opposite direction.

outward figure, to have converse with him as with one of us, and every moment that Faith was not present to see only the servant-form. When the Teacher is gone from the disciple in death, memory may bring his figure before him; but it is not on this account that the disciple believes, but because he received the condition from the God, and hence is enabled again to see, in memory's trustworthy image, the person of the God. So it is with the disciple, who knows that he would have seen nothing without the condition, since the first thing he learned to understand was that he was in Error.

But in that case is not Faith as paradoxical as the Paradox? Precisely so; how else could it have the Paradox for its object, and be happy in its relation to the Paradox? Faith is itself a miracle, and all that holds true of the Paradox also holds true of Faith. But within the framework of this miracle everything is again Socratic, yet so that the miracle is never cancelled—the miracle namely, that the eternal condition is given in time. Everything is Socratic; the relation between one contemporary and another in so far as both are believers is entirely Socratic: the one owes the other nothing, but both owe everything to the God.

*   *

I think I hear someone say: "Then it seems that the contemporary derives absolutely no advantage from his contemporaneity; and yet if we assume what you have assumed about God's appearance among men, it lies so near at hand to count the contemporary generation blessed, because it saw and heard."—"Aye, truly it lies near at hand; so near I think, that this generation has doubtless also counted itself blessed. Shall we assume that this was the case? For otherwise it was surely not happy, and our praise of this generation is merely an expression for the fact that by acting differently under the same circumstances, one might have become happy. But if this is the case, our praise may need to be qualified in a variety of ways, when we consider the matter more carefully, and may in the last analysis become altogether ambiguous. Suppose, as we sometimes read in old chronicles, that an emperor celebrated his marriage for an entire week with festivities the like of which had never before been seen, every breath of air being scented with perfume, while the ear found it constantly vibrant with music and song, so as to enhance the enjoyment of the costliest viands, set forth in richest abundance. Day and night the festivities continued, for the night was made as bright as the day by torches that illumined the scene—but whether seen by the light of day or by the illumination of the night, the queen was more beautiful and more gracious than any mortal woman; and the whole was an enchantment, wonderful as the most audacious desire in its still more audacious fulfilment. Let us assume that all this had happened in the past, and that we had to be content with the meager and fasting report of what had taken place—why should we not, humanly speaking, count the contemporaries happy? That is to say those contemporaries who saw and heard and grasped with their hands; for otherwise of what avail would it be to be contemporary? The splendors of the imperial marriage-feast and the rich abundance of its pleasures were directly accessible to sight and touch, so that anyone who was a contemporary in the stricter sense would presumably have feasted his eyes and made his

heart to be glad. But suppose the splendor had been of a
different kind, not immediately apparent to the senses,
what profit would there then be in being a contemporary,
since one would not on that account necessarily be contemporary with the splendor? Such a contemporary could
scarcely be counted happy, nor could we bless his eyes and
ears; for he was not contemporary with the splendor,
neither hearing nor seeing anything of it. And this not
because he lacked time and opportunity (in the immediate
sense), but because of something else, which could be
lacking even if he himself had been present, and favored
with opportunities for seeing and hearing to the fullest
extent, and had not permitted these opportunities (in the
immediate sense) to go unused. But what does it mean
thus to say that one can be a contemporary without being
contemporary, that one may be a contemporary and
though utilizing this advantage (in the immediate sense)
yet be a non-contemporary—what does this mean except
that it is quite impossible to be an immediate contemporary of such a Teacher and of such an event; so that the
real contemporary is not the real contemporary by virtue
of an immediate contemporaneity, but by virtue of something else? A contemporary may for all that be a non-
contemporary; the real contemporary is such not by virtue
of his immediate contemporaneity; *ergo*, it must also be
possible for a non-contemporary (in the immediate sense)
to be a contemporary, by virtue of that something which
makes the contemporary a real contemporary. But the
non-contemporary (in the immediate sense) is of course
the member of a later generation, whence it must be possible for an individual so situated to be a real contemporary. Or what do we mean by being contemporary? Is it

perhaps this kind of a contemporary that we praise, one who can speak as follows: 'I ate and drank in his presence, and he taught in our streets. I saw him often, and knew him for a common man of humble origin. Only a very few thought to find something extraordinary in him; as far as I am concerned, I could see nothing remarkable about him, and I was certainly as much of a contemporary as anybody.' Or is this what we mean by calling anyone a contemporary, and is he a contemporary to whom the God must say if they meet in another life, and he seeks to urge his contemporaneity: 'I do not know you'? And so it was in truth, just as it was equally true that such a contemporary could not have known the Teacher. Only the believer, i.e., the non-immediate contemporary, knows the Teacher, since he receives the condition from him, and therefore knows him even as he is known."—"Stop there a moment, I beg you; for if you keep on talking in this fashion I will not be able to get in a single word. You talk like a disputant for the doctorate, or better still, you talk like a book; and what is worse for you, you talk like a very particular book. For here again, whether wittingly or unwittingly, you have introduced some words into the discourse which are not your own, nor by you placed in the mouths of the speakers. The words are very well known, except that you have substituted the singular for the plural. Here are the scripture passages (for the words are taken from the Bible): 'We have eaten and drunk in thy presence, and thou hast taught in our streets'; 'I tell ye, I know not whence ye are.' However, let this pass without further comment for the present. But are you not drawing too sweeping a conclusion when you infer from the Teacher's reply to a given individual, 'I do not know you,' that this individual was not a contemporary and had not known the Teacher? If the emperor of whom you spoke had said to one who claimed contemporaneity with his splendid marriage-feast, 'I do not know you,' would the emperor thereby have proved that he was not a contemporary?"—"By no means would the emperor have proved such a thing; he would at the most have proved himself a fool, not content like Mithridates to know the name of every soldier in his army, but pretending to know every contemporary, and assuming to decide by this knowledge whether any given individual had been contemporary or not. The emperor was immediately knowable, and hence someone may very well have known the emperor, even if the emperor did not know him. But the Teacher of our hypothesis was not immediately knowable; he could be known only when he himself gave the condition. Whoever received the condition received it from the Teacher himself, and hence the Teacher must know everyone who knows him, and no one can know the Teacher except through being known by him. Are we not agreed on this point, and do you perhaps at once perceive the remoter consequences of what we have been saying? When the believer is the believer and knows the God through having received the condition from the God himself, every successor must receive the condition from the God himself in precisely the same sense, and cannot receive it at second hand; for if he did, this second hand would have to be the hand of the God himself, and in that case there is no question of a second hand. But a successor who receives the condition from the God himself is a contemporary, a real contemporary; a privilege enjoyed only by the believer, but also enjoyed by every believer."—"Indeed, now that you have pointed it out I clearly perceive the truth of this, and I already descry the far-reaching consequences. I am only surprised that I had not discovered it for myself, and I would give a great deal for the honor of having been the discoverer."—"And I would give still more if I could be sure that I had fully understood it; this concerns me far more than who discovered it. But I have not yet entirely understood it, as I shall show you presently in a later chapter, at which time I will rely on your assistance, you who have at once understood the whole. But with your permission I shall now submit what the lawyers call a brief, summarizing what I have expounded and understood up to the present time. And as I present this brief I ask you to look to your rights and to assert them; for I hereby summon you *sub poena praeclusi et perpetui silentii*. The immediate contemporaneity can serve only as an occasion. (a) It can serve as occasion for the acquirement of historical knowledge. In this respect a contemporary of the emperor's marriage-feast is far more fortunately situated than a contemporary of the Teacher; for the latter merely gets an opportunity to see the servant-form, and at most one or another mysterious deed, in relation to which he must remain uncertain whether to admire or to resent being made a fool of, since he will presumably not even wish to persuade the Teacher to do it over again, as a juggler does, in order to give the spectators a better opportunity to see how the trick is turned. (b) It may serve as an occasion for the contemporary to acquire a Socratic deepening of his self-knowledge, in which case the contemporaneity vanishes as nothing in comparison with the Eternal which he discovers within himself. (c) Finally (and this is our assumption, lest we be thrown back on Socrates), it may serve as an occasion by means of which the contemporary, as one who is in Error, receives the condition from the God, and so beholds his glory with the eyes of faith. Aye, happy such a contemporary! But such a contemporary is not in the immediate sense an eye-witness; he is contemporary as a believer, in the autopsy of Faith. But in this autopsy every non-contemporary (in the immediate sense) becomes a contemporary. If then some member of a later generation, perhaps even moved by his own romanticism, yearns to be a contemporary in the immediate sense, he only proves himself a pretender, recognizable like the false Smerdes by the absence of ears—the ears of Faith namely, though he may have asses' ears long enough to permit even a contemporary (in the immediate sense) to hear himself into being a non-contemporary. If such a man continues to romance about how splendid it is to be a contemporary (in the immediate sense), betraying a restless eagerness to be up and away, he must doubtless be allowed to go; but if you watch him you will readily see, both from the nature of his movements and the direction he takes, that he goes not to meet the Paradox with its awe and fear, but rather trips off like a dancing-master to be in time for the emperor's nuptials. And though he gives his expedition a sacred name, preaching fellowship for others so that they join the pilgrimage in crowds, he will none the less scarcely discover the holy land (in the immediate sense), since it is not to be found either on the map or on the earth; his journey is a jest, like the children's game of seeing somebody to 'grandmother's door.' And though he may give himself no rest, but runs faster than a horse can trot or a man can lie, he runs only with the lime-rod, misunderstanding himself as bird-catcher;

for if the birds do not come to him of their own accord, it will certainly not help to run after them.—In only one respect could I be tempted to count a contemporary (in the immediate sense) more fortunate than the member of some later generation. For if we assume that centuries intervene between this event and the period of a succeeding generation there will presumably have accumulated much gossip about this thing, so much foolish chatter that the untrue and confusing rumors with which the contemporary (in the immediate sense) had to contend, did not prove nearly so serious an obstacle to the realization of a right relationship. And that so much the more, since the echo of the centuries, like the echo in some of our churches, would not only have tended to surround Faith with noisy chatter, but might even have transformed Faith itself into chatter; which could not very well have happened in the first generation, when Faith must have revealed itself in all its pristine vigor, through the contrast easily distinguishable from everything else."

Interlude

Is the past more necessary than the future? or,
When the possible becomes actual, is it thereby
made more necessary than it was?

Dear reader! Let us now assume that this Teacher has
made his appearance, that he is dead and buried, and
that some time intervenes between Chapters IV and V.
Likewise it sometimes happens in a comedy that several
years elapse between two successive acts. In order to indicate this passage of time, the orchestra is occasionally made
to play a symphony or the like, foreshortening the time
by filling it with music. In a somewhat similar manner I
have thought to fill out the intervening time by a consideration of the problem set forth above. How long the
interval should be, I am content to leave to your discretion;
but if it seems agreeable to you, let us in a spirit of jest
and earnest assume that precisely 1843 years have elapsed.
You will note that I ought to proceed somewhat leisurely,
if only for the sake of the illusion; for 1843 years is an
exceptionally generous allotment of time, likely to put me
in a predicament the opposite of that in which our philosophers find themselves, whom the time usually permits
only an indication of their meaning; and the opposite also
to that of our historians, who find that not the material,
but the time, leaves them in the lurch. Hence when you
find me somewhat long-winded, repeating the same things,
"about the same things" please notice, you must remember
that it is for the sake of the illusion; and then you will no
doubt pardon my prolixity, and interpret it in a manner
more satisfactory to yourself rather than suppose that I

allowed myself to think that this matter needed consideration, even by you, in that I suspected you of not completely
understanding yourself with respect to it. And this in spite
of the fact that I do not by any means doubt that you have
completely understood and assented to the newest philosophy, which like the modern age generally seems to
suffer from a curious distraction, confusing promise with
performance, the superscription with the execution; for
what age and what philosophy was ever so wonderful and
wonderfully great as our own—in superscriptions!

1

COMING INTO EXISTENCE

In what sense is there change in that which comes into
existence? Or, what is the nature of the coming-into-
existence kind of change ($\kappa \acute{\iota} \nu \eta \sigma \iota \varsigma$)? All other change
($\dot{\alpha} \lambda \lambda o \acute{\iota} \omega \sigma \iota \varsigma$) presupposes the existence of that which
changes, even when the change consists in ceasing to exist.
But this is not the case with coming into existence. For if
the subject of coming into existence does not itself remain
unchanged during the change of coming into existence,
that which comes into existence is not *this* subject which
comes into existence, but something else. Then the ques-
tion involves a $\mu \epsilon \tau \acute{\alpha} \beta \alpha \sigma \iota \varsigma$ $\epsilon \acute{\iota} \varsigma$ $\check{\alpha} \lambda \lambda o$ $\gamma \acute{\epsilon} \nu o \varsigma$ in that the
inquirer in the given case either sees another change co-
present with the change of coming into existence, which
confuses the question for him, or he mistakes the nature
of what is coming into existence and therefore is not in
position to ask the question. If a plan in coming into existence [in being fulfilled or carried out] is in itself changed,
it is not this plan which comes into existence; but if it comes

into existence without being changed, what then is the change of coming into existence? This coming-into-existence kind of change, therefore, is not a change in essence but in being and is a transition from not existing to existing. But this non-being which the subject of coming into existence leaves behind must itself have some sort of being. Otherwise "the subject of coming into existence would not remain unchanged during the change of coming into existence," unless it had not been at all, and then the change of coming into existence would for another reason be absolutely different from every other kind of change, since it would be no change at all, for every change always presupposes something which changes. But such a being, which is nevertheless a non-being, is precisely what possibility is; and a being which is being is indeed actual being or actuality; and the change of coming into existence is a transition from possibility to actuality.

Can the necessary come into existence? Coming into existence is a change, but the necessary cannot be changed, since it always relates itself to itself and relates itself to itself in the same way. All coming into existence is a *suffering*, and the necessary cannot suffer; it cannot undergo the suffering of the actual, which is that the possible (not only the excluded possibility but also the accepted possibility) reveals itself as nothing in the moment it becomes actual, for the possible is made into nothing by the actual. Everything which comes into existence proves precisely by coming into existence that it is not necessary, for the only thing which cannot come into existence is the necessary, because the necessary *is*. ✓

Is not necessity then a synthesis of possibility and actuality? What could this mean? Possibility and actuality do not differ in essence but in being; how could there from this difference be formed a synthesis constituting necessity, which is not a determination of being but a determination of essence, since it is the essence of the necessary to be. If possibility and actuality could be united to become necessity, they would become an absolutely different essence, which is not a kind of change; and in becoming necessity or the necessary, they would become that which alone of all things excludes coming into existence, which is just as impossible as it is self-contradictory. (Compare the Aristotelian principle: "it is possible," "it is possible that not," "it is not possible."—The theory of true and false propositions—Epicurus—tends only to confuse the issue here, since essence and not being is reflected upon, and in this way no help is given with respect to the characterization of the future.)

The necessary is a category entirely by itself. Nothing ever comes into existence with necessity; likewise the necessary never comes into existence and something by coming into existence never becomes the necessary. Nothing whatever exists because it is necessary, but the necessary exists because it is necessary or because the necessary is. The actual is no more necessary than the possible, for the necessary is absolutely different from both. (Compare Aristotle's doctrine of the two kinds of possibility in relationship to the necessary. His mistake lies in his beginning with the principle that everything necessary is possible. In order to avoid having to assert contradictory and even self-contradictory predicates about the necessary, he helps himself out by two kinds of possibility, instead of discovering that his first principle is incorrect, since possibility cannot be predicated of the necessary.)

The change involved in coming into existence is actuality; the transition takes place with freedom. No coming into existence is necessary. It was not necessary before the coming into existence, for then there could not have been the coming into existence, nor after the coming into existence, for then there would not have been the coming into existence.

All coming into existence takes place with freedom, not by necessity. Nothing comes into existence by virtue of a logical ground, but only by a cause. Every cause terminates in a freely effecting cause. The illusion occasioned by the intervening causes is that the coming into existence seems to be necessary; the truth about intervening causes is that just as they themselves have come into existence they point back ultimately to a freely effecting cause. Even the possibility of deducing consequences from a law of nature gives no evidence for the necessity of any coming into existence, which is clear as soon as one reflects definitively on coming into existence. The same is the case with manifestations of freedom, provided we do not let ourselves be deceived by the manifestations of freedom but reflect upon the coming into existence.

2

THE HISTORICAL

Everything that has come into existence is *eo ipso* historical. For even if it accepts no further historical predicate, it nevertheless accepts the one decisive historical predicate: it has come into existence. That whose coming into existence is a simultaneous coming into existence (*Nebeneinander*, Space) has no other history than this. But even when viewed in this light (*en masse*), and abstracting from what an ingenious speculation calls the history of nature in a special sense, nature has a history.

But the historical is the past (for the present pressing upon the confines of the future has not yet become historical). How then can it be said that nature, though immediately present, is historical, except in the sense of the said ingenious speculation? The difficulty comes from the fact that nature is too abstract to have a dialectic with respect to time in the stricter sense. This is nature's imperfection, that it has no history in any other sense; but it is a perfection in nature that it nevertheless has this suggestion of a history, namely that it has come into existence. (This constitutes its past, the fact that it exists is its present.) On the other hand, it is the perfection of the Eternal to have no history, and of all that is, the Eternal alone has absolutely no history.

However, coming into existence may present a reduplication, i.e., the possibility of a second coming into existence within the first coming into existence. Here we have the historical in the stricter sense, subject to a dialectic with respect to time. The coming into existence which in this sphere is identical with the coming into existence of nature is a possibility, a possibility which for nature is its whole reality. But this historical coming into existence in the stricter sense is a coming into existence within a coming into existence, which should constantly be kept in mind. The more specifically historical coming into existence occurs by the operation of a relatively freely effecting cause, which in turn points ultimately to an absolutely freely effecting cause.

3

THE PAST

What has happened has happened, and cannot be undone; in this sense it does not admit of change (Chrysippus
the Stoic—Diodorus the Megarian). Is this immutability
identical with the immutability of the necessary? The immutability of the past has been brought about by a change,
namely the change of coming into existence; such an
immutability does not exclude all change, since it did not
exclude this change. All change is excluded (subjecting
the concept to a temporal dialectic) only by being excluded
in every moment. If the past is conceived as necessary, this
can happen only by virtue of forgetting that it has come
into existence; is such forgetfulness perhaps also necessary?

What has happened has happened as it happened; in
this sense it does not admit of change. But is this immutability identical with the immutability of the necessary?
The immutability of the past consists in the fact that its
actual "thus" cannot become different; but does it follow
from this that its possible "how" could not have been
realized in a different manner? The immutability of the
necessary, on the contrary, consists in its constant relating
itself to itself, and in its relating itself to itself always in
the same manner, excluding every change. It is not content with the immutability that belongs to the past, which
as we have shown is not merely subject to a dialectic with
respect to a prior change from which it emerges, but must
even suffer a dialectic with respect to a higher change
which annuls it. (Repentance, for example, which seeks to
annul an actuality.)

The future has not yet happened. But it is not *on that*

account less necessary than the past, since the past did not become necessary by coming into existence, but on the contrary proved by coming into existence that it was not necessary. If the past had become necessary it would not be possible to infer the opposite about the future, but it would rather follow that the future also was necessary. If necessity could gain a foothold at a single point, there would no longer be any distinguishing between the past and the future. To assume to predict the future (prophesy) and to assume to understand the necessity of the past are one and the same thing, and only custom makes the one seem more plausible than the other to a given generation. The past has come into existence; coming into existence is the change of actuality brought about by freedom. If the past had become necessary it would no longer belong to freedom, i.e., it would no longer belong to that by which it came into existence. Freedom would then be in a sorry case, both an object of laughter and deserving of tears, since it would be responsible for what did not belong to it, being destined to bring offspring into the world for necessity to devour. Freedom itself would be an illusion, and coming into existence no less so; freedom would be witchcraft and coming into existence a false alarm.[1]

[1] A prophesying generation despises the past, and will not listen to the testimony of the scriptures; a generation engaged in understanding the necessity of the past does not like to be reminded of the future. Both attitudes are consistent, for each would have occasion to discover in the opposite the folly of its own procedure. The Absolute Method, Hegel's discovery, is a difficulty even in Logic, aye a glittering tautology, coming to the assistance of academic superstition with many signs and wonders. In the historical sciences it is a fixed idea. The fact that the method here at once begins to become concrete, since history is the concretion of the Idea, has given Hegel an opportunity to exhibit extraordinary

4

THE APPREHENSION OF THE PAST

Nature, as the spatial order, has only an immediate existence. But everything that admits of a dialectic with respect to time is characterized by a certain duality, in that after having been present it can persist as past. The essentially historical is always the past (it is over, but whether years since or only a matter of days ago makes no

---

learning, and a rare power of organization, inducing a quite sufficient commotion in the historical material. But it has also promoted a distraction of mind in the reader, so that, perhaps precisely from respect and admiration for China and Persia, the thinkers of the middle ages, the four universal monarchies (a discovery which, as it did not escape Geert Westphaler, has also set many a Hegelian Geert Westphaler's tongue wagging), he may have forgotten to inquire whether it now really did become evident at the end, at the close of this journey of enchantment, as was repeatedly promised in the beginning, and what was of course the principal issue, for the want of which not all the glories of the world could compensate, what alone could be a sufficient reward for the unnatural tension in which one had been held—that the method was valid. Why at once become concrete, why at once begin to experiment *in concreto*? Was it not possible to answer this question in the dispassionate brevity of the language of abstraction, which has no means of distraction or enchantment, this question of what it means that the Idea becomes concrete, what is the nature of coming into existence, what is one's relationship to that which has come into existence, and so forth? Just as it surely might have been cleared up in the Logic what "transition" is and means, before going over to write three volumes describing its workings in the categories, astounding the superstitious, and making so difficult the situation of one who would gladly owe much to the superior mind and express his gratitude for what he owes, but nevertheless cannot over this forget what Hegel himself must have considered the matter of principal importance.

difference), and has as past its own actuality; for the fact
that it has happened is certain and dependable. But the
fact that it has happened is on the other hand the ground
of an uncertainty, by which the apprehension will always
be prevented from assimilating the past as if it had been
thus from all eternity. Only in terms of this conflict between certainty and uncertainty, the distinguishing mark
of all that has come into existence, and hence also of the
past, can the past be understood. When the past is understood in any other manner, the apprehension has misunderstood itself in the role of apprehension; and it has
misunderstood its object, as if anything such could be the
object of an apprehension. Every apprehension of the past
which proposes to understand it better by construing it,
has only the more thoroughly misunderstood it. (A manifestation theory instead of a construction theory is at first
sight deceptive, but the next moment we have the secondary construction and the necessary manifestation.) The
past is not necessary, since it came into existence; it did not
become necessary by coming into existence (which is a
contradiction); still less does it become necessary through
someone's apprehension of it. (Distance in time tends to
promote an intellectual illusion, just as distance in space
provokes a sensory illusion. A contemporary does not
perceive the necessity of what comes into existence, but
when centuries intervene between the event and the beholder he perceives the necessity, just as distance makes
the square tower seem round.) If the past became necessary through being apprehended, the past would be the
gainer by as much as the apprehension lost, since the latter
would come to apprehend something else, which is a poor
sort of apprehension. If the object of apprehension is

changed in the process of apprehension, the apprehension is changed into a misapprehension. Knowledge of the present does not confer necessity upon it; foreknowledge of the future gives it no necessity (Boethius); knowledge of the past confers no necessity upon the past; for no knowledge and no apprehension has anything of its own to give.

Whoever apprehends the past, *historico-philosophus,* is therefore a prophet in retrospect (Daub). That he is a prophet expresses the fact that the certainty of the past is based upon an uncertainty, an uncertainty that exists for the past in precisely the same sense that it exists for the future, being rooted in the possibility (Leibniz and the possible worlds) out of which it could not *emerge* with necessity, *nam necessariam se ipso prius sit, necesse est.* The historian thus again confronts the past, moved by the emotion which is the passionate sense for coming into existence: wonder. If the philosopher never finds occasion to wonder (and how could it occur to anyone to wonder at a necessary construction, except by a new kind of contradiction?) he has *eo ipso* nothing to do with the historical; for wherever the process of coming into existence is involved, as is the case in relation to the past, there the uncertainty attaching to the most certain of events (the uncertainty of coming into existence) can find expression only in this passion, which is as necessary to the philosopher as it is worthy of him. (Plato, Aristotle.) Even if the event is certain in the extreme, even if wonder offers its consent in advance, saying that if this had not happened it would have had to be invented (Baader), even then the passion of wonder would fall into contradiction with itself if it falsely imputed necessity, and thereby cheated itself.—

As for the Method, both the word itself and the concept sufficiently show that the progress connoted is teleological. But in every such movement there is each instant a pause (where wonder stands *in pausa* and waits upon coming into existence), the pause of coming into existence and of possibility, precisely because the τέλος lies outside. If there is only one way possible, the τέλος is not outside, but in the movement itself, and even behind it, as in the case of an immanent progression.

So much for the apprehension of the past. We have in the meanwhile presupposed that a knowledge of the past is given; how is such knowledge acquired? The historical cannot be given immediately to the senses, since the *elusiveness* of coming into existence is involved in it. The immediate impression of a natural phenomenon or of an event is not the impression of the historical, for the *coming into existence* involved cannot be sensed immediately, but only the immediate presence. But the presence of the historical includes the process of coming into existence, or else it is not the presence of the historical as such.

Immediate sensation and immediate cognition cannot deceive. This is by itself enough to show that the historical cannot be the object of either, because the historical has the elusiveness which is implicit in all coming into existence. As compared with the immediate, coming into existence has an elusiveness by which even the most dependable fact is rendered doubtful. Thus when the observer sees a star, the star becomes involved in doubt the moment he seeks to become aware of its having come into existence. It is as if reflection took the star away from the senses. So much then is clear, that the organ for the historical must have a structure analogous with the historical itself;

it must comprise a corresponding somewhat by which it may repeatedly negate in its certainty the uncertainty that corresponds to the uncertainty of coming into existence. The latter uncertainty is two-fold: the nothingness of the antecedent non-being is one side of it, while the annihilation of the possible is another, the latter being at the same time the annihilation of every other possibility. Now faith has precisely the required character; for in the certainty of belief* [Danish: *Tro, faith* or *belief*] there is always present a negated uncertainty, in every way corresponding to the uncertainty of coming into existence. Faith believes what it does not see; it does not believe that the star is there, for that it sees, but it believes that the star has come into existence. The same holds true of an event. The "what" of a happening may be known immediately, but by no means can it be known immediately that it has happened. Nor can it be known immediately that it happens, not even if it happens as we say in front of our very noses. The elusiveness pertaining to an event consists in its having happened, in which fact lies the transition from nothing, from non-being, and from the manifold possible "how." Immediate sensation and immediate cognition have no suspicion of the uncertainty with which belief approaches its object, but neither do they suspect the certainty which emerges from this uncertainty.

Immediate sensation and immediate cognition cannot deceive. This is important for the understanding of doubt, and for the assignment to belief of its proper place through a comparison with doubt. This thought underlies Greek

* *Tro* is translated here and in the following three pages as *belief* or "faith . . . in a direct and ordinary sense," as distinguished from Faith "in an eminent sense." See pp. 108-09.—H.V.H.

scepticism, strange as it may seem. Yet it should not be
so difficult to understand, nor to perceive the light that
this throws upon the nature of belief, provided one has
escaped being altogether confused by the Hegelian doctrine of a universal doubt, against which it is certainly not
necessary to preach. For what the Hegelians say about
this is of such a character as rather to encourage a modest
little doubt of how far it can be true that they have ever
doubted anything at all. Greek scepticism was of the retiring kind (ἐποχή). The Greek sceptic did not doubt by
virtue of his knowledge, but by an act of will (refusal to
give assent—μετριοπαθεῖν). From this it follows that
doubt can be overcome only by a free act, an act of will,
as every Greek sceptic would understand as soon as he had
understood himself. But he did not wish to overcome his
scepticism, precisely because he willed to doubt. For this he
will have to assume the responsibility; but let us not impute
to him the stupidity of supposing that doubt is necessary, or
the still greater stupidity of supposing that if it were, it could
ever be overcome. The Greek sceptic did not deny the validity of sensation or immediate cognition; error, he says,
has an entirely different ground, for it comes from the conclusions that I draw. If I can only refrain from drawing conclusions, I will never be deceived. If my senses, for example,
show me an object that seems round at a distance but
square near at hand, or a stick bent in the water which is
straight when taken out, the senses have not deceived me.
But I run the risk of being deceived when I draw a
conclusion about the stick or the object. Hence the sceptic
keeps his mind constantly in suspense, and it was this
frame of mind that he *willed* to maintain. In so far as
Greek scepticism has been called φιλοσοφία ζητητική,

ἀπορητική, σκεπτική, these predicates do not express its distinctive feature, for Greek scepticism had recourse to knowledge only for the sake of protecting the state of mind which was its principal concern, and therefore did not even express its negative cognitive results θετικῶς, for fear of being caught in a conclusion. The state of mind was the sceptic's chief concern. (τέλος δέ οἱ σκεπτικοί φασι τὴν ἐποχήν, ἡ σκιᾶς τρόπον ἐπακολουθεῖ ἡ ἀταραξία, Diogenes Laertius, IX, 107.)[2]—By way of contrast it now becomes easy to see that belief is not a form of knowledge, but a free act, an expression of will. It believes the fact of coming into existence, and has thus succeeded in overcoming within itself the uncertainty that corresponds to the nothingness of the antecedent non-being; it believes the "thus" of what has come into existence, and has consequently succeeded in annulling within itself the possible "how." Without denying the possibility of another "thus," this present "thus" is for belief most certain.

In so far as that which through its relation to belief becomes historical and as historical becomes the object of belief (the one corresponds to the other) has an immediate existence, and is immediately apprehended, it is not subject to error. A contemporary may then safely use his eyes and so forth, but let him look to his conclusions.

---

[2] Both Plato and Aristotle insist on the principle that immediate sensation and immediate cognition cannot deceive. Later also Descartes, who says precisely as do the Greek sceptics, that error has its root in the will, which is over-hasty in drawing conclusions. This also throws light on faith; when faith resolves to believe it runs the risk of committing itself to an error, but it nevertheless believes. There is no other road to faith; if one wishes to escape risk, it is as if one wanted to know with certainty that he can swim before going into the water.

He cannot know, as a matter of immediate cognition, that his fact has come into existence, but neither can he know it as a matter of necessity; for the very first expression for coming into existence is a breach of continuity. The moment faith believes that its fact has come into existence, has happened, it makes the event and the fact doubtful in the process of becoming, and makes its "thus" also doubtful through its relation to the possible "how" of the coming into existence. The conclusion of belief is not so much a conclusion as a resolution, and it is for this reason that belief excludes doubt. When belief concludes: this exists, *ergo*, it must have come into existence, it might appear to be making an inference from effect to cause. However, this is not quite the case; and even if it were so it must be remembered that the cognitive inference is from cause to effect, or rather, from ground to consequent (Jacobi). But it is not accurate to say that the conclusion of belief is an inference from effect to cause; I cannot sense or know immediately that what I sense or know immediately is an effect, since for the immediate apprehension it merely is. I believe that it is an effect, for in order to bring it under this category I must already have made it doubtful with the uncertainty implicit in coming into existence. When belief resolves to do this, doubt has been overcome; in that very instant the indifference of doubt has been dispelled and its equilibrium overthrown, not by knowledge but by will. Thus it will be seen that belief is the most disputable of things while in process of approximation; for the uncertainty of doubt, strong and invincible in making things ambiguous, *dis-putare*, is brought into subjection within it. But it is the least disputable when once constituted, by virtue of its new quality. Belief is the opposite of doubt. Belief and doubt are not two forms of knowledge, determinable in continuity with one another, for neither of them is a cognitive act; they are opposite passions. Belief is a sense for coming into existence, and doubt is a protest against every conclusion that transcends immediate sensation and immediate cognition. The sceptic does not, for example, deny his own existence; but he draws no conclusion from fear of being deceived. In so far as he has recourse to dialectics in order to make the opposite of any given conclusion seem equally probable, it is not on the foundation of these dialectical arguments that he sets up his scepticism. They are but outworks, human accommodations. He has no result, therefore, not even a negative result; for this would be to recognize the validity of knowledge. By an act of will he resolves to keep himself under restraint, and to refrain from every conclusion ($\phi\iota\lambda o\sigma o\phi\iota\alpha\ \dot{\epsilon}\phi\epsilon\kappa\tau\iota\kappa\dot{\eta}$).

One who is not contemporary with the historical has, instead of the immediacy of sense and cognition, in which the historical is not contained, the testimony of contemporaries, to which he stands related in the same manner as the contemporaries stand related to the said immediacy. Even if the content of the testimony has undergone in the process of communication the change which makes it historical, the non-contemporary cannot take it up into his consciousness without giving it his assent, thus making it historical for himself, unless he is to transform it into something unhistorical for himself. The immediacy of the testimony, i.e., the fact that the testimony is there, is what is given as immediately present to him; but the historicity of the present consists in its having come into existence, and the historicity of the past consists in its having once

been present through having come into existence. Whenever a successor believes the past (not its truth, which is
a matter of cognition and concerns not existence but
essence), whenever he believes that the past was once
present through having come into existence, the uncertainty which is implicit in coming into existence is
present in the past that is the object of his belief. This
uncertainty (the nothingness of the antecedent non-being
—the possible "how" corresponding to the actual "thus")
will exist for him as well as for a contemporary; his
mind will be in a state of suspense exactly as was the mind
of a contemporary. He has no longer a mere immediacy
before him; neither does he confront a necessary coming into existence, but only the "thus" of *coming into
existence*. A successor believes, to be sure, on account
of the testimony of some contemporary; but only in the
same sense as a contemporary believes on account of his
immediate sensation and immediate cognition. But no
contemporary can believe by virtue of this immediacy
alone, and neither can any successor believe solely by
virtue of the testimony to which he has access.

* *

Thus at no time does the past become necessary, just
as it was not necessary when it came into existence nor
revealed itself as necessary to the contemporary who believed it, i.e., believed that it had come into existence. For
belief and coming into existence correspond to one another, and are concerned with the two negative determinations of being, namely the past and the future, and with
the present in so far as it is conceived from the point of

view of a negative determination of being, namely as having come into existence. Necessity, on the other hand, is wholly a matter of essence, and thus it is of the essence of the necessary to exclude coming into existence. The possibility from which that which became actual once emerged still clings to it and remains with it as past, even after the lapse of centuries. Whenever a successor re-asserts its having come into existence, which he does by believing it, he evokes this potentiality anew, irrespective of whether there can be any question of his having a more specific conception of it or not.

SUPPLEMENT: APPLICATION

What has here been said applies to the historical in the direct and ordinary sense, whose only contradiction is that it has come into existence, which contradiction is implicit in all coming into existence.[3] Here again one must guard against the illusion of supposing that it is easier to understand after the event than before the event. Whoever thinks this does not yet grasp the fact that what he apprehends has come into existence; he has before him only the present content of a sensory and cognitive im-mediacy, in which coming into existence is not contained.

Let us now return to our story, and to our hypothesis

[3] The word "contradiction" must not here be taken in the frothy sense into which Hegel has beguiled himself and others and the concept—that it has the power to produce something. As long as nothing has come into existence, the contradiction is merely the impulsive power in the passion of wonder, its *nisus*; but it is not the *nisus* of the process of coming into existence itself. When the process of coming into existence has occurred, the con-tradiction is again present as the *nisus* of the wonder in the passion which reproduces the coming into existence.

that the God *has been.* As far as the direct and ordinary form of the historical is concerned, we have seen that this cannot become historical for immediate sensation or cognition, either for a contemporary or for a successor. But this historical fact which is the content of our hypothesis has a peculiar character, since it is not an ordinary historical fact, but a fact based on a self-contradiction. (This is sufficient to show that in relation to this fact there is no difference between an immediate contemporary and a successor; for over against a self-contradiction, and the risk involved in giving it assent, an immediate contemporaneity can yield no advantage.) Yet it is an historical fact, and only for the apprehension of Faith. Faith is here taken first in the direct and ordinary sense [belief], as the relationship of the mind to the historical; but secondly also in the eminent sense, the sense in which the word can be used only once, i.e., many times, but only in one relationship. From the eternal point of view, one does not *have Faith* that the God exists [eternally is], even if one assumes that he does exist. The use of the word Faith in this connection enshrines a misunderstanding. Socrates did not have faith that the God existed. What he knew about the God he arrived at by way of Recollection; the God's existence was for him by no means historical existence. If his knowledge of the God was imperfect in comparison with his who according to our supposition receives the condition from the God himself, this does not concern us here; for Faith does not have to do with essence, but with being [historical existence], and the assumption that the God is determines him eternally and not historically. The historical fact for a contemporary is that the God has *come into existence*; for the member of a later generation the historical fact is that the God has been present through *having come into existence*. Herein precisely lies the contradiction. No one can become immediately contemporary with this historical fact, as has been shown in the preceding; it is the object of Faith, since it concerns coming into existence. No question is here raised as to the true content of this; the question is if one will give assent to the God's having come into existence, by which the God's eternal essence is inflected in the dialectical determinations of coming into existence.

Our historical fact thus stands before us. It has no immediate contemporary, since it is historical in the first degree, corresponding to faith [belief] in the ordinary sense; it has no immediate contemporary in the second degree, since it is based upon a contradiction, corresponding to Faith in the eminent sense. But this last resemblance, subsisting between those who are most diversely situated temporally, cancels the difference which in respect of the first relation exists for those of diverse temporal situations. Every time the believer makes this fact an object of his Faith, every time he makes it historical for himself, he re-instates the dialectical determinations of coming into existence with respect to it. If ever so many thousands of years have intervened, if the fact came to entail ever so many consequences, it does not on that account become more necessary (and the consequences themselves, from an ultimate point of view, are only relatively necessary, since they derive from the freely effecting cause); to say nothing of the topsy-turvy notion that the fact might become necessary by reason of the consequences, the consequences being wont to seek their ground in something else, and not to constitute a ground for that of which they are the consequences. If a contemporary or a predecessor saw ever so clearly the preparations, perceived intimations and symptoms of what was about to come, the fact was nevertheless not necessary when it came into existence. That is to say, this fact is no more necessary when viewed as future, than it is necessary when viewed as past.

The Disciple at Second Hand

"Dear reader! Since by our supposition 1843 years have elapsed between the contemporary disciple and the time of this conversation, there would seem to be ample reason to raise the question of a disciple at second hand, for this relationship must often have been repeated. The question seems one, therefore, that we cannot refuse to discuss; nor does it seem that we can dismiss the demand involved in the question for an explanation of the difficulties that may offer when we seek to determine the disciple at second hand in his resemblance to, and difference from, the contemporary disciple. But in spite of this, should we not perhaps first consider whether the above question is as legitimate as it lies near at hand? For if it should appear that the question is illegitimate, or that one cannot ask such a question without stupidity, and hence forfeiting the right to charge one with stupidity who happens to be so wise as not to be able to answer it—in that case the difficulties would seem to be removed."—"Undoubtedly; for when the question cannot be asked the answer need not trouble us, and the difficulty becomes slight indeed."—"This does not quite follow; for suppose the difficulty lay in perceiving that one cannot ask such a question. Or have you perhaps already perceived this; was it this you meant by what you said in our last conversation (Chapter IV), that you had understood me and all the consequences of my proposition, while I confess that I had not yet entirely understood myself?"—"By no means was this my meaning; nor is it my opinion that the question can be dismissed, so much the less as it immediately involves a new question, whether there is not a difference between the many who consort under the head: the disciple at second hand. In other words, is it right to divide so tremendous a section of time into two such unequal parts: the generation of contemporary disciples on the one hand, and all the subsequent generations on the other?"—"You mean that there must be room for question concerning the disciple at fifth hand, at seventh hand, and so forth. But even if to please you something were to be said about this, does it follow that a discussion of all these differences, unless it be in contradiction with itself, may not properly be comprised under a single head, over against the class: the contemporary disciple? Or would our discussion be justified if it imitated your example, in its simplicity following in the steps of your cunning, so as to transform the problem of the disciple at second hand into an entirely different problem, by which, instead of assenting to or dissenting from my proposal, you would find opportunity to trick me by raising a new question? But since you probably do not wish to continue this conversation from fear of its degenerating into sophistry and bickering, I will break it off at this point; but from the exposition I now intend to place before you, you will observe that notice has been taken of the remarks that have passed between us."

1

The class of disciples at second hand considered with respect to the differences comprised within it

In this section we do not reflect upon the relation between the secondary disciple and the contemporary dis-

ciple, but the differences considered are such as to leave
intact the identity which the internally different exhibits
over against something external; for the variation which is
only a variation within a class remains subordinate to the
identity which constitutes the class. For this reason it is not
arbitrary to cut off the discussion where we please; the
relative differences here in question constitute no sorites,
from which a new quality may be made to emerge by a
coup de mains, since they are all comprised within a determinate common quality. A sorites would arise only if
we subjected the concept of contemporaneity to a false
dialectic, for example by showing that in a certain sense
no one could be a contemporary, since no one could be
contemporary with every moment or phase; or by asking
where contemporaneity leaves off and non-contempora-
neity begins, whether there may not exist a twilight zone
subject to bargaining, of which the prating understanding
might say: to a certain degree, and so forth. All such inhuman profundities lead nowhere, or perhaps in our day
they may lead to a reputation for genuine speculative insight; for the despised sophism, the devil only knows
how, has become the wretched secret of genuine speculation, and the to-a-certain-degree mode of thought (that
travesty on tolerance which mediates everything without
petty scrupulosity), regarded as negative by the ancients,
has now become positive; and what the ancients regarded
as positive, the passion for distinctions, has now become
a childish folly.

Opposites stand revealed most clearly when they are
juxtaposed, and hence we choose for discussion here the
first generation of secondary disciples and the last, i.e.,
that which limits the given *spatium*, the 1843 years. We

shall make our exposition as brief as possible, since we do not speak historically but algebraically, and have no wish to distract or beguile the mind by the enchantments of the manifold. On the contrary, we shall strive constantly to remember to hold fast the common likeness subsisting beneath the differences discussed, as over against the contemporary disciple (not until we come to the next paragraph will we have occasion to note more precisely that the question of the disciple at second hand is at bottom illegitimate); and we shall take care to see that the differences do not swell to such proportions as to confuse everything.

A. THE FIRST GENERATION OF SECONDARY DISCIPLES

This generation enjoys the (relative) advantage of being nearer to an immediate certainty, of being nearer to the attainment of an exact and reliable account of what happened, from witnesses whose reliability is subject to collateral control. We have already in Chapter IV calculated the value of this immediate certainty. To be somewhat nearer to it is doubtless an illusory advantage; for he who is not so near to immediate certainty as to be immediately certain is absolutely separated from it. But suppose we try to estimate the value of this relative difference, that which marks the first generation of secondary disciples over against later ones; how great a value shall we assign to it? We can evaluate it only by comparing it with the advantage enjoyed by a contemporary. But his advantage, the advantage namely of immediate certainty in the strict sense, we have already shown in Chapter IV to be ambiguous (*anceps*—dangerous), and we shall show this further in the next paragraph.—Suppose there lived a man in the

immediately succeeding generation who combined in his
own person a tyrant's power with a tyrant's passion, and
suppose that this man had somehow conceived the idea of
concentrating his entire time and energy upon the problem
of bringing the truth to light on this point, would this
constitute him a disciple? Suppose he possessed himself of
all the contemporary witnesses still living, together with
the immediate circle of their associates; suppose he subjected them one by one to the most searching inquisition,
shutting them up in prison like the seventy interpreters,
starving them to make them tell the truth, confronting
them with one another in the craftiest possible manner, all
for the sake of making sure by every possible means of a
reliable account—would the possession of this account constitute him a disciple? Must not the God rather smile at
him, because he thought to arrogate to himself in this manner what cannot be purchased for money, nor yet seized
by violence? Even if the fact we speak of were a simple
historical fact, difficulties would not fail to present themselves as soon as he tried to realize an absolute agreement
in all petty details, which would be of extreme importance
to him, because the passion of faith, i.e., the passion with
the intensity of faith, had been misdirected upon the
merely historical as its object. It is a familiar fact that the
most conscientious and truthful of witnesses are the first
to involve themselves in contradiction when subjected to
inquisitorial treatment and questioned in the light of an
inquisitor's fixed idea; while it is the prerogative of a
hardened criminal, on account of the precision which an
evil conscience tends to enforce, not to contradict himself
in his lie. But leaving this aside, the fact of which we speak
is not a simple historical fact: of what advantage then is

all this precision? If he succeeded in bringing to pass a complicated account, consistent to the letter and to the minute, he would beyond all doubt be deceived. He would have obtained a certainty even greater than was possible for a contemporary observer, one who saw and heard; for the latter would quickly discover that he sometimes failed to see what was there, and sometimes saw what was not there, and so with his hearing. And besides, a contemporary would constantly be reminded that he did not see or hear the God immediately, but merely a humble human being who said of himself that he was the God; in other words, he would constantly be reminded that the fact in question was based upon a self-contradiction. Would this man then gain anything by reason of the reliability of his account? Historically speaking yes, but otherwise not; for all talk of the God's earthly beauty, when he was after all only in the form of a servant, an individual human being like one of us, the cause of offense; all talk of his immediately manifest divinity, though divinity is not an immediate characteristic, and the Teacher must first develop in the learner the most profound self-reflection, the sense of sin, as a condition for the understanding; all talk of the immediate miraculousness of his deeds, though a miracle does not exist for immediate apprehension, but only for faith, if it be true that whoever does not believe does not see the miracle—all such talk is here as everywhere galimatias, an attempt to substitute idle words for serious consideration.

This generation has the relative advantage of being nearer to the shock produced by the impact of our fact. This shock and its reverberations will help to arouse the attention. The significance of such an aroused attention (which may also issue in taking offense) has already been evaluated in Chapter IV. The being somewhat nearer to it in comparison with later generations, well, suppose we call it an advantage; its value can only be relative to the doubtful advantage enjoyed by an immediate contemporary. The advantage is entirely dialectical, like the aroused attention itself. It consists in having one's attention aroused, whether the result is that one believes or is offended. The aroused attention is by no means partial to faith, as if faith followed from the attention by a simple consequence. The advantage is that a state of mind is induced in which the crucial nature of the decision confronting the individual becomes more clearly evident. This is an advantage, and the only one of any account; aye, so significant is it that it is fearful, by no means an easy and comfortable convenience. Unless in consequence of a stupid insensibility this fact should some time deteriorate into a meaningless human conventionality, each subsequent generation will exhibit the same proportion of offense as the first; for there is no immediacy by the aid of which anyone could come any nearer to it. One may be educated up to this fact as much as you please, it will be of no avail. On the contrary, and especially if the educator is himself accomplished in this direction, it may help one to become a well-drilled chatterer, in whose mind there is no suspicion of the possibility of offense, nor any room for faith.

B. THE LAST GENERATION

This generation is far removed from the initial shock, but it has on the other hand the consequences to lean upon, the proof of probability afforded by the results. It has before it, as immediate datum, the consequences with which this fact must doubtless have invested everything; it has an obvious recourse to a demonstration of probability, from which however no immediate transition to Faith is possible, since as we have shown Faith is by no means partial to probability; to make such an assertion about Faith is to slander it.[1] If this fact came into the world as the Absolute

[1] The idea, in whatever concrete form it may be understood, of attaching a demonstration of probability to the improbable (to prove—that it is probable? but in that case the concept is altered; to prove that it is improbable? but in that case it is a contradiction to use probability for the purpose) is so stupid when seriously conceived, that it would seem impossible for it to be entertained; but as jest and banter it is in my view extraordinarily amusing; to practise in this narrow turning is a very entertaining pastime.—A good man wishes to serve humanity by presenting a probability-proof, so as to help it accept the improbable. He is successful beyond all measure; deeply moved, he receives congratulations and addresses of thanksgiving, not only from the quality, who know how to appreciate the proof as experts, but also from the general public— and alas! the good man has precisely ruined everything.—Or a man has a conviction; the content of this conviction is the absurd, the improbable. The same man is not a little vain. The following procedure is adopted. In as quiet and sympathetic a manner as possible you prompt him to an expression of his conviction. Since he suspects nothing wrong, he presents it in sharply defined outlines. When he has finished, you come down upon him with an attack calculated to be as irritating as possible for his vanity. He is embarrassed, abashed, apologetic, "to think that he could entertain so absurd an opinion." Instead of replying calmly: "Honored sir, you speak like a fool; of course it is absurd, as it ought to be, in spite of all objections, which I have thought through myself in a far more terrible shape than anyone else could bring them home to me; in spite of which I have deliberately chosen to believe the improbable"—instead of replying thus, he seeks to bring a probability-demonstration to bear. Now you come to his assistance, you permit yourself to be vanquished, and finally wind up about as follows: "Ah, now I see it; why, nothing could be more probable!" And

Paradox, nothing that happens subsequently can avail to change this. The consequences will in all eternity remain the consequences of a paradox, and hence in an ultimate view will be precisely as improbable as the Paradox itself; unless it is to be supposed that the consequences, which as such are derivative, have retroactive power to transform the Paradox, which would be about as reasonable as to suppose that a son had retroactive power to transform his own father. Even if the consequences be conceived in a purely logical relation to their cause, and hence under the form of immanence, it still remains true that they can be conceived only as identical and homogeneous with their cause; least of all will they have a transforming power. To have the consequences as a datum is then precisely as dubious an advantage as to have an immediate certainty; whoever takes the consequences immediately to his credit is deceived, precisely as one who takes the immediate certainty for Faith.

The advantage of the consequences would seem to lie in a gradual *naturalization* of this fact. If such is the case, i.e., if such a thing is conceivable, the later generation has even a direct advantage over the contemporary generation; and

---

then you embrace him; if you wish to carry the jest very far you kiss him, and thank him *ob meliorem informationem*. In saying farewell you look once more into the depths of his romantic eyes, and part from him as from a friend and brother in life and death, a congenial soul whom you have learned to understand for ever. Such banter is justified; for if the man had not been vain, I would have stood revealed as a fool over against the sincere earnestness of his conviction.—What Epicurus says about the individual's relationship to death (though his view contains but a sorry comfort) holds of the relation between the probable and the improbable: when I am, it (death) is not, and when it (death) is, I am not.

a man would surely have to be very stupid if he could speak of the consequences in this sense, and yet rave about how fortunate the contemporaries were. Under the assumption of naturalization, it will be possible for a later generation to appropriate the fact without the slightest embarrassment, without sensing anything of the ambiguity of the aroused attention, from which offense may issue as well as faith. However, this fact is no respecter of the drillmaster's discipline; it is too proud to desire a disciple whose willingness to attach himself to the cause is based upon the favorable turn that events have taken; it disdains naturalization, whether under the protection of a king or a professor. It is and remains the Paradox, and cannot be assimilated by any speculation. This fact exists for Faith alone. Faith may indeed become the *second nature* in a man, but the man in whom it becomes a second nature must surely have had a *first* nature, since Faith became the second. If the fact in question is *naturalized*, this may be expressed in relation to the individual by saying that the individual is born with faith, i.e., with his second nature. If we begin in this manner all sorts of galimatias will simultaneously begin to jubilate; for now the flood of nonsense has broken through and nothing can stop it. This particular nonsense will naturally have been discovered by the process of making an advance; for in Socrates' view there was certainly a genuine meaning, though we left it behind in order to discover the hypothesis here set forth; such galimatias as that just described would doubtless feel deeply insulted if anyone refused to concede that it had advanced far beyond Socrates. There is meaning even in a doctrine of transmigration; but the doctrine that a man may be born with his second nature, a second nature involving a reference to a temporally dated historical fact, is a veritable *non plus ultra* of absurdity. From the Socratic point of view the individual has an existence prior to his coming into being and remembers himself, so that the Recollection here involved is his preexistence, and not a recollection about his preexistence. His nature (his one nature, for here there is no question of a first and second nature) is determined in continuity with itself. But in our project, on the contrary, everything is forward-looking and historical, so that the notion of being born with faith is as plausible as the notion of being born twenty-four years old. Were it really possible to find an individual born with Faith, he would constitute a prodigy, more notable even than the marvel told of by the barber in *The Busy Man*, the birth in the Neuen-Buden; even though barbers and "busy" men be inclined to regard him as a precious little darling, the crowning triumph of philosophical speculation.—Or is it perhaps the case that the individual is born with both natures simultaneously; please to note, not with two natures which supplement one another and together form an ordinary human nature, but with two complete human natures, one of which presupposes the intermediation of an historical event. If this is the case, everything which we have proposed in our first chapter is confounded, nor do we stand at the Socratic order of things, but we stand before a confusion which not even Socrates would have been able to master. It would be a confusion in the forward direction having much in common with that invented by Apollonius of Tyana in the backward direction. Apollonius was not content like Socrates to remember himself as being before he came into existence (the eternity and continuity of the consciousness is the fundamental meaning of the Socratic thought), but was quick to make an advance; he remembered who he was before he became himself. If this fact has been naturalized, birth is no longer merely birth, but is at the same time a *new birth*, so that one who has never before been in existence is born anew—in being born the first time.—In the individual life the hypothesis of naturalization is expressed in the principle that the individual is born with faith; in the life of the race it must be expressed in the proposition that the human race, after the introduction of this fact, has become an entirely different race, though determined in continuity with the first. In that event the race ought to adopt a new name; for there is indeed nothing inhuman about faith as we have proposed to conceive it, as a birth within a birth (the new birth); but if it were as the proposed objection would conceive it, it would be a fabulous monstrosity.

The advantage afforded by the consequences is dubious for still another reason, in so far as the consequences do not follow directly, as simple consequences. Let us assess the advantage of the consequences at its highest maximum, and assume that this fact has completely transformed the world, that it has interpenetrated even the smallest detail of life with its omnipresence—how has this come to pass? Surely not all at once, but by a succession of steps; and how have these steps been taken? By each particular generation again coming into relationship with this fact. This intermediary determination must be brought under control, so that the entire virtue of the consequences can redound to one's advantage only by means of a conversion. Or may not a misunderstanding also have consequences, may not a lie also be powerful? And has it not happened so to each generation? If now the previous generations collectively propose to bequeath to the last the whole splendid array of consequences without further ado, will not the consequences constitute a misunderstanding? Or is not Venice built over the sea, even if it became so solidly built up that a generation finally came upon the scene that did not notice it; and would it not be a sad misunderstanding if this last generation made the mistake of permitting the piles to rot and the city to sink? But consequences founded on a paradox are humanly speaking built over a yawning chasm, and their total content, which can be transmitted to the individual only with the express understanding that they rest upon a paradox, are not to be appropriated as a settled estate, for their entire value trembles in the balance.

C. COMPARISON

We shall not pursue these considerations further, but leave it to each one in particular to practise for himself the art of coming back to this thought from the most diverse angles, using his imagination to hit upon the strangest cases of relativity in difference and situation, in order thereupon to cast up the account. Thus the quantitative is confined within its limits, and within these limits it has unrestricted scope. It is the quantitative that gives to life its manifold variety, ever weaving its motley tapestry; it is that sister of Destiny who sat spinning at the wheel. But Thought is the other sister, whose task it is to cut the thread; which, leaving the figure, should be done every time the quantitative attempts to create a new quality.

The first generation of secondary disciples has the advantage that the difficulty is patently there; for it is always an advantage, an alleviation of a difficult task, that it is made to appear difficult. If the last generation, beholding the first, and seeing it almost sink under its burden of awe and fear, were to find it in its heart to say: "It is impossible to understand why they should take it so hard, for the whole is not heavier than that one could easily take it up and run with it," there will doubtless be someone to answer: "You are welcome to run with it if you like; but you ought at all events make sure that what you run with really is that of which we are speaking; for there is no disputing the fact that it is easy enough to run with the wind."

The last generation has the advantage of a greater ease; but as soon as it discovers that this ease is precisely the danger which breeds the difficulty, this new difficulty will correspond to the difficulty of the fear confronting the first generation, and it will be gripped as primitively by awe and fear as the first generation of secondary disciples.

2

The problem of the disciple at second hand

Before taking up the problem itself, let us first present one or two considerations by way of orientation. (a) If our fact is assumed to be a simple historical fact, contemporaneity is a *desideratum*. It is an advantage to be a contemporary in the more precise sense described in Chapter IV, or to be as near to such contemporaneity as possible, or to be in a position to check the reliability of contemporary witnesses, and so forth. Every historical fact is merely relative, and hence it is in order for time, the relative power, to decide the relative fortunes of men with respect to contemporaneity; such a fact has no greater significance, and only childishness or stupidity could so exaggerate its importance as to make it absolute. (b) If the fact in question is an eternal fact, every age is equally near; but not, it should be noted, in Faith; for Faith and the historical are correlative concepts, and it is only by an accommodation to a less exact usage that I employ in this connection the word "fact," which is derived from the historical realm. (c) If the fact in question is an absolute fact, or to determine it still more precisely, if it is the fact we have described, it would be a contradiction to suppose that time had any power to differentiate the fortunes of men with respect to it, that is to say, in any decisive sense. Whatever can be essentially differentiated by time is *eo ipso* not the Absolute; this would be to make the Absolute itself a *casus* in life, or a *status* relative to other things. But though the Absolute is declinable in all the *casibus* of life, it remains itself ever the same; and though it enters continually into relations with other things, it constantly remains *status absolutus*. But the absolute fact is also an historical fact. Unless we are careful to insist on this point our entire hypothesis is nullified; for then we speak only of an eternal fact. The absolute fact is an historical fact, and as such it is the object of Faith. The historical aspect must indeed be accentuated, but not in such a way that it becomes decisive for the individuals, for then we stand at the alternative described in (a), though when so understood it involves a contradiction; for a simple historical fact is not absolute, and has no power to force an absolute decision. But neither may the historical aspect of our fact be eliminated, for then we have only an eternal fact.—Now just as the historical gives occasion for the contemporary to become a disciple, but only it must be noted through receiving the condition from the God himself, since otherwise we speak Socratically, so the testimony of contemporaries gives occasion for each successor to become a disciple, but only it must be noted through receiving the condition from the God himself.

Now we are ready to begin. From the God himself everyone receives the condition who by virtue of the condition becomes the disciple. If this is the case (and this has been expounded in the foregoing, where it was shown that the immediate contemporaneity is merely an occasion, but not in the sense that the condition was presupposed as already present), what becomes of the problem of the disciple at second hand? For whoever has what he has from the God himself clearly has it at first hand; and he who does not have it from the God himself is not a disciple.

Let us assume that it is otherwise, that the contemporary generation of disciples had received the condition from the God, and that the subsequent generations were to receive it from these contemporaries—what would follow? We shall not distract the attention by reflecting upon the historical pusillanimity with which the contemporary accounts would presumably be sought after, as if everything depended on that, thus introducing a new contradition and a new confusion (for if we once begin in this manner, the confusions will be inexhaustible). No, if the contemporary disciple gives the condition to the successor, the latter will come to believe in him. He receives the condition from him, and thus the contemporary becomes the object of Faith for the successor; for whoever gives the individual this condition is *eo ipso* (cf. the preceding) the object of Faith, and the God.

Such a meaningless consequence will surely deter thought from making this assumption. If on the contrary the successor also receives the condition from the God, the

Socratic relationships will return, of course within the total difference which is constituted by the fact in question, and by the individual's (the contemporary's and the successor's) particular relationship to the God. The above meaningless consequence on the other hand is unthinkable, in a different sense than when we say of the fact in question and of the individual's particular relationship to the God, that it is unthinkable. Our hypothetical assumption of this fact and of the individual's particular relationship to the God contains no self-contradiction, and thought is free to occupy itself therewith as with the strangest proposal possible. But the meaningless consequence developed above contains a self-contradiction; it does not rest content with positing an absurdity, the content of our hypothesis, but within this absurdity it brings forth a self-contradiction, namely that the God is the God for the contemporary, but that the contemporary is the God for a third party. Only through placing the God in particular relationship with the individual did our project go beyond Socrates; but who would dare to appear before Socrates with the nonsense that a human being is a God in his relation to another human being? The nature of the relationship between one human being and another is something that Socrates understood with a heroism of soul which it requires courage even to appreciate. And yet it is necessary to acquire the same understanding within the framework of what has here been assumed, namely the understanding that one human being, in so far as he is a believer, owes nothing to another but everything to the God. It will doubtless be readily perceived that this understanding is not easy, and especially not easy constantly to preserve (for to understand it once for all without meeting the concrete objections that present themselves in life, i.e., to imagine that one has understood it, is not difficult); and he who will make a beginning of practising himself in this understanding will often enough catch himself in a misunderstanding and will have need of the utmost circumspection if he proposes to enter into communication with others. But if he has understood it, he will also understand that there is not and never can be a disciple at second hand; for the believer, and he alone is a disciple, is always in possession of the autopsy of Faith; he does not see through the eyes of another, and he sees only what every believer sees—with the eyes of Faith.

What then can a contemporary do for a successor? (a) He can inform him that he has himself believed this fact, which is not in the strict sense a communication (as expressed in the absence of any immediate contemporaneity, and in the circumstance that the fact is based upon a contradiction), but merely affords an occasion. For when I say that this or that has happened, I make an historical communication; but when I say: "I believe and have believed that so-and-so has taken place, *although it is a folly to the understanding and an offense to the human heart*," then I have simultaneously done everything in my power to prevent anyone else from determining his own attitude in immediate continuity with mine, asking to be excused from all companionship, since every individual is compelled to make up his own mind in precisely the same manner. (b) In this form he can relate the content of the fact. But this content exists only for Faith, in the same sense that colors exist only for sight and sounds for hearing. In this form, then, the content can be related; in any other form he merely indulges in empty words, perhaps misleading the successor to determine himself in continuity with the inanity.

In what sense may the credibility of a contemporary witness interest a successor? Not with respect to whether he really has had Faith, as he has testified of himself. This does not concern a successor in the least; such knowledge would profit him nothing; it can neither help him nor hurt him with respect to becoming a believer. Only one who receives the condition from the God is a believer. (This corresponds exactly to the requirement that man must renounce his reason, and on the other hand discloses the only form of authority that corresponds to Faith.) If any-one proposes to believe, i.e., imagines himself to believe, because many good and upright people living here on the hill have believed, i.e., have said that they believed (for no man can control the profession of another further than this; even if the other has endured, borne, suffered all for the Faith, an outsider cannot get beyond what he says about himself, for a lie can be stretched precisely as far as the truth—in the eyes of men, but not in the sight of God), then he is a fool, and it is essentially indifferent whether he believes on account of his own and perhaps a widely held opinion about what good and upright people believe, or believes a Münchausen. If the credibility of a contemporary is to have any interest for him—and alas! one may be sure that this will create a tremendous sensa-tion, and give occasion for the writing of folios; for this counterfeit earnestness, which asks whether so-and-so is trustworthy instead of whether the inquirer himself has faith, is an excellent mask for spiritual indolence, and for town gossip on a European scale—if the credibility of such a witness is to have any significance it must be with respect to the historical fact. But what historical fact? The historical fact which can become an object only for Faith, and which one human being cannot communicate to another, i.e., which can indeed be communicated to another but not so that the other believes it; and which if communicated in the form of Faith is so communicated as to prevent the other, so far as possible, from accepting it immediately. If the fact spoken of were a simple historical fact, the accuracy of the historical sources would be of great importance. Here this is not the case, for Faith cannot be distilled from even the nicest accuracy of detail. The historical fact that the God has been in human form is the essence of the matter; the rest of the historical detail is not even as important as if we had to do with a human being instead of with the God. Jurists say that a capital crime submerges all lesser crimes, and so it is with Faith. Its absurdity makes all petty difficulties vanish. Inconsistencies which would otherwise be disconcerting do not count for anything here; they make no difference whatsoever. But it does make a difference on the contrary, if someone by petty calculation should try to auction off faith to the highest bidder; it makes so much difference as to prevent him from ever becoming a believer. If the contemporary generation had left nothing behind them but these words: "We have believed that in such and such a year the God appeared among us in the humble figure of a servant, that he lived and taught in our community, and finally died," it would be more than enough. The contemporary generation would have done all that was necessary; for this little advertisement, this *nota bene* on a page of universal history, would be sufficient to afford an occasion for a successor, and the most voluminous account can in all eternity do nothing more.

If we wish to express the relation subsisting between a contemporary and his successor in the briefest possible compass, but without sacrificing accuracy to brevity, we may say: The successor believes *by means of* (this expresses the occasional) the testimony of the contemporary, and *in virtue of* the condition he himself receives from the God.— The testimony of the contemporary provides an occasion for the successor, just as the immediate contemporaneity provides an occasion for the contemporary. And if the testimony is what it ought to be, namely the testimony of a believer, it will give occasion for precisely the same ambiguity of the aroused attention as the witness himself has experienced, occasioned by the immediate contemporaneity. If the testimony is not of this nature, then it is *either* by an historian, and does not deal essentially with the object of Faith, as when a contemporary historian who was not a believer recounts one or another fact; *or* it is by a philosopher, and does not deal with the object of Faith. The believer on the other hand communicates his testimony in such form as to forbid immediate acceptance; for the words: I believe—in spite of the Reason and my own powers of invention, present a very serious counter-consideration.

There is no disciple at second hand. The first and the last are essentially on the same plane, only that a later generation finds its occasion in the testimony of a contemporary generation, while the contemporary generation finds this occasion in its own immediate contemporaneity, and in so far owes nothing to any other generation. But this immediate contemporaneity is merely an occasion, which can scarcely be expressed more emphatically than in the proposition that the disciple, if he understood himself, must wish that the immediate contemporaneity should cease, by the God's leaving the earth.

*   *

But I think I hear someone say: "It is very strange; I have now read your exposition through to the end, and really not without a certain degree of interest, noting with pleasure that there was no catchword, no invisible script. But how you twist and turn, so that, just as Saft always ended up in the pantry, you inevitably always manage to introduce some little word or phrase that is not your own, and which awakens disturbing recollections. This thought, that it is profitable for the disciple that the God should again leave the earth, is taken from the New Testament; it is found in the Gospel of John. However, whether this procedure of yours is intentional or not, whether you have perhaps desired to give this remark a special significance by clothing it in this form or not, as the case now stands it would seem that the advantage of the contemporary, which I was originally inclined to estimate very highly, is considerably reduced, since there can be no question of a disciple at second hand; which in plain English is as much as to say that all are essentially alike. But not only so; for the immediate contemporaneity viewed as an advantage seems by your last remark so dubious that the most that can be said for it is that it is better that it should cease. This would seem to indicate that it is an intermediate situation, having its significance indeed, and not eliminable without, as you would say, turning back to the Socratic order of things, but nevertheless without absolute significance for the contemporary; he is not deprived of anything essential by its cessation, but rather profits by it; although if it had not been he loses all, and returns to the Socratic order of things."—"Well said, I would reply, did not modesty forbid; for you speak as if it were myself. It is precisely as you say, the immediate contemporaneity is by no means a decisive advantage. This is readily seen if we think it through, and are not merely prompted by curiosity; provided we are not in too much of a hurry, provided we are not overly desirous, aye, perhaps in desire already standing on tip-toe in readiness to risk our lives to be first to tell remarkable news, like the barber in ancient Greece; and provided we are not so stupid as to consider such a death to be the death of a martyr. The immediate contemporaneity is so far from being an advantage that the contemporary must precisely desire its cessation, lest he be tempted to devote himself to seeing and hearing with his bodily eyes and ears, which is all a waste of effort and a grievous, aye a dangerous toil. But these considerations, as you have doubtless observed, belong in another place, in connection with the problem of what advantage a contemporary believer, after having become a believer, might have of his contemporaneity; while here we speak only of how far the immediate contemporaneity makes it easier to become a believer. A successor cannot be so tempted, for he is confined to the testimony of contemporaries, which in so far as it is the testimony of believers, has the prohibitive form of Faith. If the successor therefore understands himself he will wish that the contemporary testimony be not altogether too voluminous, and above all not filling so many books that the world can scarce contain them. There is in the immediate contemporaneity an unrest, which does not cease until the word goes forth that it is finished. But the succeeding tranquillity must not be such as to do away with the historical, for then everything will be Socratic."—"In this manner then equality seems to have been achieved, and the differences between the parties involved brought back to a fundamental likeness."—"Such is also my opinion; but you should take into consideration the fact that it is the God himself who effects the reconciliation. Is it thinkable that the God would enter into a covenant with a few, such that this their covenant with him established a difference between them and all other men so unjust as to cry to heaven for vengeance? That would be to bring strife instead of peace. Is it conceivable that the God would permit an accident of time to decide to whom he would grant his favor? Or is it not rather worthy of the God to make his covenant with men equally difficult for every human being in every time and place; equally difficult, since no man is able to give himself the condition, nor yet is to receive it from another, thus introducing new strife; equally difficult but also equally easy, since the God grants the condition. This is why I looked upon my project in the beginning as a godly one (in so far as an hypothesis can be viewed in this light), and still so consider it, though not on that account being indifferent to any human objection; on the contrary I now ask you once more, if you have any valid objection, to bring it forward."—"How festive you suddenly become! Even if the case did not demand it, one would almost have to make some objection for the sake of the festiveness; unless it should be regarded as more festive to omit it, and your solemn challenge is merely intended indirectly to enjoin silence. But that the nature of the objection may at least be such as not to disturb this festive mood, I will draw it from the festivity by which it seems to me that a later generation will distinguish itself from the contemporary generation. I recognize indeed that the contemporary generation must profoundly feel and suffer the pain entailed by the coming into being of such a Paradox, or as you have put it, the God's implantation of himself in human life. But gradually the new order of things will presumably struggle its way through to victory; and then at last will come the happy generation which garners with songs of joy the fruits of the seed sowed in the first generation with so many tears. Now this triumphant generation, which passes through life with song and clang, is surely different from the first and earlier ones?"—"Aye, undoubtedly it is different, and perhaps so different as not to retain the resemblance which makes it necessary for us to take it into consideration; it may be lacking in the condition which could cause its difference to disconcert our efforts to establish equality. But can such a triumphant generation, which goes through life as you say with song and clang, by which if my memory does not fail me you intend to remind me of the sophomoric and ale-Norse translation of a scripture passage by a not unknown genius—can this generation actually be a believing generation? Verily, if Faith ever gets the notion of marching forward triumphantly *en masse*, it will not be necessary to license the singing of songs of mockery, for it would not help to forbid them to all. Even if men were stricken dumb, this mad procession would draw upon itself a shrill laughter, like the mocking nature-tones on the island of Ceylon; for a faith that celebrates its triumph is the most ridiculous thing conceivable. If the contemporary generation of believers

found no time to triumph, neither will any later generation; for the task is always the same, and Faith is always
militant. But as long as there is struggle there is always
a possibility of defeat, and with respect to Faith it is therefore well not to triumph before the time, that is to say, in
time; for when will there be found time to compose songs
of triumph or occasion to sing them? If such a thing were
to happen it would be as if an army drawn up in battle
array, instead of marching forward to meet the enemy,
were to march home again in triumph to their barracks in
the city—even if no human being laughed at this, even if
the entire contemporary generation sympathized with this
abracadabra, would not the stifled laughter of the universe
break forth where it was least expected? What would the
behavior of such a so-called believer be but an intensifica-
tion of the offense committed by the contemporary believer
(compare Chapter II) who begged of the God—in vain,
since the God would not—that he refrain from exposing
himself to humiliation and contempt? For this later so-
called believer was not only himself unwilling to bear
humiliation and contempt, unwilling to strive as the
world's fool, but *was* willing to believe when this could
be done with song and clang. To such a man the God
will not, nay cannot say, as to the contemporary in question: And so you love only the omnipotent wonder-worker,
but not Him who humbled himself to become your equal!
But here I will break off. Even if I were a better dialectician
than I am, there would still be a limit to my powers; at
bottom it is an immovable firmness with respect to the
absolute, and with respect to absolute distinctions, that
makes a man a good dialectician. This is something that
our age has altogether overlooked, in and by its repudia-

tion of the principle of contradiction, failing to perceive what Aristotle nevertheless pointed out, namely that the proposition: the principle of contradiction is annulled, itself rests upon the principle of contradiction, since otherwise the opposite proposition, that it is not annulled, is equally true. One further remark I wish to make, however, with respect to your many animadversions, all pointing to my having introduced borrowed expressions in the course of my exposition. That such is the case I do not deny, nor will I now conceal from you that it was done purposely, and that in the next section of this piece, if I ever write such a section, it is my intention to call the whole by its right name, and to clothe the problem in its historical costume. If I ever write a next section; for an author of pieces such as I am has no seriousness of purpose, as you will doubtless hear said about me; why then should I now at the end feign a seriousness I do not have, in order to please men by making what is perhaps a great promise? It is a frivolous matter, namely, to write a piece—but to promise the System is a serious thing; many a man has become serious both in his own eyes and in those of others by making such a promise. However, what the historical costume of the following section will be is not hard to see. It is well known that Christianity is the only historical phenomenon which in spite of the historical, nay precisely by means of the historical, has intended itself to be for the single individual the point of departure for his eternal consciousness, has intended to interest him otherwise than merely historically, has intended to base his eternal happiness on his relationship to something historical. No system of philosophy, addressing itself only to thought, no mythology, addressing itself solely to the imagination, no historical knowledge, addressing itself to the memory, has ever had this idea: of which it may be said with all possible ambiguity in this connection, that it did not arise in the heart of any man. But this is something I have to a certain extent wished to forget, and, making use of the unlimited freedom of an hypothesis, have assumed that the whole was a curious conceit of my own; which I did not wish to abandon, however, until I had thought it through. The monks never finished telling the history of the world because they always began with the creation; if in dealing with the relations between philosophy and Christianity we begin by first recounting what has previously been said, how will it ever be possible—not to finish but to begin; for history continues to grow. If we have to begin first with 'that great thinker and sage, *executor Novi Testamenti*, Pontius Pilate,' who in his own way has been of considerable service to Christianity and to philosophy, even if he did not discover the principle of mediation; and if before beginning with him we must wait for one or another decisive contribution (perhaps the System), for which the banns have several times already been published *ex cathedra*; in that case how will we ever come to begin?"

MORAL

The projected hypothesis indisputably makes an advance upon Socrates, which is apparent at every point. Whether it is therefore more true than the Socratic doctrine is an entirely different question, which cannot be decided in the same breath, since we have here assumed a new organ: Faith; a new presupposition: the consciousness of Sin; a new decision: the Moment; and a new Teacher: the God in Time. Without these I certainly never would have dared present myself for inspection before that master of Irony, admired through the centuries, whom I approach with a palpitating enthusiasm that yields to none. But to make an advance upon Socrates and yet say essentially the same things as he, only not nearly so well—that at least is not Socratic.

COMMENTARY

Commentary

BY NIELS THULSTRUP

THE COMMENTARY presents the most important variations of Sören Kierkegaard's draft and manuscript from the published work. In addition, summary accounts are given of Kierkegaard's knowledge of various philosophers, philosophical and theological schools, and issues of concern to him in *Philosophical Fragments*. In these accounts the main emphasis is placed upon clarification of his relationship to German Speculative Idealism and its various exponents, including the Danish Hegelians. The accounts usually consist of pointing out the particular works and the presuppositions used by Kierkegaard and are not a sketch of the general historical background. As far as possible, reference is made to Kierkegaard's actual sources, which in certain instances are not identical with the primary sources.

Except where noted otherwise, Biblical quotations in English are from the Revised Standard Version and in Danish from the authorized Danish translation of 1819, which Kierkegaard used. References to Plato's works are to the third and last Jowett edition (New York: Random House, I-II, 1937) and in the Stephens pagination. The Oxford *Aristotle*, I-XII, ed. W. D. Ross (London: Oxford University Press, 1908-1952) is used throughout the Commentary. Quotations from Hegel and other writers are from the available English translations. Quotations from Kierkegaard's other formal writings are also from the available English translations. English translations of selections from Kierkegaard's *Papirer* (*Journals*) and other Danish or German works not yet in translation are, unless otherwise indicated, by Howard V. Hong.

A complete survey of all the literature has not been attempted. Emphasis has been placed upon the more recent main works and special studies of Kierkegaard's thought and its historical context. Beyond this there is only mention of selected recent monographs on the thinkers, schools, or problems referred to. Indebtedness to commonly used general reference works is acknowledged although no particularized references are given.

In the preparation of this Commentary the following have been of significant help: A. B. Drachmann's notes to *Philosophiske Smuler* (sv iv, 15-27 of the appendix), the textual explanations in F. J. Billeskov Jansen, *Sören Kierkegaards Værker i Udvalg* (Copenhagen: 1950), iv, 153-63, Emanuel Hirsch's notes to his translation, *Philosophische Brocken* (Cologne: Diederichs, 1952), pp. 165-90. For certain portions David Swenson's notes to his English translation have also been useful and in some instances have been included verbatim. It must be observed that the great indebtedness of the present Commentary to its predecessors is not lessened by the declared or unexpressed lack of unity on particulars. Likewise it must be observed that no explanation has been entered without rechecking.

A survey of Kierkegaard research in Scandinavia has been made by Aage Kabell in *Kierkegaard-Studiet i Norden* (Copenhagen: Hagerup, 1948) and by Aage Henriksen in *Methods and Results of Kierkegaard-Studies in Scandinavia,* Publications of The Kierkegaard Society, 1 (Copenhagen: Munksgaard, 1951). In "Studiet af Kierkegaard udenfor Skandinavien 1945-1952" (*Dansk teologisk Tidskrift*, 1953, pp. 65-80) and in "Kierkegaard-Studiet i Skandinavien 1945-52" (*Edda*, 1954, pp. 79-122, and in *Theology Today*, 1955, pp. 297-312) I have given a critical survey. Mention should also be made of R. Jolivet's "Sören Kierkegaard Bibliography" in I. M. Bochenski, ed., *Bibliographische Einführingen in das Studium der Philosophie* (Bern: Francke Verlag, 1948) and to E. Ortmann Nielsen (with the assistance of Niels Thulstrup), *Sören Kierkegaard, Bidrag til en Bibliografi* (Copenhagen: Munksgaard, 1951). The periodical *S. Kierkegaardiana* (Copenhagen: Munksgaard, 1955ff.) brings information about the most recent literature.

In the Commentary the following abbreviations are used:

sv (with reference to volume and page): *Sören Kierkegaards Samlede Værker* [*Collected Works*], 1-xv, second edition, edited by A. B. Drachmann, J. L. Heiberg, and H. O. Lange (Copenhagen: Gyldendal, 1920-1936).

Pap.: *Sören Kierkegaards Papirer* [*Journals*], 1-xi, edited by P. A. Heiberg, V. Kuhr, and E. Torsting (Copenhagen: Gyldendal, 1909-1948).

Breve og Aktstykker: *Breve og Aktstykker* [*Letters and Documents*] *vedrörende Sören Kierkegaard*, 1-11, edited by Niels Thulstrup (Copenhagen: Munksgaard, 1953-1954).

Ktl.: *Fortegnelse over Dr. Sören A. Kierkegaards efterladte Bogsamling* [*Catalog of the Books in the Estate of Dr. Sören A. Kierkegaard*] . . . (Copenhagen: 1856). Critical edition edited by Niels Thulstrup, *Katalog over Sören Kierkegaards Bibliotek* (Copenhagen: Munksgaard, 1957).

W.a.A.: *Georg Wilhelm Friedrich Hegels Werke*, Vollständige Ausgabe durch einen Verein von Freunden des Verewigten, 1-xviii (1832-1840). J.A., together with volume and page number, refers to the later Jubiläumsausgabe of Hegel's works (Stuttgart: Frommanns Verlag, 1927ff.). Quotations from Hegel are in the most available English translation, to which page reference is given following references to the two German editions.

Full bibliographical data on English books and the publication dates of works in other languages are given when they are first mentioned. Thereafter reference is usually only by author and title.

In the Commentary references to particular portions of the text of *Philosophical Fragments* are by page-numbers of the present edition followed by the cue-words in italics.

COMMENTARY ON THE TITLE-PAGE AND MOTTO

Title-page. This page of *Philosophical Fragments*, which appeared June 13, 1844, originally looked somewhat different. Originally it read: *Philosophiske Piecer* [Philosophical Pieces] by S. Kierkegaard, No. 1. Then *Piecer* was changed to *Smuler* [*Fragments*] and the sub-title *"eller en Smule Philosophie"* [*or a Fragment of Philosophy*] was added. Originally the problem had this formulation: "How do I arrive at an historical point of departure for my eternal consciousness; how can such a point of departure have more than historical interest; how can I base my salvation upon historical knowledge? —A dogmatic-philosophical problem." This was changed to: "Is an historical point of departure possible for an eternal consciousness; how can such a point of departure have any other than a merely historical interest; is it possible to base an eternal happiness upon historical knowledge?" Whereas the change from *Pieces* to *Fragments* and the elimination of "No. 1" were certainly due to the fact that Kierkegaard had given up a plan to have the book appear as the first in a special series, the changes in the formulation of the problem are an indication that the problem is not only the author's private, personal problem but a fundamental and universal one. Inasmuch as Sören Kierkegaard is the author, according to the draft of the title-page, this can only mean that the work represents his own views. By using the pseudonym *Johannes Climacus* and listing himself as responsible only for publication he has significantly removed himself from the work and its reader. To this end major formal changes were also made in the Preface (see below).

In "A First and Last Declaration" in *Concluding Unscientific Postscript* (Princeton: Princeton University Press, 1941, pp. 552ff.), after having pointed out that in a legal and literary sense the responsibility for the pseudonymous authorship is his, Kierkegaard writes: "For this reason my name as editor was promptly placed on the title-page of the *Fragments* (1844), because the absolute importance of the subject for reality required the expression of dutiful observance, that there should be named a responsible person to accept what reality might propose. The Preface to the *Postscript* (p. 3) says in humorous form: 'The work [*Fragments*] was permitted to enter the world unnoticed, without fuss or fury, without the shedding of ink or blood. It was neither reviewed nor mentioned anywhere. No learned outcry was raised to mislead the expectant multitude; no shouts of warning from our literary sentinels served to put the reading public on its guard; everything happened with due decency and decorum.'" The actual disappointment is detectable behind the words. Kierkegaard's later explanations of pseudonymity in *Philosophical Fragments* are at variance with the actual situation. In writing *Synspunktet for min Forfattervirksomhed* (*The Point of View for my Activity as an Author*; Oxford: Oxford University Press, 1939), written August-October 1848, but first published by his brother P. C. Kierkegaard in 1859, Kierkegaard, apparently forgetful of his name on the title-page as editor of *Philosophical Fragments*, carries out (pp. 13-14), in concurrence with this forgetting, his schematic distinction between the esthetic and the religious productivity with the *Postscript* as the turning point. It may be noted that E. Hirsch, who has most thoroughly investigated the problem of pseudonymity in *Philosophical Fragments* (in *Kierkegaard-Studien*, II, 672ff. according to the continuous pagination) maintains that Kierkegaard's later explanation (in connection with the concept "indirect communication") is completely misleading. Yet it would be more accurate to say that Kierkegaard's later explanations are an expression partly of his self-understanding at the different times when these explanations were written, and partly of how he at these times desired to be understood by his reader.

If this double expressiveness of autobiographical writing holds true of Kierkegaard's, there is no difficulty in understanding the reasons for variance between the factual situations and later comments on them.

Title-page. *Johannes Climacus.* Johannes Climacus, who was born before 579 and who died about 649, was a monk in the famed monastery on Sinai. He received his surname after his work Κλῖμαξ τον παραδείσου (Latin: *Scala paradisi*, Jacob's ladder). In thirty chapters or steps, a popular, simple presentation is made first of what the monks should guard against (Chapters I-XXIII) and then of the virtues they ought to strive for in order to approach the perfect life (Chapters XXIV-XXX). The work won wide circulation and numerous translations are known (in English: St. Johannes Climacus, *The Ladder of Divine Ascent*; New York: Harper, 1959). Apparently Kierkegaard had not known Johannes Climacus' work, but in his reading of de Wette, *Lærebog i den Christelige Sædelære og sammes Historie* (translated into Danish by C. E. Scharling in 1835; Ktl., 871), while preparing for his examinations in 1839 (cf. *Pap.* II A 335 and 469 and elsewhere) he had come across various quotations from the Greek ascetic writer, and the name had captured his interest to such a degree that he used it as a symbol ("Hegel is a Johannes Climacus who did not, like the giants, storm heaven by setting mountain upon mountain but entered by means of his syllogisms." *Pap.* II A 335) and later as a pseudonym. In 1842-1843 Kierkegaard wrote the incomplete *Johannes Climacus eller de omnibus dubitandum est* (*Pap.* IV B 1, pp. 103-50 with supplement; English translation, *Johannes Climacus or De Omnibus Dubitandum Est*, London: A. and C. Black, 1958), and the name is first used as a pseudonym on the title-page of *Philosophical Fragments* and later for the author of *Concluding Unscientific Postscript*, which appeared February 28, 1846. When Kierkegaard uses the pseudonym Climacus (and later Anti-Climacus) he has in mind essentially the meaning "climax," ascent and ascending, both as logical progression upwards and as the steadily rising emphasis upon the Christian categories as distinctive from others. In a significant entry in the *Journal*, most likely from the end of July 1849 (*Pap.* x¹ A 510, p. 329) Kierkegaard writes that "the pseudonym [used for *The Sickness unto Death*, which had just been delivered to the printer] is called Johannes Anticlimacus in contrast to Climacus, who declared himself not to be a Christian [*Postscript*, p. 19]. Anticlimacus is the opposite extreme in being a Christian to an extraordinary degree, but I myself manage to be no more than a very ordinary Christian." A following entry (x¹ A 517) reads: "Anti-Climacus has something in common with Climacus, but the difference is in Johannes Climacus' having placed himself so low that he even declares himself not to be a Christian and Anti-Climacus' supposing himself to be a Christian to an extraordinary degree, . . . I considered myself above Joh. Climacus and below Anti-Climacus."

Title-page. *Is an historical point of departure possible* etc. In the first draft of the work (*Pap.* v B 1) the problem is formulated in this way: "How do I arrive at an historical point of departure for my eternal consciousness; how can such a point of departure have more than historical interest?" This is explained further (*Pap.* v B 1,2): "This is and remains the main problem with respect to the relationship between Christianity and philosophy. Lessing is the only one who has dealt with this. But Lessing knew considerably more what the issue is about than the common herd of modern philosophers." Kierkegaard continues (*Pap.* v B 1, 3) by saying, "Lessing uses the word *leap* as if its being an expression or a thought were a matter of indifference; I understand it as a thought." (*Samtl. W.,* vi) Apparently Kierkegaard's attention had been directed to Lessing's *Über den Beweis des Geistes und der Kraft* (1777) through his reading of the translation (Ktl. 803-04) of D. F.

Strauss's *Die Christliche Glaubenslehre*, I-II (1840-1841), translated into Danish by his relative, Hans Bröchner, later professor of philosophy. Strauss says "Even suppose that the
Biblical narrative were established on the level of historical
evidence, on the same level as the most indubitable historical
facts (and the proof of the authenticity of the Biblical books
has in later times been made at least more precisely and fully),
even then those who know the nature of the historical world
would not be able to avoid seeing that the so-called certainty
in this sphere is only a high degree of probability, never
absolute certainty, and consequently remains in a permanent
misrelationship to religious faith, which requires unconditional
certainty on the basis of which it can live and die. When will
one cease—so exclaims Lessing in this connection—wanting to
suspend nothing less than the totality of the eternal by a
thread. . . . Accidental historical events, Lessing says in another
place [Strauss apparently refers to Lessing's *Eine Duplik*,
Werke, VI, 380] can never prove the necessary truths of reason.
. . . If, however, I have no historical objections to Christ's
resurrection from the dead, must I therefore (dogmatically)
hold to be true that precisely this resurrected Christ has been
the Son of God? That the Christ, against whose resurrection I
cannot bring any historical objection of importance, has on
these grounds claimed to be the Son of God and that his
disciples have therefore regarded him as the Son of God—
this I willingly and cordially believe, for these truths, as truths
of one and the same class, follow quite naturally from each
other. But now from this historical truth to leap over into an
entirely different class of truths and to require me to reform-
ulate all my metaphysical and moral concepts to conform to
it, and to require me, because I cannot present any believable
witness against Christ's resurrection, to change all my fundamental ideas of the nature of God accordingly—if *this* is not
μετάβασις, then I do not know what Aristotle understood by

this word. But now, then, one answers: but this very Christ, who, you must admit, in the historical sense awakened from the dead and arose, has himself said that God had a son, like unto God in essence, and that he was this son. This would be good enough, if it were only historically certain that Christ said this. If one pressed me further and said: it is even more than historically certain, for the inspired writers of the account, who could not commit errors, give assurance of this —then is this also historically certain, that these writers of the accounts were inspired and could not commit errors. All this is a forbidding, deep chasm which I cannot cross over, however frequently and seriously I have attempted the leap." (From I, 148-50, of the translation which Kierkegaard used.) Strauss, who has here used the pertinent passage from *Über den Beweis des Geistes und der Kraft* almost word for word, refers again to volume VI of Lessing's works. Kierkegaard, as mentioned, does the same, but in his edition of Lessing, *Gotthold Ephraim Lessing's sämmtliche Schriften*, I-XXXII (Berlin: 1825-1828; Ktl. 1747-62) the two works mentioned are printed in volume V. Therefore it is natural to suppose that Kierkegaard obtained Lessing's works after reading *Die christliche Glaubenslehre* by Strauss (whose *Leben Jesu*, translated into Danish by F. Schaldemose on the basis of the fourth edition and published in two volumes in 1842-1843, Kierkegaard did not own and hardly read). This supposition is strengthened by the fact that in the *Postscript*, especially the section "Something about Lessing," Kierkegaard is clearly oriented in Lessing's polemical situation and quotes directly from his works.

Title-page. *eternal consciousness*. The expression here signifies the consciousness of the Eternal, more sharply defined as the religious consciousness, and in the strictest sense the Christian faith, which is linked to an historical point of departure, the Moment in time, the Christ-revelation. The two last questions, *how can such a point of departure have any other than a merely historical interest* and *is it possible to base an eternal happiness upon historical knowledge* are, like the first question, answered in the work itself: the historical point of departure can have more than historical interest only when it signifies the moment of revelation, for otherwise one remains in "the Socratic," and one cannot base an eternal happiness upon merely historical knowledge; only through faith in the paradoxical revelation, the faith which is not some human production but the gift of revelation, can a human being come to "an eternal happiness."

p. 2   *Motto. Better well hung than ill wed.* Kierkegaard took his motto from Shakespeare's *Twelfth Night*, Act I, Scene v (clown speaking to Maria): "Many a good hanging prevents a bad marriage." Most likely Kierkegaard remembered this reply from his frequent reading of Schlegel and Tieck's translation, *Was ihr wollt, Shakespeares dramatische Werke* (1841), v, 116: "Gut gehängt ist besser, als schlecht verheiratet." The meaning of the motto is explained in the preface to *Concluding Unscientific Postscript* (p. 3): "Undisturbed, and in compliance with his own motto: 'Better well hung than ill wed,' the well-hung [crucified with Christ] author has been left hanging. . . . Better so, better well hung than by an unfortunate marriage brought into systematic relationship with all the world."

COMMENTARY ON THE PREFACE

pp. 3-7   The Preface, just like the formulation of the problem on the title-page, originally bore a personal stamp and was written in Kierkegaard's own name. It read as follows: "My intention in this undertaking is not at all polemical, to defend something or to attack something. This explanation, which I give *bona fide*, is without any irony (otherwise it would be an objective irony which even an infant or an animal can produce), is without any mental reservation, and is *in optima forma*, which seems to make the explanation worse for me: 'I have not succeeded in uniting basic learning with independent thought, thus satisfying the requirements of both, which I wanted to do and which ought to be possible for one whose claim to belong within the field of scholarship is legitimate.' Therefore my choice is made in accordance with this consciousness; I pack my little bundle together and declare myself unauthorized to have any opinion of scholarly significance, the honor of which is not my due, inasmuch as scholarly modesty ought to be virginal like that of a woman, zealous against all looseness, and inasmuch as I should prefer for the sake of my own honor and of the sacredness of scholarship to lead a modest life outside of scholarship rather than to participate in it foolishly. Therefore I resign, recommending myself in the best way, and take my place in pamphlet-literature, whereby I give up every claim of participating in scholarly efforts or of meriting even a relative justification for being regarded as a link or transition, as a preparer or a concluding participator, as a cooperator or as a voluntary follower. My mind is not for such things; I feel like a poor lodger who has a little room in the attic of a huge building which is constantly being enlarged and beautified while to his terror he thinks he discovers that the foundation is cracking [changed to: *thinks he discovers a misunderstanding which, however, no one is concerned about*]; I feel like a spider which preserves its life by remaining overlooked in the corner while it shakes within because of presentiments of a storm [changed to: *fearful intimations*]. So let me remain. I shall not intrude upon scholarship or fraternize with its worshippers or offend any man. My thinking and its fate are matters of the greatest indifference to everyone, with the exception of myself. Whatever I do, I do *proprio marte, propriis auspiciis, proprio stipendio*, in short, as a proprietor, insofar as a person can be one without possessing anything or looking for anything. This I do sincerely, not Sophistically, if Aristotle is at all correct in his explanation that the art of Sophistry is that whereby one makes money; I do it honorably, for it is not my intention to defraud anyone. Insofar as I must in my poor way consider a single thinker, I shall quote him honestly as well as I can [remark added: *for here there is the difficulty of making observations about Plato and Aristotle without understanding them*]. As far as particular expressions are concerned, I shall adhere to my old practice of placing in quotation marks everything which I know does not belong to me and everything whose author I do not know. My relinquishing of erudition is not a shell-game, and even though it hurts to do so, I am consoled by the fact that those who covet learning, like those who covet wealth, fall into various snares and temptations which I can easily imagine, for if that poor course of study 'for one Drachma,' which I have completed, has already ensnared me in many ways, what temptations await one [changed to: *the many*] who is to take 'the big course for 50 Drachmas'?" (*Pap.* v b 24) This original preface was altered and expanded (*Pap.* v b 25-39) into its present form.

p. 3, l. 1   *proprio Marte* etc. By one's own hand, on one's own behalf, and at one's own expense (a similar expression is used by Cicero in his *Phillipics*, ii, 37, 95). Cf. *Pap.* v b 24, p. 84.

p. 3, l. 9   *Holberg's magister.* In Holberg's *Jacob von Tyboe eller den stortalende Soldat* (1725), in addition to the main character, the ludicrous officer Jacob von Tyboe, there appears a ludicrous Magister Stygotius, who boasts to the beautiful Leonora that he will defend his thesis: "I walk in the footsteps of the ancients, of which there will be proof the day after tomorrow when I, God willing, shall defend my thesis." His thesis, a very short work, common at the time, treats of "De alicubitate" ("one-or-another-place-ness") and "will be followed by five others" (iii, 4). Kierkegaard most likely remembered the reply from the presentation of the comedy in the Royal Theater, where the famous T. L. Phister and C. N. Rosenkilde (much admired by Kierkegaard) acted.

the noble Roman. Sallust, who writes in *Jugurtha*, IV, that "it was by merit, not by baseness" (*magis merito quam ignavia*; Kierkegaard understood *merito* to mean *on the basis of my merits*) that he had changed his principles and no longer would serve the state but rather record the events of the future. (C. Sallusti Crispi *Opera*, ed. F. Kritzius, 1834, II, 22; Ktl. 1269-70; *Sallust*; New York: Putnam, 1921; Loeb Classics, XXII, 2, p. 183). *p. 3, l. 14*

serve the system. Of course, the Hegelian system. *p. 3, l. 14*

ex animi sententia. By inclination. *p. 3, l. 16*

ἀπραγμοσύνη. Abstention from participation in public life. Xenophon (*Memorabilia*, III, 11, 16; New York: Putnam, 1913; Loeb Classics, p. 249) uses the term in connection with Socrates. According to Plutarch's report ("Solon," XX; New York: Putnam, 1914; Loeb Classics, p. 457; cf. Aristotle, *Atheniensium Respublica, Works*, X, 8:5) Solon had laid down the law for Athens that every Athenian who refused to take part in civil factions and internal disputes should lose his civic rights. Most likely it was this provision which Kierkegaard had in mind, presumably from his school lessons. But he may have remembered it from his reading of Plutarch, whose works he owned both in Greek and in various German and Danish translations (see Ktl. 1172-1200). Also in K. F. Becker's *Verdenshistorie* (1841ff., I, 213), which he owned in J. Riise's translation (Ktl. 1872-83), Solon's law is referred to: "Most remarkable is Solon's law, under which everyone who did not take part *pro* or *contra* in a revolution should be declared dishonorable and be exiled." *p. 3, l. 18*

nolite perturbare. Do not disturb my circles. Kierkegaard uses the generally known formulation of Archimedes' famous reply to the Roman soldier who killed him in the conquest of Syracuse in 212 B.C. In *Valerius Maximus* (VIII, 7, 7) the reply *p. 4, l. 1* reads: "Noli, inquit, obsecro istum disturbare." Kierkegaard owned (Ktl. 1296) F. Hoffmann's translation of *Valerius Maximus: Sammlung merkwürdiger Reden und Thaten* (1828-1829), in which (pp. 514-15) the scene is described.

p. 4, l. 3 *Philip threatened to lay siege.* . . . After his victory at Chæronea in 338 B.C., Philip undertook a victory march through the whole of Greece in order to bind its city-states to him, and apparently it was on this occasion that the episode of the famous Cynic philosopher Diogenes of Sinope (ca. 413-323 B.C.) took place. Kierkegaard gives the report almost verbatim from the German translation, which he owned, of the works of Lucian of Samos (*Lucians Schriften*, Aus dem Griechischen übersetzt, 1769, 1, 29-30; Ktl. 1135-38).

p. 4, l. 12 *Aristotle.* From Kierkegaard's *Journals* (*Pap.* IV A 63) it appears that his source is W. G. Tennemann, *Geschichte der Philosophie* (1798), 1, 356, note 66 (hereafter this work will be referred to only by author, volume, and page). Kierkegaard writes in his journal: "If anyone wants to call my fragment of wisdom Sophistic, I must point out that it lacks at least one characteristic which belongs, according to Plato's and Aristotle's definitions—that one makes money by it." Aristotle says this in *De Sophisticis Elenchis* or *On Sophistic Fallacies* (*Works*, 1, 171^b, 28), which is cited by Tennemann in the note mentioned above.

p. 4, l. 21 *Salomon Goldkalb.* In J. L. Heiberg's play *Kong Salomon og Jörgen Hattemager* (1825) the wealthy Baron Goldkalb is expected to come to Köbenhavn from Frankfurt by way of Korsör. When the Jewish merchant Salomon Goldkalb of Hamburg arrives in Korsör, through the similarity of names he is taken for the Baron and is received with pomp and ceremony. (Heiberg, *Poetiske Skrifter*, 1862, v, 171-280.) It is not improbable that Kierkegaard is making a direct allusion to H. L. Martensen.

p. 4, l. 27 *a new era* etc. In 1837 H. L. Martensen published his theological dissertation, *De autonomia conscientiae sui humanae, in theologiam dogmaticam nostri temporis introducta*. In 1834-1836 while on a study tour abroad he had been greatly impressed by Franz von Baader of Munich and by him directed to the study of Eckhart, Tauler, and Jacob Böhme. Because he endorsed Anselm's principle (*credo ut intelligam*; I believe in order that I may understand), Martensen in this study sought to discredit the principle of autonomy which he found to have been dominant in modern philosophy from Descartes to Hegel (with the exception of Leibniz). In 1841 Martensen's work was translated into Danish by L. V. Petersen under the title *Den menneskelige Selvbevidstheds Autonomie i vor Tids dogmatiske Theologie*. In his Preface the translator said that "This is the first work to appear in this country in the new speculative trend and heralds the era in theology which we now recognize as having already begun." Kierkegaard owned the work both in Latin and in Danish (Ktl. 648 and 651). As late as 1849 he wrote in his *Journals* (*Pap.* x² A 155, p. 117): "It is now over ten years since Martensen returned home from foreign travels, bringing with him the newest German philosophy and creating quite a sensation with this novelty; he has always been actually more of a reporter and correspondent than a seminal thinker. It was a positional philosophy which enchanted youth and opened up the prospect of swallowing everything in half a year. He is making quite a splash, and in the meantime young students [the translator, L. V. Petersen, was a theological student in 1841] take the opportunity to inform the public in print that with Martensen begins a new era, epoch, epoch and era, *etc.* . . . . The bad thing here is to permit young men to do such things, whereby all relationships are turned around." Mention may be made of Martensen's older colleague H. N. Clausen (most closely aligned with Schleiermacher), who in his memoirs (*Optegnelser om mit Levneds og min Tids Historie*, 1877, pp. 210ff.) took a very dim view of the enthusiasm with which theological students toward the close of the 1830's had received and had tried to appropriate the speculative theology. He wrote of Hegel's terrorizing the spiritual life and of the fanaticism of his followers. For a discussion of Martensen's book and its reception in Denmark see Skat Arildsen, *H. L. Martensen* (Copenhagen: Gad, 1932), I, 119-41.

p. 4, l. 28   *quantum satis.* A sufficient amount.

p. 4, l. 6   *The current circus season. Philosophical Fragments* was published July 13, 1844, and the Preface must have been written some weeks before. The comparison between the clowning side-shows at Dyrehave amusement park and the speculative way of thought requires no further explanation. Furthermore, Kierkegaard had frequently taken trips to the northern part of Sjælland in the spring of 1844. On April 27 he was in Dyrehave and in nearby Nyholte during May and a number of times in June.

p. 4, l. 8   *flopping over and over.* To change into its opposite. In his critique of Kant's doctrine of cosmological antinomies (*Critique of Pure Reason*) Hegel remarks (W.a.A., III, 217; J.A., IV, 227; *Science of Logic*; New York: Macmillan, 1951; I, 205) that "A deeper insight into the antinomous or, rather, into the dialectic nature of Reason shows, however, that *every* concept is a unity of opposite moments, which could therefore be asserted in the shape of an antinomy. Thus, Becoming, Determinate Being, and so on, and other concepts, could each furnish its particular antinomy, and as many antinomies could be set up as concepts were yielded." Inasmuch as Hegel hypostatizes the concepts, *der Begriff*, which is understood as a unity of contrasts, he seeks to unite formal logic and epistemology in his speculative logic, which treats of what is usually called metaphysics (cf. Hegel's expression of this in W.a.A., III, 6; J.A., IV, 16; *Science of Logic*, I, 36), and demonstrates the identity of the laws of thought and the laws of being.

Thought and being therefore move ahead by means of the contradictions immanent in the concept, whereby there is a change at some particular moment. In other words, the concept can be called a living tendency in existence, and it is by means of his doctrine of the concept as a unity of contrasts that Hegel introduces movement into logic, which Kierkegaard criticizes in many places, especially in the *Postscript* (pp. 99ff.) on the presupposition that formal logic and epistemology are not identical and that traditional logical principles stand firm in spite of Hegel.

As a particularly clear example of how Hegel has the concepts "flop over," reference may be made to his famous treatment of *Herrschaft und Knechtschaft* (*lordship and bondage*) in *Phänomenolgie des Geistes* (W.a.A., II, 140-50; J.A., II, 148-58; *The Phenomenology of Mind*, 2nd ed.; New York: Macmillan, 1931; pp. 228-40). The doctrine of the concept as the unity of contrasts is basic in his philosophical system as a whole and in its parts. In Hegel research this doctrine is frequently discussed. See G. R. G. Mure, *A Study of Hegel's Logic* (Oxford: Clarendon, 1950), especially pp. 151-66; Kuno Fischer, *Geschichte der neuern Philosophie* (2nd ed., 1911), VIII, 527-76; Nicolai Hartmann, *Die Philosophie des deutschen Idealismus* (1929), II, especially pp. 258ff.; Willy Moog, *Hegel und die Hegelsche Schule* (1930), pp. 260-77; Ivan Iljin, *Die Philosophie Hegels als kontemplative Gotteslehre* (1946), pp. 151-66; Theodor Litt, *Hegel, Versuch einer kritischen Erneuerung* (1953), especially pp. 275ff. The most complete treatment is found in Henri Niel, *De la médiation dans la philosophie de Hegel* (1945). V. Kuhr's *Modsigelsens Grundsætning* (in *Kierkegaard Studier*, II, 1915) is a concentrated philosophical-historical study of the battle in Denmark over the principles of logic between J. L. Heiberg and H. L. Martensen on one side and F. C. Sibbern and J. P. Mynster on the other. The controversy began in 1839, at which time Kierkegaard did not take part. In a journal-entry from the spring of 1844 (*Pap.* v a 68) one can see how Kierkegaard at that time (when he was writing *Philosophical Fragments*) had achieved clarity concerning the principles of logic and had rejected the Hegelian doctrine of the concept which can "flop over" into its opposite.

p. 5, l. 10   *noise-making busybody (Rabalderfjog).* The expression was first used by Jens Baggesen in *Andet Brev til Udgiveren af Nyeste Københavns Skilderie*, printed in *Danske Værker* (1836, vii, 20; Ktl. 1509-20), later in 1831 by Henrik Hertz in *Fire Poetiske Epistler fra Knud Sjællandsfar (Digte fra forskjellige Perioder*, 1862, iii, 149).

p. 5, l. 17   *Fredericia.* Cf. *Pap.* v b 28 and 35, 2. It has not been possible to determine whether or not this refers to a particular fire; yet it is quite probable, inasmuch as Kierkegaard was a diligent newspaper reader.

p. 6, l. 11   *dancing . . . to the honor of God.* Perhaps an allusion to the story of David, who danced before the Ark of the Covenant (II Samuel 6:14-16).

p. 6, l. 15   *communio bonorum.* Here, the community of goods.

p. 6, l. 17   *the priest at the altar.* An allusion to I Corinthians 9:13.

p. 6, l. 30   *scarcely enough for the course.* Kierkegaard employs freely the expression from Plato's dialogue *Cratylus* (New York: Random House, 1937; i, 173; p. 384 in the Stephens pagination) where Socrates ironically says to Hermogenes: "If I had not been poor, I might have heard the fifty-drachma course of the great Prodicus, which is a complete education in grammar and language—these are his own words—and then I should have been able to answer your questions about the correctness of names. But, indeed, I have only heard the single drachma course, and therefore, I do not know the truth about such matters. . . ." (Hereafter reference to Plato in this translation will be given only by page according to the standard Stephens pagination which is noted marginally in the Random House

edition and in other scholarly editions of Plato.) Concerning
Prodicus, see the note to page 14.

per deos obsecro. I swear by the gods.   *p. 7, l. 5*

for I will not dance. In the first draft of the Preface (*Pap.*   *p. 7, l. 6*
V B 29, p. 86) it reads: "for in this sense I will not dance."

Propositio. Proposal or, more accurately here, provisional   *p. 9*
point of departure. In the manuscript it originally read "Position I," since Kierkegaard had thought of the main divisions
as *"Propositio," "Positio,"* and "Historical Costume" (*Pap.* V B
1, 12). Accordingly *Positio* was thereupon divided into "Position I" and "Position II." After *A* the original manuscript read
as follows (*Pap.* V B 3, 2): "It is well known that Christianity
is the only historical phenomenon which in spite of the historical, nay, precisely by means of the historical, has intended
itself to be for the single individual the point of departure
for his eternal consciousness, has intended to interest him otherwise than merely historically, has intended to base his eternal
happiness on his relationship to something merely historical.
No philosophy, no mythology, no historical knowledge has had
this idea; therefore one may ask whether it is a recommenda-
tion or an objection that it has not arisen in the heart of any
man, for these three are the spheres which would yield analogies to this self-contradictory doubleness, if such were to be
found. In the meantime we have forgotten this and shall
continue to forget it, as if Christianity had never existed;
instead, making use of the unlimited freedom of a hypothesis,
we shall assume that this question has entered our heads and
that we are unwilling to give it up until the answer has been
found. The monks never finished telling the history of the
world because each one began with creation; if in dealing with
the relations between philosophy and Christianity we begin
by first recounting what has previously been said, how will it
ever be possible—not to finish—no, how shall one ever begin,
for this history continues to grow. If we have to begin with

that thinker and sage, *Executor novi Testamenti, Pontius Pilate*, and before we begin must wait for the decisive work announced by one or another assistant professor or publisher—what then?" In the final revision this selection in somewhat altered form was shifted to the end of the work (p. 137), where it reads: "If I ever write a next section, it is my intention to call the whole by its right name, and to clothe the problem in its historical costume." The so-called Position II should then be: "One in ignorance who knows historically what it is he is asking about but seeks the answer" (*Pap.* VB 10), but this became the *Propositio*: "The question is asked in ignorance, by one who does not even know what can have led him to ask it." The position is thereby clearly given as that of the pseudonymous writer, Johannes Climacus, who stands outside Christianity, and not as Kierkegaard's own. Consequently Position II finally became the *Propositio*, and the original Position I is treated in the *Postscript*, where Climacus clothes "the Problem in its historical costume," for the treatment of the problem in *Philosophical Fragments* is entirely systematic. The changes instituted here, just as in the Preface, signify partly that Kierkegaard in his relationship to the reader moves into the background and partly that the conceptual development takes on the character of a hypothesis, "A Project of Thought," as it is called.

COMMENTARY TO CHAPTER I

p. 11   *A Project of Thought*. Cf. *Pap.* VB 40, 7, where it appears that additions were made to the portion quoted in the note above: "In the meantime we have forgotten and shall continue to forget what has been said here, as if Christianity had never existed; instead, making use of the unlimited freedom of a hypothesis, we shall assume that the whole was a curious conceit of our own, which we do not wish to abandon, however, until we have tested it." Concerning this Kierkegaard noted in the margin: "to be placed at the end of Chapter v so that the first part ends with these words."

How far does the Truth admit of being learned? The phrase *p. 11, l. 1* *the Truth* does not mean the same in Platonic (Socratic) thought on the one hand and in the New Testament and for Kierkegaard on the other. One can speak of descriptive truth in Plato, which consists in the substantial correspondence of our judgments with the state of things which they are presumed to characterize. Truth can also be understood as a characteristic of being: when something is what it ought to be, it is true. In such a case there is ontological truth, and according to Plato ontological truths are unchangeable. Here we find the tradition of the Eleatic Parmenides: ontological truths are not known through sense-observation and experience (cf. *Theaetetus*, pp. 185f.) but through thought, the highest function of the soul, of the human spirit. Through thought it becomes clear that the Truth is present in man, is a priori, innate. In a preëxistence our souls have contemplated the Truth, ontological truth, and when in their earthly existence men strive after knowledge of the Truth, they should reflect within themselves and will find Truth through recollection (ἀνάμνησις) and thereby participate in the immaterial world of Ideas from which the soul has come and for which it seeks.

In the New Testament the word is used with many meanings. There, as in the Old Testament, it may be used for what stands fast, what holds good, what one can depend upon. Secondly, it can signify the factual state of things and the truth of statements (here the usage is most reminiscent of Plato's understanding of descriptive truth). The term can also be used for right doctrine and faith, and finally in the Johannine writings it has the meaning of genuineness, divine reality, revelation. In the New Testament, and not only in the Johannine writings, this revelation is identical with the person of Jesus Christ as an historical figure. According to the New

Testament this Truth is not within every human being but has come to the world at a particular time.

In this work Kierkegaard takes as his point of departure the Platonic understanding of truth as ontological and immanent and then proceeds to give the term its New Testament content and to draw the consequences of this, as is evident from what follows. The concept of truth is developed more sharply in the *Postscript*, with the conclusion that truth from the Socratic point of view is subjectivity, inwardness, but from the Christian viewpoint subjectivity is untruth (pp. 206, etc.). Concerning the usage in the New Testament, see Rudolf Bultmann, *Theology of the New Testament* (New York: Scribner's, 1951-1955); Bultmann's article in *Theologisches Wörterbuch zum Neuen Testament* (2nd ed., 1949) 1, 239-51; C. H. Dodd, *The Interpretation of the Fourth Gospel* (Cambridge: Cambridge University Press, 1953), pp. 170ff.; C. Ritter, *The Essence of Plato's Philosophy* (London: Allen and Unwin, 1933); Johannes Hirschberger, *The History of Philosophy* (Milwaukee: Bruce, 1958); Johannes Slök, *Platon* (1953) and Paul Friedländer, *Platon*, 2nd ed. (1954), 1, pp. 233ff. The concept of truth in the Climacus-writings is treated by Emanuel Hirsch, among others, in *Kierkegaard-Studien* (1933) 11, 768ff. A contemporary theological study is Emil Brunner, *Wahrheit als Begegnung* (*The Divine-human Encounter*; Philadelphia: Westminster, 1943).

Especially while working on his thesis (*Om Begrebet Ironi*) Kierkegaard had read the works of Plato. For his final examination in high school he had read the dialogues *Crito* and *Euthyphro* in Greek (cf. *Breve og Aktstykker*, 1953, 1, No. v), but our first definite indication of Kierkegaard's having read Plato comes in July 1840 (*Pap.* III A 5), and the particular reference is to the *Meno*. From then on Plato is so frequently mentioned both in the *Journals* and in the works that Kierkegaard's thorough reading of and reflections over Greek Idealism in its earliest and perfect formulation are clearly evident. Here we shall only mention the editions and translations of Plato which Kierkegaard owned and what secondary works he used for his study (only those which had appeared before the publication of *Philosophical Fragments* in the summer of 1844): *Platonis Opera quae exstant*, ed. F. Astius, I-XI (1819-1832) and the appended *Lexicon Platonicum*, I-III (1835-1838), also by Astius; *Platons Werke*, I-VI (1817-1828), translated into German by Friedrich W. Schleiermacher; *Udvalgte Dialoger af Platon*, I-III (1830-1838), translated into Danish by C. J. Heise; *Timæus* and *Critias* (1841), translated into German by F. W. Wagner; and *Unterredungen über die Gesetze*, I-II, translated into German by J. G. Schulthesz, revised by S. Vögelin (1842; Ktl. 1144-70).

Kierkegaard had read about Plato in general or specialized histories of philosophy which he owned. These were: F. Ast, *Grundriss einer Geschichte der Philosophie* (1807; Ktl. 385); J. Bruckeri, *Historia critica philosophiae*, I-V (1767; Ktl. 446-50); J. Gronovius, *Compendium historiæ philosophicæ antiquæ*, ed. M. J. C. Wolf (1706; Ktl. 519), but Kierkegaard does not seem to have made extensive use of any of these three works. He made much greater use of Hegel's *Vorlesungen über die Geschichte der Philosophie*, ed. K. L. Michelet, I-III (1836; Ktl. 557-59). Of less significance for Kierkegaard were such works as K. L. Kannegiesser, *Abriss der Geschichte der Philosophie* (1837; Ktl. 593); W. T. Krug, *Allgemeines Handwörterbuch der philosophischen Wissenschaften nebst ihrer Litteratur und Geschichte*, I-V (1827-1829; Ktl. 604-08); and J. C. Lossius, *Neues philosophisches allgemeines Real-Lexicon*, I-III (1803; Ktl. 631-33). Kierkegaard had carefully read G. O. Marbach, *Geschichte der griechischen Philosophie* (1838; Ktl. 642), as well as L. Preller, *Historia philosophiae graeco-romanae* (1838; Ktl. 726), and H. Ritter, *Geschichte der Philosophie alter Zeit*, 2nd ed., I-IV (1836; *Ktl.* 735-38). W. G. Tennemann, *Geschichte der Philosophie*, i-xi (1798-1819; Ktl. 815-26), was a special object of Kierkegaard's careful study. Apart from philosophers whom Kierkegaard studied directly, the extensive work of Tennemann was his main authority. J. G. Walch, *Philosophisches Lexicon*, edited by J. C. Hennings, i-ii (1775; Ktl. 863-64), was of lesser significance, and the most complete contemporary research, E. Zeller, *Die Philosophie der Griechen* (1844ff.; Ktl. 913-14), Kierkegaard obtained and read toward the end of 1852 (*Pap.* x⁶c 6).

Kierkegaard was especially concerned with the Socratic question, and the auction-listing of his library does not contain much of specialized research on Plato. Mention may be made of F. Hermann, *Geschichte und System der platonischen Philosophie*, i (1839; Ktl. 576), and F. A. Trendelenburg, *Platonis de ideis et numeris doctrina ex Aristotele illustrata* (1826; Ktl. 842). Not least because of the important role Poul Möller played for Kierkegaard, mention must be made of his *Udkast til Forelæsinger over den ældre Philosophies Historie,* printed in Möller's *Efterladte Skrifter*, 1st ed. (1839; Ktl. 1574-76). The significance of this work must not be underestimated, even though it was not thoroughly worked out by Möller.

Kierkegaard's relationship to Plato (Greek philosophical Idealism) is the main theme in J. Himmelstrup's *Sören Kierkegaard's Opfattelse af Sokrates* (1924); Hermann Diem, *Philosophie und Christentum bei Sören Kierkegaard* (1929), see also Diem, *Die Existenzdialektik von Sören Kierkegaard* (1951; *Kierkegaard's Dialectic of Existence*; Edinburgh: Oliver and Boyd, 1959); Sören Holm, *Sören Kierkegaards Historiefilosofi* (1952); and Johs. Slök, *Die Anthropologie Kierkegaards* (Copenhagen: 1954).

In his *Vorlesungen über die Geschichte der Philosophie*, ii, Hegel had given a presentation of the Platonic (Socratic) epistemology which corresponds closely to Kierkegaard's formulation of it in *Philosophical Fragments*. It appears clearly in the following quotation (W.a.A., xiv, 74ff.; J.A., xviii, 74ff.; *Hegel's Lectures on the History of Philosophy*; New York: Humanities Press, 1955; i, 410-11): "This direction of consciousness back into itself takes the form—very markedly in Plato—of asserting that man can learn nothing, virtue included, and that not because the latter has no relation to science. For the good does not come from without, Socrates shows; it cannot be taught, but is implied in the nature of mind. That is to say, man cannot passively receive anything that is given from without like the wax that is moulded to a form, for everything is latent in the mind of man, and he only seems to learn it. Certainly everything begins from without, but this is only the beginning; the truth is that this is only an impulse towards the development of spirit. All that has value to men, the eternal, the self-existent, is contained in man himself, and has to develop from himself. To learn here only means to receive knowledge of what is externally determined. This external comes indeed through experience, but the universal therein belongs to thought, not to the subjective and bad, but to the objective and true. The universal in the opposition of subjective and objective, is that which is as subjective as it is objective; the subjective is only a particular, the objective is similarly only a particular as regards the subjective, but the universal is the unity of both. According to the Socratic principle, nothing has any value to men to which the spirit does not testify. Man in it is free, is at home with himself, and that is the subjectivity of spirit. As it is said in the Bible, 'Flesh of my flesh, and bone of my bone,' that which is held by me as truth and right is spirit of my spirit. But what spirit derives from itself must come from it as from the spirit which acts in a universal manner, and not from its passions, likings, and arbitrary desires. These, too, certainly come from something inward which is 'implanted in us by nature,' but which is only in a natural way our own, for it belongs to the particular; high above it is true thought, the Notion, the rational. Socrates opposed to the contingent and particular inward, that universal, true inward of thought. And Socrates awakened this real conscience, for he not only said that man is the measure of all things, but man as thinking is the measure of all things. With Plato we shall, later on, find it formulated that what man seems to receive he only remembers." (Cf. especially the *Postscript*, pp. 209-06.)

In his presentation of Plato's teaching Hegel also emphasizes (*ibid.*, II, 32-33) the same characteristic feature which Kierkegaard points out: "The source through which we become conscious of the divine is the same as that already seen in Socrates (Vol. I, pp. 410, 411). The spirit of man contains reality in itself, and in order to learn what is divine he must develop it out of himself and bring it to consciousness. With the Socratics this discussion respecting the immanent nature of knowledge in the mind of man takes the form of a question as to whether virtue can be taught or not, and with the sophist Protagoras of asking whether feeling is the truth, which is allied with the question of the content of scientific knowledge, and with the distinction between that and opinion. But Plato goes on to say that the process by which we come to know is not, properly speaking, learning, for that which we appear to learn we really only recollect. Plato often comes back to this subject, but in particular he treats of the point in the Meno, in which he asserts (p. 81, 84 Steph.; pp. 349, 355, 356 Bekk.) that nothing can, properly speaking, be learned, for learning is just a recollection of what we already possess, to which the perplexity in which our minds are placed, merely acts as stimulus. Plato here gives the question a speculative significance, in which the reality of knowledge, and not the empirical view of the acquisition of knowledge, is dealt with. For learning, according to the immediate ordinary conception of it, expresses the taking up of what is foreign into thinking consciousness, a mechanical mode of union and the filling of an empty space with things which are foreign and indifferent to this space itself. An external method of effecting increase such as this, in which the soul appears to be a *tabula rasa*, and which resembles the idea we form of growth going on in the living body through the addition of particles, is dead, and is incompatible with the nature of mind, which is subjectivity, unity, being and remaining at home with itself. But Plato presents the true nature of consciousness in asserting that it is mind in which, as mind, that is already present which becomes object to consciousness, or which it explicitly becomes. This is the Notion of the true universal in its movement; of the species which is in itself its own Becoming, in that it is already implicitly what it explicitly becomes—a process in which it does not come outside of itself. Mind is this absolute species, whose process is only the continual return into itself; thus nothing is for it which it is not in itself. According to this, the process of learning is not that something foreign enters in, but that the mind's own essence becomes actualized, or it comes to the knowledge of this last."

A little farther on Hegel characterizes Plato's teaching in this way (*op.cit.*, II, 34): "Ideas of individual, temporal, transitory things undoubtedly come from without, but not the universal thoughts which, as the true, have their root in the mind and belong to its nature; by this means all authority is destroyed."

Emanuel Hirsch, who in his Commentary (see the German translation of *Fragments*, pp. 168-70) on this portion cites the passages from Hegel quoted here, observes that Kierkegaard regards the principles lying at the basis of the Socratic-Platonic epistemology as having been taken over by Hegel, and that Kierkegaard, since he distinguishes between the Christian and the Socratic, also makes a distinction with reference to the Hegelian, and in this way he intends "to meet at root-level the speculative orthodoxy developed by conservative Christian Hegelians." However correct this is, it is not the whole truth of the matter. In *Philosophical Fragments* Kierkegaard distinguishes the Christian view not only with reference to Plato, Hegel, and the right-wing Hegelians, but with reference to every possible form of Idealistic philosophy, including a Rousseauistic primitive naturalism and a scientific humanism, as well as the view of one like Schleiermacher, who in *Der Christliche Glaube* (2nd ed., para. 13; *The Christian Faith*; Edinburgh: T. and T. Clark, 1956; para. 13, p. 62) says: "The appearance of the Redeemer in history is, as divine revelation, neither an absolutely supernatural nor an absolutely suprarational thing," a proposition which cannot at all be united with the Christian understanding which is expressed in *Philosophical Fragments*. Hegel's view in *System der Philosophie* (para. 573, W.a.A., VII, 2, p. 453; J.A., x, 459) that "the content of philosophy and of religion is the same" and consequently that, as in Schleiermacher also, revelation in the most rigorous sense is not emphasized, is a consistent outcome of philosophical Idealism. In this view the historical revelation can only be illusion or a manifestation, or, as R. Bultmann thinks (most clearly expressed in *Jesus* [1926]; cf. his *Theology of the New Testament*, especially para. 4): Jesus proclaimed nothing essentially new; he was the bearer of the Word, not the Word of God itself.

Inasmuch as Kierkegaard works systematically, not historically, he does not make fine distinctions among the four Platonic dialogues (referred to in the next sentence in the text) from the early and middle periods. Nor does he distinguish between Socrates and Plato. In the *Postscript* (pp. 184-85) he himself gives this explanation: ". . . a difficulty in the plan of the *Fragments* . . . had its ground in the fact that I did not wish at once to make the case as difficult dialectically as it is, because in our age terminologies and the like are turned so topsy-turvy that it is almost impossible to secure oneself against confusion. In order, if possible, to exhibit clearly the difference between the Socratic position (which was supposed to be the philosophical, the pagan-philosophical position) and the experimentally evoked thought-determination which really makes an advance beyond the Socratic, I carried the Socratic back to the principle that all knowledge is recollection. This is, in a way, commonly assumed, and only for one who with a specialized interest concerns himself with the Socratic, returning again and again to the sources, only for him would it be of importance on this point to distinguish between Socrates and Plato. The proposition does indeed belong to both, only that Socrates is always departing from it, in order to exist. By holding Socrates down to the proposition that all knowledge is recollection, he becomes a speculative philosopher instead of an existential thinker, for whom existence is the essential thing. The recollection-principle belongs to speculative philosophy, and recollection is immanence, and speculatively and eternally there is no paradox."

There is a remarkable entry in Kierkegaard's *Journals*, July 10, 1840 (*Pap.* III A 5), of special importance here for an understanding of his placing Plato and Speculative Idealism together: "It is a thought just as beautiful as profound and sound which Plato expresses when he says that all knowledge is recollection, for how sad it would be if that which should bring peace to a human being, that in which he really can find rest, were external to him . . . and if the only means of consolation, this external knowledge (*sit venia verbo*), with its incessant and noisy din, came to drown out the inward need which never became satisfied. This point of view reminds one of that which in modern philosophy has found expression in the observation that all philosophy is a self-reflection on what already is given in consciousness, only that this view is more speculative and Plato's view more pious." Reference is clearly made here to J. L. Heiberg's Hegelian work, *Om Philosophiens Betydning for den nuværende Tid,* which appeared in 1833. There it says (quoted from *Prosaiske Skrifter,* 1861, 1, 434): "It is a matter . . . simply of opening our eyes for what we already see without knowing it."—On Kierkegaard's reflections over the phrase "Knowledge is recollection," see J. Himmelstrup, *Sören Kierkegaards Opfattelse af Sokrates* (Copenhagen: 1924), pp. 84ff.

p. 11, l. 5 *Protagoras, Gorgias, Meno, Euthydemus.* Inasmuch as Kierkegaard is writing "algebraically" or systematically, he gives no indication here that Plato treats the concept of the good and virtue as insight (the knowledge which alone can lead to the right ethical view and mode of action) in different ways in the four dialogues named. In the dialogue with his name as title, Protagoras, the most renowned of the Sophists, initially asserts that ethical goodness, virtue, can be *taught,* for example, through his instruction, but it becomes clear that he is a thoroughgoing relativist who has no concept of the absolute good, does not really know what goodness is. In opposition Socrates affirms that virtue may be *learned,* that goodness rests upon knowledge; it cannot be *taught* through Sophistic instruction; only with the knowledge that there is an absolute good can one realize it. In this dialogue there is only the formal definition of what ethical knowledge of the good is and what virtue is, the realization of this knowledge. In the dialogue *Gorgias* this point of departure is used in a discussion of the nature and value of rhetoric, and the conclusion is that it is not an art, only a routine, which in practice, for example, can lead a person only to a position of external power. But in its basic relativism Sophistic instruction in rhetoric cannot teach anyone the far more important knowledge and realization of the absolute good. Rhetoric first achieves its proper role when it is placed in the service of the absolute good. In *Protagoras* also it is maintained that man of himself can know and by his own powers realize the good. In the dialogue *Euthydemus*, most likely named after an historical Sophist just as *Protagoras* and *Gorgias* were, it is again emphasized that knowledge of the good is possible and that this knowledge is self-knowledge. It is, however, first in the *Meno*, which Kierkegaard refers to specifically here, that we find a sharper development of the implications of essential knowledge as self-knowledge, which is recollection, since the soul is immortal, and of man's ability to gain clarity of knowledge, even the ignorant slave whom Socrates uses to demonstrate the validity of the doctrine. The teacher, in this case Socrates, does not bring to the pupil, the learner, something which he did not possess before. The teacher remains merely the accidental occasion which aids the person in coming to self-knowledge.

"*pugnacious proposition.*" Kierkegaard's translation is more   *p. 11, l. 11*
accurate than "rene Ordklöverier" ("pure hair-splitting") in the Danish translation of Plato and than "tiresome dispute" in the Jowett translation (*Meno*, 80). Kierkegaard follows Plato almost literally up to "for what to seek." The modern Danish translation treats the problem as an unreal, only apparent, problem.

The pathos of the Greek consciousness. The phrase is em-   *p. 11, l. 25*
ployed here in the sense of basic conviction, fundamental view.

immortality of the soul. The doctrine of the immortality of   *p. 11, l. 26*
the soul, which Plato develops particularly in the *Phaedo*, is not treated further here by Kierkegaard. It is first treated thoroughly in the *Postscript* (pp. 152ff.). See also *The Book on Adler* (*Pap.* VII² B 235, pp. 82-83) and pp. 696-98 in my commentary to the German edition of 1951. The English translation, under the title *Authority and Revelation* (Princeton: Princeton University Press, 1955), omits the pages referred to. Of the special Platonic studies reference is made especially to H. Barth, *Die Seele in der Philosophie Platons* (1921); see

also Carl Stange, *Die Unsterblichkeit der Seele* (1925). The controversy which arose in Germany in the 1830's over the question of immortality Kierkegaard knew essentially through Poul Möller's critical paper, "Tanker over Muligheden af Beviser for Menneskets Udödelighed med Hensyn til den nyeste derhen hörende Literatur," which was first printed in *Maanedsskrift for Litteratur* (xvii, 1837; reprinted in Poul Möller's *Efterladte Skrifter*, 3rd ed., 1856, v, 38-140).

p. 12, note   *possible variations in the soul's preëxistent state.* Presumably Kierkegaard is here thinking primarily of Pythagoras's teaching of metempsychosis and the Orphic doctrine of the preëxistence of the soul, which was adopted by Plato and of which we find expression in the dialogue *Meno* (81) mentioned by Kierkegaard, but afterwards S. K. proceeds to discuss other types of this doctrine.

p. 12, note   *an older and more recent speculation.* The manuscript originally read (*Pap.* v b 40,8) : "The contradictions of existence are explained by positing a *pre-* according to the needs (Alexandrians); the contradictions of existence are explained by positing one or another *post-* (wandering among the stars)." Kierkegaard's knowledge of the Alexandrian thinkers (of most importance here is Origen) came primarily from Tennemann, vi, which (pp. 376-438) provides a survey of this school in the history of thought. The expressions "an eternal creation" and "an eternal procession from the Father" are found in Origen (cf., for example, the references and quotations in E. R. Redepenning, *Origines*, 1846, ii, especially pp. 277ff.). Kierkegaard most likely is thinking also of the somewhat earlier thought influenced by the neo-Platonic emanation theory whose fundamentally timeless character is appropriately described by the word *eternal* in Kierkegaard. It is possible, as A. B. Drachmann mentions in his note, that by "an older speculation" Kierkegaard also has in mind John Scotus Erigena and Eckhart, whom he knew especially by way of G. O.

Marbach, *Geschichte der Philosophie des Mittelalters* (1841; Ktl. 643; cf. *Pap.* IV c 59 *etc.*) and H. L. Martensen, *Mester Eckart, Et Bidrag til at oplyse Middelalderens Mystik*, which appeared in the summer of 1840 (cf. especially pp. 100ff. and also Skat Arildsen, *H. L. Martensen*, 1932, I, 165-87). By "modern speculation" Kierkegaard probably means Franz von Baader in particular, Schelling, and not least Hegel himself. Kierkegaard owned and knew the essential part of Baader's authorship (cf. Ktl. 393-418), of which special mention is made here of *Fermenta Cognitionis*, published in 1822-1824 (now in the Royal Library, Copenhagen), *Vorlesungen über religieuse Philosophie* (I, 1827), *Vorlesungen über speculative Dogmatik* (1828), and *Über den Begriff des Gut—oder positiv und des Nichtgut—oder negative-gewordenen endlichen Geistes* (1829). Already in June 1836 (*Pap.* I A 174) Kierkegaard had read *Vorlesungen über speculative Dogmatik*, on which he had taken notes (*Pap.* I c 27-33; cf. particularly c 31 on the problem of the origin of evil and its entry into the world), and on March 19, 1837, Kierkegaard copied an older journal-entry (*Pap.* II A 31) in which the problem of the origin of sin is discussed, and in November of the same year he referred to Martensen's series of lectures, *Prolegomena til den speculative Dogmatik* (*Pap.* II c 12-24), where reference is made also to Baader (II c 13). In *Philosophical Fragments* Kierkegaard may be thinking particularly of Baader's development in *Fermenta Cognitionis* (1824, *Sämmtliche Werke*, 1851, II, 319-64), where he presents his doctrine of the Fall: first Lucifer's rebellion, then the first fall of the originally androgynous Adam when he desired a feminine companion, and finally Adam's last fall when following the differentiation of the sexes he united with Eve. Franz von Baader's theory of the three falls is treated, for example, in David Baumgardt, *Franz von Baader und die philosophische Romantik* (1927, especially pp. 275ff.), H. Spreckelmeyer's monograph, *Die philosophische Deutung des Sündenfalls bei*

Franz von Baader (1938); and Eugène Susini, *Franz von Baader et le romantisme mystique* (1942, II, especially pp. 299ff., 358ff. and 368ff.). Kierkegaard's relationship to Baader is investigated by T. Bohlin, among others, in his *Kierkegaards dogmatiska åskådning* (1925, pp. 50ff.) and by Richard Hejll in "Sören Kierkegaard och mystiken" in *Edda* (1938, pp. 350-93). The area is touched upon by Arild Christensen in the article "Felix-culpa Motive hos Sören Kierkegaard," *Meddelelser fra Sören Kierkegaards Selskabet* (1954, V, I, pp. 18-20).

Of Schelling's works Kierkegaard owned (Ktl. 763-67) only *Philosophische Schriften*, I (1809), *Vorlesungen über die Methode des academischen Studium* (3rd ed., 1830), *Bruno* (2nd printing, 1842), and *Erste Vorlesung in Berlin* (1841). As is known, from Nov. 22 to Feb. 4, 1842, Kierkegaard attended Schelling's Berlin lectures on *Philosophie der Offenbarung* (cf. *Pap.* III c 27 and the letters from his stay in Berlin printed in *Breve og Aktstykker*, I, 1953, particularly numbers 49, 51, 54, 61, 62, 68, 69, and 70, together with the Commentary in Volume II, 1954), but he does not seem to have known H. E. G. Paulus' reports of the lectures in *Die endlich offenbar gewordene positive Philosophie der Offenbarung* (1843), which was published without Schelling's cooperation, indeed in spite of his attempt to secure a police-order against it (cf. Kuno Fischer's account in *Geschichte der neuern Philosophie*, 3rd printing, 1902, VII, 263ff.). Schelling acknowledged that the book contained a verbatim account of the Berlin lectures, but the first authorized edition of these lectures was arranged by his son, K. F. A. Schelling, in 1856. When Emanuel Hirsch in his Commentary upon *Philosophical Fragments* frequently refers to and quotes the Paulus edition, the reader is not therefore to think that Kierkegaard was acquainted with it. As early as 1837 (*Pap.* II A 31) Kierkegaard mentions Schelling and the *Journals* from 1840 (*Pap.* III A 34) read: "The observation that Hegel is a parenthesis in Schelling seems more and

more to be true, and one only waits for it to be terminated."
In 1844 Kierkegaard most likely read Karl Rosenkranz, *Schelling*. Kierkegaard obtained Schelling's *Vorlesungen* on April
30, 1843 (Ktl. 766; cf. *Pap.* IV A 185 and 232). After Dec. 19,
1843, when following the appearance of J. L. Heiberg's annual,
Urania, with its discussion of *Repetition* Kierkegaard made a
copious draft of a polemic (*Pap.* IV B, 100-17), he wrote (IV B
117, p. 290) about Schelling's conception of movement and
freedom in relationship to Hegel's view (cf. *Pap.* IV B 118, 7).
Pap. IV C 46 contains a reminiscence of the Berlin lectures.
The discussion of Schelling in *The Concept of Dread* (Princeton: Princeton University Press, 1946; p. 53) fits in with the
abovementioned book by Rosenkranz and with the journal-entry, *Pap.* V C 5. In *Philosophical Fragments* Kierkegaard
surely is especially aware of Schelling's thought-development in
the sixteenth lecture on *Philosophie der Offenbarung* (*F. W. J.
von Schelling's sämmtliche Werke*, 1858, III², 337ff.), which he
had heard in Berlin. Schelling's special demonology, which
came later in the same series of lectures, could hardly have
been known by Kierkegaard. Schelling's doctrine of preëxistence and the origin of evil in *Philosophie der Offenbarung* is
reproduced, for example, in Kuno Fischer's work mentioned
above, especially pp. 794ff., and in H. Knittermeyer's *Schelling
und die romantische Schule* (1929), in which there is also a
discussion of the relationship between Schelling's and Baader's
theories (especially pp. 376ff.). See also V. Jankélévitch,
*L'odyssée de la conscience dans la dernière philosophie de
Schelling* (1933), particularly pp. 45ff. A brief presentation in
Danish of Schelling's later philosophy is found in C. I. Scharling, *Grundtvig og Romantiken* (1947), pp. 213-41. There is
as yet no study devoted to the relationship between Kierkegaard and Schelling.

Kierkegaard's characterization of modern speculation applies
to Hegel also. Apparently Kierkegaard came relatively late

to the reading of Hegel's own works, which he obtained in
the well-known first collected edition, brought out by Hegel's
friends and colleagues between 1832 and 1842 in eighteen
volumes under the main title: *Georg Wilhelm Friedrich Hegels
Werke*, Vollständige Ausgabe durch einen Verein von Freunden des Verewigten. Not all these volumes are listed in the
auction catalog, but it can be established that Kierkegaard
knew at least some of the missing volumes. Most likely Kierkegaard began to study Hegel while preparing his dissertation
Om Begrebet Ironi [*The Concept of Irony*, English translation
being done presently by Lee M. Capel] in which there is clear
evidence not only of his reading of Hegel's larger works but
also the shorter studies (see notes in sv xiii and especially
Emanuel Hirsch, *Kierkegaard-Studien*, ii, 591). Yet it is
doubtful that Kierkegaard had already read Hegel's *Wissenschaft der Logik* (*Science of Logic*, i-ii; New York: Macmillan,
1951) and *Vorlesungen über die Philosophie der Religion*
(*Lectures on the Philosophy of Religion*, i-iii; London: Kegan
Paul, 1895). Evidently one of the first things to engage Kierkegaard was Hegel's understanding of Christianity, which is
clearly and briefly expressed in *Vorlesungen über die Philosophie der Geschichte*, which appeared in 1837 (*the Philosophy
of History*; New York: Colonial Press, 1900). There is a
quotation from this work in *Pap.* ii a 282, probably written in
the latter part of 1838. In Hegel's interpretation of Christianity
the historical Christ-revelation is central, but its decisive significance according to Hegel is not in its *Einmaligkeit*, to use a
modern expression, but in its being a representative, illustrative
demonstration of the unity of the spirit of God and the spirit
of man, of the reconciliation of the infinite and the finite, the
reconciliation which is also brought about in Hegel's own
speculative thought. The revelation in history, in time, becomes,
if not superfluous to Hegel, at least not of absolute, essential
significance. In relationship to Hegel's thought, Kierkegaard's

category, *the Eternal*, is also of significance. In Hegel's *Vorlesungen über die Philosophie der Religion* (*Lectures on the Philosophy of Religion*) it is also clear concerning Christ's death that it "exhibits the absolute history of the Divine Idea, what has implicitly taken place and takes place eternally" (W.a.A., xii, 302-03; J.A., xvi, 302-03; *Philosophy of Religion*, iii, 94).

It is well known that Kierkegaard's relationship to Hegel occupies a central place in Kierkegaard-research. Of the most important works mention may be made here to: Reidar Thomte, *Kierkegaard's Philosophy of Religion* (Princeton: Princeton University Press, 1948); James Collins, *The Mind of Kierkegaard* (1953); Herman Diem, *Kierkegaard's Dialectic of Existence* (1959); Hans Reuter, *S. Kierkegaards religionsphilosophische Gedanken im Verhältnis zu Hegels religionsphilosophische System* (1914); Victor Kuhr, *Modsigelsens Grundsætning* (1915); T. Bohlin, *Sören Kierkegaards etiska åskådning* (1918); J. Himmelstrup, *Sören Kierkegaards Opfattelse af Sokrates* (1924), in German, *Sören Kierkegaards Sokratesauffassung* (1927); Hermann Diem, *Philosophie und Christentum bei Sören Kierkegaard* (1929); Emanuel Hirsch, *Kierkegaard-Studien* (1931-1933); A. Dempf, *Kierkegaards Folgen* (1935); V. Lindström, *Stadiernas teologi* (1943); T. Bohlin, *Kierkegaards tro och andra Kierkegaard-studier* (1944); M. Bense, *Hegel und Kierkegaard* (1948); Karl Löwith, *Von Hegel zu Nietzsche* (1950); Sören Holm, *Sören Kierkegaards Historiefilosofi* (1952). In addition to the more comprehensive works on Hegel listed on page 159, reference is also made to special studies of his philosophy of religion: J. M. Sterret, *Studies in Hegel's Philosophy of Religion* (New York: Appleton, 1890); J. Werner, *Hegels Offenbarungsbegriff* (1887); H. Richert, *Hegels Religionsphilosophie* (1900); E. Ott, *Die Religionsphilosophie Hegels* (1904); H. Reese, *Hegel über das Auftreten der christlichen Religion in der Weltgeschichte* (1909); W. Lütgert, *Die Religion des deutschen Idealismus und ihr Ende*, III (1925); W. Schulz, *Die Grundprobleme der Religionsphilosophie Hegels und der Theologie Schleiermachers* (1937); G. E. Müller, *Hegel über Offenbarung, Kirche und Christentum* (1939); Erik Schmidt, *Hegels Lehre von Gott* (1952); and of the special treatments of his philosophy of history reference may be made to P. Barth, *Die Geschichtsphilosophie Hegels* . . . (1890); F. Brunstäd, *Untersuchungen zu Hegels Geschichtsphilosophie* (1909); G. Lasson, *Hegel als Geschichtsphilosoph* (1920); K. Leese, *Die Geschichtsphilosophie Hegels* (1922). See also Introduction by N. Thulstrup to Kierkegaard's *Postscript*, II (Copenhagen, 1961).

p. 12, note   *On another planet* etc. Kierkegaard evidently is thinking particularly of Origen's doctrine, according to which there will be a succession of worlds in which the soul will have a higher or lower place, depending upon merit.

p. 12, l. 6   *the role of midwife.* Kierkegaard presumably is thinking especially of Socrates' characterization of himself in *Theaetetus* (148-51), which he cites a little further on.

p. 12, note   *criticism in our age.* Kierkegaard alludes here to the presentations of Socrates found in the strongly Hegel-influenced works of H. T. Rötscher, *Aristophanes und sein Zeitalter* (1827), and P. W. Forchhammer, *Die Athener und Sokrates, die Gesetzlichen und der Revolutionär* (1837). In his thesis, *Om Begrebet Ironi med stadigt Hensyn til Socrates*, which he defended September 29, 1841, Kierkegaard at many points (especially sv XIII, 232ff.) takes account of Rötscher's book and Forchhammer's study (sv XIII, 269ff.; cf. *Pap.* III B 30). But he may also have in mind Hegel's own representation of Socrates in *Vorlesungen über die Geschichte der Philosophie* (W.a.A., XIV, 42-122; J.A., XVIII, 42-122; *Lectures on the History of Philosophy*, I-III; New York: Humanities Press, 1955; I, 384-487). In his thesis Kierkegaard makes Hegel's conception of Socrates the object of special consideration (sv XIII, 321-37) and remarks [translation from Lee M. Capel's ms. of *The Concept*

of Irony] "that according to Hegel the Socratic teaching was
negative, had the negative as its end, that it was calculated to
render vacillating and not to render secure, that in Socrates
the negative is not immanent in a positivity but self-purposive,
all this clearly follows . . . from a multitude of observations
. . . but it becomes even more obvious from the way Hegel
discusses the Aristophanic conception of Socrates. He remarks
on page 85 [abovementioned edition of Hegel and pp. 426-427
in English translation] that it is Aristophanes who has conceived the Socratic philosophy from the negative side, whereby
everything existent disappears in the indeterminate universal.
He adds that it does not even occur to him to justify or excuse
Aristophanes." In his book *Sören Kierkegaards Opfattelse af
Sokrates* (1924) J. Himmelstrup has treated (especially pp.
61-84 and pp. 252-307) Kierkegaard's conception in relationship to Hegel's and also the most important contemporary
interpretations of the problem of Socrates.

 reflect upon the absolute. The absolute relationship.   *p. 13, l. 1*

 half-truths . . . the System. In the given context the thought   *p. 13, l. 3*
must be that according to Hegel speculative thought and
revelation have the same content (see quotation in the middle
of page 170) and that therefore the speculative thinker, the
system-builder, supposes that by using his approach he is able
to occupy a higher position above his associates than is, strictly
speaking, humanly possible, because he thinks he is able to
bring truth in its adequate form, the conceptual form, to others
who have not advanced so far. If, then, the System is developed
from these presuppositions, it may be said to suffer from half-
truths, from a deficiency of consistent analysis of the tenability
of these presuppositions, and from a lack of understanding of
the implications of the System as it stands but which would
be undone if the presuppositions were investigated. Understood in this way, Kierkegaard is characterizing not only the

Hegelian System as given but also the untenable presuppositions upon which it is built.

p. 13, l. 5   *the God.* See translator's Foreword and note to p. 18 for discussion of the expressions *God* and *the God.*

p. 13, l. 6   *Plato's Apology.* Especially pp. 21ff., where Socrates tells of the Delphic Oracle's characterization of him as the wisest man, one who "knows that his wisdom is in truth worth nothing" (23) and: "now, when, as I conceive and imagine, God orders me to fulfil the philosopher's mission of searching into myself and other men ..." (28). In the *Theaetetus* (148 and elsewhere) Socrates speaks considerably about his art of midwifery.

p. 13, l. 10   μαιѵεσθαί. To aid in delivery.

p. 13, l. 27   *Diogenes Laertius.* Kierkegaard owned and used the ancient Greek historian-of-philosophy's anecdotal work both in Greek (H. G. Huebner's edition, 1833; Ktl. 1109) and in a Danish translation, *Diogen Laërtses filosofiske Historie ...* , by Börge Riisbrigh (1731-1809, Professor of Philosophy, University of Copenhagen, where he represented the Wolff-Baumgarten school), edited by B. Thorlacius (1775-1829, Professor of Latin), I-II (1812; Ktl. 1110-11). This contains the story (II, 19-21; Diogenes Laertius, *Lives of Eminent Philosophers*, I-II; New York: Putnam, 1925; Loeb Classics, I, 149-51) of Socrates: "Duris makes him out to have been a slave and to have been employed on stone-work. . . ." but "that he discussed moral questions in the workshops and the market-place, being convinced that the study of nature is no concern of ours; and that he claimed that his enquiries embraced whatso'er is good or evil in an house. . . ."

p. 14, l. 3   *nor will one reach the concept of a Revelation.* The polemic is continually directed especially against the Hegelians' attempt to affirm an unbroken line, a harmony between the purely human and the Christian, but it cannot be said with certainty whether or not Kierkegaard's disdain in this passage has a special occasion or is directed toward anyone in particular.

his self-knowledge is a knowledge of God. Since Kierkegaard   *p. 14, l. 6*
points out that this is the Socratic (the Idealistic) view, and
since he says "a knowledge of God" and not simply "knowledge
of God," it is clear that he does not recognize it as genuine
knowledge of God and that, consistently, he does not here
recognize a natural theology. The most pregnant expression
of the Idealistic view is probably that of J. L. Heiberg: "For
thought rises to the heights, when it descends into itself"
(in *Cantate ved Universtitetets aarlige Fest i Anledning af
Reformationens Indförelse samt Rectorskiftet 1839*, quoted
from *Poetiske Skrifter*, 1862, IX, III).

mediated. Reconciled, having entered into a higher unity.   *p. 14, l. 18*
Kierkegaard continually employs this term for the Hegelian
Vermittlung, although Hegel himself does not use it. Cf.,
however, the English translations "mediation" and "self-
mediating" in, for example, Hegel's *Science of Logic*, II, 479,
485, 486.

commune naufragium. A common shipwreck (is easy to   *p. 14, l. 19*
endure).

client. Among the Romans a free-man who lived under   *p. 14, l. 21*
the protection of his wealthy patron.

one fool, when he goes astray. In an old Danish children's   *p. 14, l. 24*
game the "fool" is the name both of the piece or card which
bears the picture of a fool and of the person who draws it
and who therefore loses a point and must "go" as one who
has the lowest card. From this comes the mode of speaking
which Kierkegaard uses here, whereby Hegel and the Hegelians are clearly characterized.

Prodicus. A Sophist mentioned in many places in Plato (for   *p. 14, l. 28*
example, *Theaetetus*, 151; *Protagoras*, 341; *Charmides*, 163;
Meno, 96; *Cratylus*, 384). In a few of these places Socrates calls
himself a pupil of Prodicus, but of course this is not to be
taken seriously. Prodicus is the originator of the famous alle-
gory of Heracles at the crossways, which is related in Xeno-

phon's *Memorabilia* (II, 1, 21ff.; New York: Putnam's 1923; Loeb Classics, pp. 95ff.).

p. 14, l. 29   *Plato in sentimental enthusiasm.* Kierkegaard presumably has in mind not only the *Phaedo*, especially the closing portions (118), but Plato's entire poetic idealization of Socrates in the dialogues.

p. 14, l. 32   εὐκαταφορία εἰς πάθος. Disposition to passion. The expression is used by the Stoics. Kierkegaard gets it from Tennemann, IV, 129, note. In *Pap.* IV A 44 it reads: "This is what I desire in a man: εὐκαταφορία εἰς πάθος, which the Stoics use in a bad sense." In working out the manuscript of *Philosophical Fragments* he evidently looked up the passage again (*Pap.* V B 3, 4). Tennemann presents (pp. 124ff.) the Stoic Zeno's doctrine of the passions: "Passions are, according to their sources, wrong and falsified perceptions of the good and the evil" and according to Zeno there are "four main kinds of passions . . . pleasure and sadness, desire and fear," but the passions are only a passing error which must be regarded as a sickness in the soul, and "a weakness is related to these illnesses so that the soul has not even the power to withstand their inclinations but willingly gives way to them. Thus they are a sickliness (ἀρρωστήματα)." In the note it is explained that of such dispositions to passion Chrysippus had used the expression which Kierkegaard borrows here.

p. 15, note   *Clitophon . . . not believed to be genuine.* The investigation of the genuineness of the Platonic dialogues, which began essentially with Schleiermacher's analyses and was continued in a radical way by F. Ast in *Platons Leben und Schriften* (1816) and, among others, by K. F. Hermann, *Geschichte und System der Platonischen Philosophie* (1839), was in large measure known by Kierkegaard when he was working on *Om Begrebet Ironi*; and in observing the exclusion of *Clitophon* as not being genuine he is merely following the estimate commonly held also in contemporary Plato scholarship. Now the very portion Kierkegaard refers to is used as an argument against the genuineness of the dialogue: "In content *Clitophon* is entirely unPlatonic. It proceeds to criticize Socrates as one who can only stimulate to goodness but either will not or cannot explain what he means by it and thereby has the most discouraging effect upon those in whom he has aroused interest and who now want to go further" (Carsten Höeg, "Indledning til Kleitofon," *Platons Skrifter*, x, 200). In J. Himmelstrup, *Sören Kierkegaards Opfattelse af Sokrates* (1924), especially pp. 252ff. and 275ff., there is an account of Kierkegaard's relationship to the historical and critical Plato-research of his time.

which Socrates fearlessly expressed. In Plato's *Apology* (41)   *p. 15, l. 18*
Socrates says after the sentence has been given: "Above all, I shall then be able to continue my search into true and false knowledge; as in this world, so also in the next; and I shall find out who is wise, and who pretends to be wise, and is not."

the Eternal. The concept is here defined as the timeless, the   *p. 16, l. 1*
continuously present and unchangeable. Here, and throughout the work, Kierkegaard purposely employs the terminology of Greek Idealism and of Speculative Idealism (especially Hegel's). Hegel defines eternity as the timeless present, "zeit-lose Gegenwart" (W.a.A., 1, 225; J.A., 1, 97); Schelling defines it as the "beständiges Nun" (*Vom Ich als Prinzip der Philoso-phie* . . . , 1795, pp. 105ff.). Both of these definitions are expressions of the same understanding of the Eternal as is found, for example, in Augustine (*Confessions*, Chapter xi, 10), in Aristotle (*Physica*, ii, 221b), and in Plato (especially clear in the *Timaeus*, 37-38). The origin of this view is undoubtedly the Eleatics. Kierkegaard's concept of the Eternal is investigated by V. Lindström, *Stadiernas Teologi* (1943), especially pp. 76-88; Sören Holm, *Sören Kierkegaards Historiefilosofi* (1952), especially pp. 21-30; Per Lönning, *Samtidighedens Situation* (Oslo: Forlaget Land og Kirke, 1954), especially pp. 59-69; and

Johannes Slök, *Die Anthropologie Kierkegaards* (Copenhagen: Rosenkilde og Bagger, 1954), especially pp. 52-77. It is of special interest to compare this Greek concept of the Eternal with that in the Old and New Testaments. Significant modern studies are: Oscar Cullmann, *Christ and Time* (Philadelphia: Westminster, 1950); Walter Stromseth, *The Time-Eternity Correlation in Western Theology* (ms. doctoral thesis, Yale University, 1960); and Thorlief Boman, *Das hebräische Denken im Vergleich mit dem Griechischen* (1952). Important contributions to the debate (especially on Cullmann's book) can be found, for example, in Karl Barth, *Church Dogmatics* (Edinburgh: T. and T. Clark, 1960), III, 2, especially pp. 437ff. and in Paul Althaus, *Die Letzten Dinge* (1949), especially pp. 337ff.

p. 16, l. 4   *ubi et nusquam.* Everywhere and nowhere.

At this point, where Kierkegaard for the first time presents in very brief form his anthropology and Christology, there is a good occasion to give a brief summary of his knowledge of dogmatics.

As a child, Kierkegaard had studied Nicolai E. Balle's (1744-1816) well-known *Lærebog i den Evangelisk-christelige Religion*, prepared for use in the Danish schools. It came out in 1791 and was approved in 1794 for introduction in all schools. Only in 1856 was it displaced. Balle's *Lærebog*, as it is still commonly called, presents a predominantly orthodox view of Christianity, and the same is the case with the more copious work which Kierkegaard studied in the Borgerdydsskole, Nikolai Fogtmann's *Lærebog i den christelige Religion* (1823), as well as S. B. Hersleb's definitely anti-rationalist *Lærebog i Bibelhistorie*, which first appeared in 1812. It is not certain whether or not Kierkegaard's teacher of religion, Ludvig Christian Müller (1806-1851), who together with Kierkegaard's brother P. C. Kierkegaard and others belonged to the close circle around Jacob C. Lindberg and N. F. S. Grundtvig, and S. C. W. Bindesböll (1798-1871), who most closely represented

Mynster's view of Christianity, exercised any noteworthy influence upon Kierkegaard in his later school years. It is, however,
a well-known fact that Kierkegaard's father's rigorous understanding of Christianity and Mynster's sermons were of decisive significance.

During the winter semester of 1833-1834 and the summer
semester of 1834 H. N. Clausen delivered lectures on dogmatics.
The young student Sören Kierkegaard was so interested in
them that on the basis of his own or another student's notes he
made a full résumé of most of them (unprinted; cf. *Pap.* I C 19;
surveyed and described by Valdemar Ammundsen, *Sören Kierkegaards Ungdom*, 1912, pp. 82ff.). According to the view of
theology to which Kierkegaard gives expression in the draft of
a letter, June 1, 1835 (*Breve og Aktstykker*, 1953, I, No. 3,
pp. 35-36; cf. *Pap.* I A 72), H. N. Clausen to him evidently
represented rationalism, "which on the whole cuts a rather
poor figure." In the same letter-draft we find his view of orthodoxy at the time: "I grew up, so to speak, in orthodoxy; but as
soon as I began to think for myself the prodigious colossus
gradually began to totter. I call it a prodigious colossus ad-
visedly, for on the whole it is very consistent and in the course
of centuries the various parts have fused so tightly together
that it is difficult to quarrel with it. . . . I had to leave the
fundamental structure *in dubio* for a time. The moment that
was changed, the whole thing naturally assumed another
form." In the spring of 1834 Kierkegaard studied with H. L.
Martensen as tutor, who at that time was a Bachelor of Theology, and together with him went through Schleiermacher's
Der Christliche Glaube in the well-known revised second edition of 1830 (cf. *Pap.* I A 4, 273, and especially I C 20-24), and in
the summer of 1836 he read and made notes on Franz von
Baader, *Vorlesungen über speculative Dogmatik* (cf. *Pap.* I A
174 and I C 27-33). After December 14 of the same year he
grappled with the Hegel-dominated second edition (1827) of

P. Marheineke's *Die Grundlehren der christlichen Dogmatik als Wissenschaft* (cf. *Pap.* I c 25-26), and in the winter semester of 1837-1838 he attended Martensen's lectures on *Prolegomena til den speculative Dogmatik* (cf. *Pap.* II c 12-24), although he apparently did not attend the sequel *Foredrag over den speculative Dogmatik*, given during the summer semester of 1838 and winter semester of 1838-1839, but made use of a fellow-student's notes (*Pap.* II c 25-28). Also in 1838 he read F. C. Baur, *Die Christliche Lehre von der Versöhnung* (1838), at least in part, and there are journal entries which quite likely have to do with H. N. Clausen's lectures on dogmatics during the winter semester of 1839-1840 and the summer semester of 1840 (*Pap.* II c 34-35). While preparing for his examinations he probably made special use of Karl Hase's well-known *Hutterus redivivus oder Dogmatik der evangelisch-lutherischen Kirche*, which he owned in the fourth printing of 1839 (Ktl. 581).

In addition to the works mentioned, he owned and knew various other works in dogmatics, of which only the most important up to the time *Philosophical Fragments* was published (1844) are listed here. H. N. Clausen, *Udvikling af de christelige Hovedlaerdomme* (1844); J. P. Mynster, *Betragtning over de christelige Troeslaerdomme* (2nd printing, 1837); and P. Marheineke, *Lehrbuch des christlichen Glaubens und Lebens für denkende Christen* (2nd printing, 1836, which Kierkegaard owned also in Danish; Ktl. 646) are popular works; whereas K. G. Bretschneider, *Handbuch der Dogmatik*, I-II (4th printing, 1838); August Hahn, *Lehrbuch des christlichen Glaubens* (1828); and A. D. C. Twesten, *Vorlesungen über die Dogmatik der evangelisch-lutherischen Kirche*, I-II (4th printing, 1837-1838) are more scholarly productions. In addition to these books, comprehensive works on doctrine, there are listed in the auction catalog many special studies, theses, etc., which need not be mentioned here.

Kierkegaard's early study of dogmatics is treated especially in Valdemar Ammundsen, *Sören Kierkegaards Ungdom* (1912), pp. 77-107, and in Emanuel Hirsch, *Kierkegaard-Studien* (1933), II, 457-602, where there is also a treatment of Kierkegaard's reading of papers in German theological journals. T. Bohlin in his *Kierkegaards dogmatiska åskådning* (1925), pp. 1-59, is essentially a study of the general background of Kierkegaard's dogmatics in Danish and German theology.

Kierkegaard's terminology in dogmatics is by and large the traditional orthodox terminology, and his allusions particularly to the New Testament are numerous. It is hardly necessary to point out the prototype and borrowing in every instance. It was clearly Kierkegaard's intention to permit the different traditional categories of dogmatics to develop naturally and consistently, and they all receive their vindication from the fundamental category, the Moment in time, which is understood as the fullness of time in Jesus Christ and the single individual's rebirth in faith.

the Moment in time. In this context it means the moment of   *p. 16, l. 5* revelation. As is evident in *The Concept of Dread* (see especially pp. 74ff.), published at the same time as *Philosophical Fragments*, the concept "the Moment," which has many meanings in Kierkegaard, is linked to what Plato sets forth in the *Parmenides* (especially 156). An account of Kierkegaard's relationship to Plato with respect to this concept is best given in connection with the relevant portion of *The Concept of Dread* (Princeton: Princeton University Press, 1944). In addition, see Johannes Slök, *Forsynstanken* (1947), pp. 96ff., and Hermann Diem, *Philosophie und Christentum bei Sören Kierkegaard* (1929), pp. 201ff., also his *Kierkegaard's Dialectic of Existence*.

the Eternal . . . came into existence. The divine Truth was   *p. 16, l. 8* revealed in that Moment and was apprehended by man. According to the Socratic viewpoint, the moment is accidental, essentially an indifferent point of departure in time. Here it acquires decisive significance.

p. 16, l. 28   *departing from it* [the Truth]. As is evident even more clearly from what follows, it is of great importance to Kierkegaard to affirm man's originally right relationship to the Truth and his own responsibility for his current condition.

p. 17, l. 27   *give him the condition.* Here Kierkegaard clearly gives allegiance to the evangelical-Reformation doctrine of *testimonium Spiritus Sancti internum*, the inner witness of the Holy Spirit, but not to the various alterations of this doctrine in experience-theology (Ritschl, for example). See also pages 79-80 and note.

p. 18, l. 12   *by the God himself.* Kierkegaard consciously writes "Platonically" here and therefore does not say "by God" but "by the God." This word-usage is followed throughout almost the entire work. If, however, one reads the modern Danish translation of Plato's works, the *Apology*, for example, he will not be able to detect the similarity of language in Kierkegaard and Plato. Jowett in the English translation (cf. *Theaetetus*, 150, referred to on p. 13) uses *the God*; whereas Cornford frequently uses *heaven*, etc.

Correspondingly one will most frequently be able to understand Kierkegaard's Biblical allusions if he uses the authorized Danish translation of 1819. Therefore, unless otherwise indicated, quotations of the Bible in Danish are from this translation and in English from RSV. In addition to this Danish translation, Kierkegaard possessed and occasionally used Luther's German translation, as well as Christian Kalkar's and J. C. Lindberg's varying independent Danish translations. In one place he clearly seems to have used Sebastian Castellio's Latin translation, which he had in the edition of 1778.

p. 18, l. 13   *he is already created.* The idea of creation is advanced here as self-evident. The substance and the significance of creation in Kierkegaard's thought is investigated and emphasized particularly by V. Lindström in *Stadiernas teologi* (1943), pp. 57-67, 106-13, 133-39, and *passim*. Lindström points out the differences particularly between Kierkegaard's view and that of Brunner as it is formulated in *Man in Revolt* (New York: Scribner's, 1939). Of the major recent contributions mention may be made of Karl Barth, *Church Dogmatics*, III, 1-2, and Regin Prenter, *Dogmatik: Skabelse og Genlösning* (1951-1953), German translation, *Schöpfung und Erlösung* (1959-60).

this state . . . "Sin." Kierkegaard's concept of sin here, in   *p. 19, l. 8*
The Concept of Dread (especially Chapter 1), and in *The Sickness unto Death* has been investigated particularly by T. Bohlin, who in *Kierkegaards dogmatiska åskådning* (1925), pp. 204-24 and *passim*, and also in *Kierkegaards tro* (1944), especially pp. 94ff., maintains that *sin* in the Climacus-works becomes an intellectualized and, according to the Christian view, distorted metaphysical necessity. This view, although somewhat differently formulated, was also held in the earlier Kierkegaard-research: F. Petersen, *Dr. Sören Kierkegaards Christendomsforkyndelse* (1877), *passim*; N. Teisen, *Om Sören Kierkegaards Betydning som kristelig Tænker* (1903); and A. B. Drachmann, *Hedenskab og Christendom hos Sören Kierkegaard*, in *Udvalgte Afhandlinger* (1911) pp. 124-41. Many students of Kierkegaard cannot share this view. Of these the most important are: Hermann Diem, *Philosophie und Christentum bei Sören Kierkegaard* (1929), especially pp. 223ff., and *Kierkegaard's Dialectic of Existence, passim*; Emanuel Hirsch, *Kierkegaard-Studien* (1933), II, 695ff.; and V. Lindström, *Stadiernas teologi* (1943), *passim*.

It seems that the scholars have not pointed out with sufficient clearness that everything in this and the following portion of *Philosophical Fragments*, both the particularly stressed idea of creation and the point that man by meeting Christ ("the God himself") is in "this state . . . Sin," is thought and written not in a "world-historical" perspective of traditional dogmatics, although the traditional dogmatic expressions are used in large measure, but in the category of "the Moment." If this is overlooked, one reads *Philosophical Fragments* as something other than it is intended to be, or, as is written later in the work (pp. 98-99), in another connection: "If the object of apprehension is changed in the process of apprehension, the apprehension is changed into a misapprehension."

p. 19, l. 18   *freedom.* Kierkegaard's concept of freedom, which is never to be interpreted as unengaged freedom of choice, *libertas indifferentiae, liberum arbitrium,* has this primary meaning: the capacity in the choice between good and evil to choose the good. If a man has actually chosen not the good (what this consists of is thereby determined more closely) but the evil, there is then unfreedom in the new situation. This view is developed in other contexts, in addition to the one here, particularly in *The Concept of Dread* (pp. 96ff.) where the problem is dealt with in terms of philosophical anthropology. Cf. Sören Holm, *Schopenhauers Ethik* (1932), pp. 299-304. Kierkegaard's concept of freedom has frequently been the object of investigation, usually in connection with an analysis of his concept of faith and his concept of sin, as in the works mentioned in the previous note. No doubt the most important recent special study is Gregor Malantschuk, "Frihedens Dialektik hos Sören Kierkegaard," in *Dansk teologisk Tidsskrift* (1949), pp. 193-207; cf. Thulstrup, "Kierkegaard-Studiet i Skandinavien 1945-1952," in *Edda* (1954), especially pp. 107ff., and in *Theology Today* (1955). It would be fruitful but too far afield here to undertake a comparison of Kierkegaard's concept of freedom not least with Kant's and Hegel's, particularly as developed in Kant, *The Critique of Pure Reason,* and in Hegel with special clarity in *The Phenomenology of Mind* and in *The Philosophy of Law.*

p. 21, l. 8   *the slave of sin.* The expression comes from John 8:34: ". . . everyone who commits sin is a slave to sin."

"The vicious and the virtuous," etc. A somewhat inaccurate   *p. 21, note*
quotation from Aristotle's *Nicomachean Ethics*, Bk. III, Ch. v,
14, *Works*, IX, 1114^b.

the *"flying arrow"* of the sceptics. In Tennemann, I, 150-209,   *p. 21, note*
Kierkegaard had read about Eleatic philosophy, which denies
the reality of motion. Tennemann presents the famous example
of the flying arrow in this way: "If we imagine an arrow
flying through space at great speed, it has to be in a different
place every moment and, because it occupies this place, it is
at rest every moment. One would therefore have to imagine
it as standing still and being in motion at the same time, which
is contradictory." The presentation follows Aristotle's *Physics,
Works*, II, 239^b. It clearly appears in various places, including
Repetition (Princeton: Princeton University Press, 1941), p. 3,
that Kierkegaard had read Hegel's treatment of the Eleatics
and Zeno in *Vorlesungen über die Geschichte der Philosophie*
(W.a.A., XIII, 280-327; J.A., XVII, 296-343; *History of Philosophy*, I, 239-77). In the *Journals* (*Pap.* IV c 49) it is evident that
Kierkegaard had also read in *Diogenes Laertius* (IX, II, para.
99, B. Riisbrigh's translation, 1812, I, 445) how the Sceptics
denied motion (Loeb Classics, IX, 72, vol. II, 485): "Furthermore, they find Xenophanes, Zeno of Elea, and Democritus to
be sceptics: Xenophanes because he says, 'Clear truth hath no
man seen nor e'er shall know,' and Zeno because he would
destroy motion, saying 'a moving body moves neither where it
is nor where it is not.' . . . ." The example of the flying arrow
does not seem to have been used by the Sceptics.

Fullness of Time. Galatians 4:4: "But when the time had   *p. 22, l. 25*
fully come, God sent forth his Son. . . ."

quicken the steps toward that which lies before. The thought   *p. 23, l. 22*
here is assuredly formulated according to Philippians 3:13ff.

that simple man of wisdom. Socrates, who in the *Apology*   *p. 24, l. 15*
(41) says: "If indeed when the pilgrim arrives in the world
below, he is delivered from the professors of justice in this

world, and finds the true judges who are said to give judgment there, Minos and Rhadamanthus and Aeacus, and Trip-
tolemus, and other sons of God who were righteous in their
own life, that pilgrimage will be worth making."

p. 25, l. 17   *he thinks that God exists in and with his own existence.* It
is possible that this is an allusion to Descartes' thought as
developed in *Meditations*, III. In 1842-1843, when Kierkegaard
wrote the draft of *Johannes Climacus eller De omnibus dubitandum est* (*Pap.* IV B 1-17), he studied Descartes and read
Spinoza's *Principia philosophiae Cartesianae* as well as Hegel's
treatment of Descartes' philosophy in *Vorlesungen über die
Geschichte der Philosophie* (W.a.A., XV, 331-67; J.A., XIX, 331-
67; *History of Philosophy*, II, 220-51), but most likely Kierkegaard simply intends to express the same thought which earlier
(p. 14) reads: "In the Socratic view each individual is his own
center, and the entire world centers in him, because his self-
knowledge is a knowledge of God."

p. 25, l. 27   *so incensed with Socrates* etc. In the *Theaetetus* (151) Socra-
tes says what Kierkegaard alludes to and partially quotes: "For
I have actually known some who were ready to bite me when
I deprived them of a darling folly. . . ."

p. 26, l. 20   *I hide my head in shame.* In Kierkegaard's manuscript (*Pap.*
V B 40, 9) there originally appeared this addition: "but Sophistic
I certainly am not, if Aristotle is correct in saying that Sophistic
knowledge is that whereby one earns money."

p. 27, l. 9   *pass-me-by* (*Huus-forbi*). In the aforementioned child's game
(*Gnavspillet*) there is a piece called the house (*Huset*), and
one who does not bid says pass-me-by (*Huus-forbi*).

COMMENTARY TO CHAPTER II

p. 28, l. 1   *Let us briefly consider Socrates.* Whereas in the previous
chapter Kierkegaard speaks of Socrates as a principle, here he
speaks of him as a person. Whereas in his thesis, *Om Begrebet
Ironi* (*The Concept of Irony*), Kierkegaard goes through the

primary sources of knowledge about the historical Socrates (Xenophon, Plato, and Aristotle), and arrives at the original conclusion that the caricature by Aristophanes comes the closest to the truth (cf. sv XIII, 231-59), here he gives a description which begins in neutral terms and closes almost in expressions of enthusiasm. In J. Himmelstrup, *Sören Kierkegaards Opfattelse af Sokrates* (1924), particularly pp. 91ff. and 116ff., an account is given of the changes in Kierkegaard's view of Socrates. Correspondingly Jesus Christ, "the God in time," "the Servant," is discussed as a person, but without mention of the name.

the autopathetic and the sympathetic. Socrates is influenced just as much as he influences others. The phrase actually means self-suffering and sympathizing. *p. 28, l. 18*

he would accept neither praise nor honors nor money etc. The particular reference is most likely to Plato's *Apology* (19ff.). *p. 28, l. 19*

our age is positive. This could very well be one of Kierkegaard's not infrequent ironical remarks about the Hegelians, who with the aid of the Hegelian dialectical method supposed themselves able to know the highest truth and thereby, as it were, to achieve positivity. But it is not improbable that Kierkegaard had in mind Schelling's *Philosophie der Offenbarung*, which Schelling himself had characterized as the positive philosophy in contrast to his earlier thought, akin to Hegel's, which then was called the negative philosophy. Cf. the title of H. E. G. Paulus's previously mentioned edition of Schelling's Berlin lectures, *Die endlich offenbar gewordene positive Philosophie der Offenbarung . . .* (1843). *p. 29, l. 1*

divine jealousy. According to the common Greek conception, if in pride men attempt to go beyond the established boundary between the human and the divine, they are destroyed by Nemesis, the divine jealousy. See S. Ranulf, *The Jealousy of* *p. 29, l. 6 the Gods and Criminal Law at Athens*, I-II (London: Williams and Norgate, 1933-1934).

p. 29, l. 16   *Alcibiades.* In Plato's *Symposium* (215), Alcibiades, enamoured of Socrates, says: "When we hear any other speaker, even a very good one, he produces absolutely no effect upon us, or not much, whereas the mere fragments of you and your words, even at second-hand, and however imperfectly repeated, amaze and possess the souls of every man, woman, and child who comes within hearing of them. And if I were not afraid that you would think me hopelessly drunk, I would have sworn as well as spoken to the influence which they have always had and still have over me. For my heart leaps within me more than that of any Corybantian reveller, and my eyes rain tears when I hear them."

p. 29, l. 17   *Corybantic.* The Corybantes were priests of the Phrygian goddess Cybele, whom they worshipped ecstatically with music and with great noise.

p. 29, l. 27   *the coldness of his irony.* The expression, which Kierkegaard has permitted to stand, betokens an evaluation of Socrates which, in spite of the significantly more positive interpretation, still retains a mark of his earlier conception. Nevertheless, in a marginal note in the manuscript (*Pap.* VB 4, 3) Kierkegaard himself poses the question: "I wonder if Socrates really was so cold; I wonder if it did not grieve him that Alcibiades could not understand him."

p. 30, l. 3   *exercises all the arts of seduction in order to be seduced.* In the *Symposium* (216-18) Alcibiades himself tells of having tried it on Socrates.

p. 30, l. 10   ἀκίνητος πάντα κινεῖ. Unmoved itself, it moves all things. In his *Metaphysics* (*Works*, VIII, Book Λ, 7-8; 1071bff.) Aristotle develops his doctrine of God, his theology, in the following way. If everything which is in motion is moved by something else, it can take place in one of two ways. The second can in turn be moved by a third and so on, or there is a "first mover" not moved by something else. Such a first unmoved-mover must be presupposed and is, according to Aristotle, identical with God, who is pure actuality, pure reason, without any residue of potentiality as in all the rest of the universe, in which potentiality is the principle of motion. In this way God becomes for Aristotle the one who, unmoved himself, moves all things.

Kierkegaard did not get the expression from a reading of Aristotle's *Metaphysics* but from a secondary source. In the *Journal* of 1843 he writes (*Pap.* IV A 157): "Insofar as all philosophy is able to conceive of the relationship of the divine to the human, Aristotle has already expressed it felicitously when he says that God moves all things but is himself ἀκίνητος. (So far as I can remember, Schelling pointed this out in Berlin.) It is really the abstract concept of unchangeableness, and his influence is therefore a magnetic charm something like the sirens' song. Thus all rationalism ends in superstition." According to H. E. G. Paulus's report (p. 405; see note on p. 177), Schelling in Berlin had called the Aristotelian divinity "das bewegt, ohne selbst bewegt zu werden." But Kierkegaard, when he wrote this entry, had also read in Tennemann, III, 159ff.: "This first moving one cannot again be moved by another; it has to move without being moved (τὸ πρῶτον κινοῦν ἀκίνητον). Kierkegaard quotes Schelling more freely than Paulus. His notebook (unpublished; *Pap.* III c 27), in connection with Schelling's criticism of Hegel's concept of God, reads: "This is reminiscent of Aristotle, who taught that God worked ὡς τέλος, himself ἀκίνητος."—On Aristotle's theology see W. D. Ross, *Aristotle* (London: Methuen, 1945), pp. 179ff., and H. von Arnim, *Die Entstehung der Gotteslehre des Aristoteles* (1931). From the next sentences it is evident that Kierkegaard's concept of God is quite different from Aristotle's. A clear presentation of the Christian conception of

God as formed through the years is given by G. Aulén in his *Den kristna Gudsbilden* (2nd printing, 1941).

p. 30, l. 14

what else . . . but love? Here Kierkegaard emphasizes precisely the same characteristic of Christian love—agape—as does Anders Nygren in his motif-analysis, *Agape and Eros* (Philadelphia: Westminster, 1953). God's love is intrinsic and outgoing.

p. 30, l. 16

His resolve, which stands in no equal reciprocal relation to the occasion. Here Kierkegaard may be aiming polemically at Anselm of Canterbury's *Cur Deus Homo* (1098), in which the logical and metaphysical necessity of the Incarnation is maintained, because God's righteousness requires either punishment or satisfaction for man's sin. If man were to be punished as he deserves, God's eternal resolution of salvation could not be fulfilled—therefore satisfaction must be made. Man ought to make this satisfaction, but is unable to. God alone is able to do this, and therefore God became man: *nemo potest nisi Deus, nemo debet nisi homo, ergo Deus homo.* This view, formulated as the so-called objective theory of the Atonement, is presented in Kierkegaard's commonly used handbook in dogmatics: Karl Hase, *Hutterus redivivus* (4th printing, 1839; Ktl. 581; here quoted from the third printing, 1836, pp. 251-52, with Hase's abbreviations spelled out): "By the sin of mankind the majesty of God has been infinitely wronged. In accordance with his love he wanted to forgive; in accordance with his justice he could not. Only an infinite, i.e., divine, being could compensate infinitely for an infinite wrong, but again it had to be a man, so that the atonement would come from mankind. Therefore God himself became man, and by taking the guilt on himself and by atoning through his death the God-man gave infinite atonement to the divine."

Naturally Kierkegaard also knew Anselm and his theory from sources other than Hase—Martensen, for example, in his

lectures during the winter semester 1837-1838 dealt with
Anselm (cf. *Pap.* II c 14 and 22), but it is more reasonable to
assume that Kierkegaard's discussion here is polemically
oriented against Hegel. His *Vorlesungen über die Philosophie
der Religion* (W.a.A., XI, 269; J.A., XV, 285; *Philosophy of
Religion*, I, 276) states that the Fall "is not merely a kind of
accidental history, but rather the everlasting necessary history
of mankind." Redemption, too (the word *Versöhnung* is used
by Hegel in all fields of philosophy, often in the sense of
Vermittlung, which Kierkegaard most frequently calls *mediation*), Hegel maintains, takes place, as do all historical events,
by necessity. God's spirit and the spirit of man are actually
one, the *Vorlesungen über die Philosophie der Geschichte*
(W.a.A., IX, 394, J.A., XI, 416; *Philosophy of History*, p. 415)
declares with exceptional brevity and clarity: "this implicit
unity exists in the first place only for the thinking speculative
consciousness; but it must also exist for the sensuous, representative consciousness—it must become an object for the
World—it must *appear*, and that in the sensuous form appropriate to Spirit, which is the human. *Christ has appeared*—a
Man who is God—God who is Man; and thereby peace and
reconciliation have accrued to the World." Kierkegaard, however, maintains that the necessity of the Christ-revelation
cannot be drawn from the fact of sin.

the very learned Polos. A pupil of the Sophist Gorgias. In   *p. 32, l. 9*
the dialogue *Gorgias* (490) it is Callicles who, very irritated by
Socrates and his use of examples from ordinary life, says, "You
talk about meats, and drinks and physicians and other nonsense; I am not speaking of them."

Themistocles. Kierkegaard freely recounts Themistocles'   *p. 32, l. 22*
words to Xerxes (Plutarch's *Levnetsbeskrivelser*, translated by
S. Tetens, 1803, II, 59-60; Ktl. 1197-1200; in Loeb Classics, XXIX,
3, vol. II, 79).

For love is exultant [Danish: *overende*] . . . , *but it is tri-*   *p. 33, l. 6 umphant* [Danish: *triumpherende*]. . . . In Rome an *ovation* was the more modest form of receiving a victor (he paraded on foot); a *triumph* was the more splendid form (the victor came in riding). Therefore in Danish: *overe* and *triumphere* (*exultant* and *triumphant*).

p. 33, l. 27   *the shadow of death over the grave.* Perhaps an allusion to the assumption that one can tell when someone walks over his grave.

p. 35, l. 10   *base coinage . . . Caesar . . . God.* The expression is based upon Matthew 22:19-21. " 'Show me the money for the tax.' And they brought him a coin. And Jesus said to them, 'Whose likeness and inscription is this?' They said, 'Caesar's.' Then he said to them, 'Render therefore unto Caesar the things that are Caesar's and to God the things that are God's.' "

p. 35, l. 15   *with the flute-players* etc. The allusion is presumably to the raising of Jairus' daughter, as recounted in Matthew 9:23. The Greek text reads ἰδὼν τοὺς αὐλητὰς καὶ τὸν ὄχλον θορυβούμενον, which Kierkegaard (and also the recent Danish translators) renders more felicitously than is done in the 1819 Danish translation which Kierkegaard had.

p. 35, l. 23   *The union might be brought about by an elevation.* Kierkegaard distinguishes here between love as Eros (A) and as Agape (B) in the very way Nygren does in his work mentioned above, but Nygren's approach is purely descriptive and Kierkegaard's is constructive.

p. 35, l. 26   *a thousand years are as one day.* II Peter 3:8: "with the Lord one day is as a thousand years, and a thousand years as one day."

p. 36, l. 30   *garb more glorious than that of Solomon.* Matthew 6:29: "Yet I tell you, even Solomon in all his glory was not arrayed like one of these" [the lilies of the field].

p. 37, l. 11   *no man could see the God and live.* Exodus 33:20: " 'But,' he said, 'you cannot see my face; for man shall not see me and live.' "

sorrow in heaven as well as joy. The expression is taken   *p. 37, l. 18*
partially from Luke 15:7: "I tell you, there will be more joy
before the angels of God over one sinner who repents."

decisive significance(—). The parenthesis signifies the re-   *p. 37, l. 26*
curring thought (as on p. 34): "(and if not we return to
Socrates even if we think to advance beyond him). . . ."

the Truth makes him free. Cf. John 8:32: "and you will   *p. 38, l. 14*
know the truth, and the truth will make you free."

"but not merely in the sense which Socrates so beautifully   *p. 38, l. 18*
expounds." Socrates in the *Symposium* (210) recounts Dioti-
mas's discourse: ". . . and after laws and institutions he will
go on to the sciences, that he may see their beauty, being not
like a servant in love with one youth or man or institution,
himself a slave mean and narrow-minded, but drawing towards
and contemplating the vast sea of beauty, he will create many
fair and noble thoughts and notions in boundless love of
wisdom; until on that shore he grows and waxes strong, and
at last the vision is revealed to him of a single science, which
is the science of beauty everywhere." Shortly before this it
reads (209): "And he who in youth has the seed of these
[wisdom and virtue, temperance and justice] implanted in
him and is himself inspired, when he comes to maturity desires to beget and generate. He wanders about seeking beauty
that he may beget offspring—for in deformity he will beget
nothing—and naturally embraces the beautiful rather than
the deformed body. Above all when he finds a fair and noble
and well-nurtured soul he embraces the two in one person
and to such a one is full of speech about virtue and the nature
and pursuits of a good man; and he tries to educate him; and
at the touch of the beautiful which is ever present to his
memory, even when absent, he brings forth that which he has
conceived long before, and in company with him tends that
which he brings forth; and they are married by a far nearer
tie and have a closer friendship than those who beget mortal

children, for the children who are their common offspring are
fairer and more immortal. Who, when he thinks of Homer
and Hesiod and other great poets, would not emulate them in
the creation of children such as theirs, which have preserved
their memory and given them everlasting glory?"

p. 39, l. 19   *this servant-form is no mere outer garment.* Not something
put on. Kierkegaard is expressly opposed to Docetism, which
denies Christ's true humanity.

p. 39, l. 21   *the filmy summer-cloak of Socrates.* In Plato's *Symposium*
(220) Alcibiades tells that in the expedition to Potidaea Socrates was very hardy: "There was a severe frost, for the winter
in that region is really tremendous, and everybody else either
remained indoors, or if they went out had on an amazing
quantity of clothes, and were well shod, and had their feet
swathed in felt and fleeces; in the midst of this, Socrates with
his bare feet on the ice and in his ordinary dress marched
better than the other soldiers who had shoes. . . ."

p. 39, l. 31   *he has not a resting place for his head.* Luke 9:58: "And
Jesus said to him, 'Foxes have holes, and birds of the air have
nests; but the Son of man has nowhere to lay his head.'"

p. 40, l. 2   *than if angels guided him.* Matthew 4:6: "for it is written
[Psalm 91:11-12]:

> He will give his angels charge of you, and
> On their hands they will bear you up,
> lest you strike your foot against a stone."

p. 40, l. 5   *yet his eye rests upon mankind with deep concern.* Cf., for
example, Matthew 9:36: "When he saw the crowds, he had
compassion for them, because they were harassed and helpless,
like sheep without a shepherd."

p. 40, l. 28   *forsaken in death.* Matthew 27:46: "My God, my God, why
hast thou forsaken me?"

p. 40, l. 28   *behold the man.* Pilate's words to the Jews concerning Jesus
(I John 19:5).

p. 41, l. 13   *more filled with tears than those of a repentant woman.*

Luke 7:37ff.: ". . . a woman of the city, who was a sinner, . . . and standing behind him at his feet, weeping, she began to wet his feet with her tears, and wiped them with the hair of her head. . . ."

a woman whose heart's sole choice. Mary (Luke 10:39-42).   *p. 41, l. 18*

Man, what have I to do with thee? The expression is based *p. 41, l. 25* on Jesus' words to Mary, his mother. John 2:4.

Get thee hence, for thou art Satan. The expression is taken *p. 41, l. 25* from Matthew 4:10 and 16:23.

her heart is pierced by the sword. The expression comes *p. 42, l. 6* from Luke 2:35: "and a sword will pierce through your own soul also."

sorrowful unto death. Matthew 26:38: "My soul is very *p. 42, l. 11* sorrowful, even unto death."

bitter cup. Cf. Matthew 26:39: "this cup."   *p. 42, l. 15*

bitter refreshment. Cf. Matthew 27:48: "A sponge, filled . . . *p. 42, l. 17* with vinegar."

the misunderstanding of the beloved. That men, instead of *p. 42, l. 18* loving Jesus, put him on the cross.

in this way. The crucifixion and the misunderstanding on *p. 42, l. 22* the part of the beloved.

to bring men to the most crucial and terrible decision. For *p. 42, l. 23* every individual human being, who must either be offended or come to Faith.

falsely poetizing his love away. In all likelihood the meaning *p. 42, l. 25* here is that the *poet* will not interpret the crucifixion and the decision between offense and Faith, which men are compelled to face, as an act of love intended as the salvation of men but rather as an act of God's wrath with perdition as the consequence.

when new wine is poured in old leather bottles. Matthew *p. 43, l. 1* 9:17.

the mountains tremble at the voice of God. Probably an *p. 43, l. 10* allusion to the account of the Sinai-revelation. Exodus 19:16ff.

p. 43, l. 24   *flute-playing.* A reference to Plato's *Apology* (27) in which Socrates defends himself against Meletus' charge of atheism: "Did ever any man believe in horsemanship, and not in horses? or in flute-playing and not in flute-players? No, my friend. . . . But now please to answer the next question: Can a man believe in spiritual and divine agencies, and not in spirits or demigods?"

p. 43, l. 26   *as if it owed its existence to humanity at large.* Without pinning this down to particular expressions, it is clear that Kierkegaard in this little portion is attacking D. F. Strauss's and especially Ludwig Feuerbach's left-wing Hegelian explanations of Christianity. Strauss had certainly not denied the historicity of Jesus in his *Das Leben Jesu* (*The Life of Jesus*; London: Allen, 6th edition, 1913), but he did strip the person of Jesus of religious significance. According to Strauss the gospel accounts are mythological constructions whose decisive significance is their picturesque presentation of the unity of the spirit of God and the spirit of man, the unity which for this speculative view manifests itself not in a single individual person but in all humanity. Feuerbach maintained, more radically, in his *Das Wesen des Christenthums* (1841; *The Essence of Christianity*; New York: Harper, 1957), which appeared only five years after Strauss's main work, that all religion is human illusion, poetry, a projection of the dream-wish. When in religion men believe they know God, in actuality they know their own being but imagine it to be incarnated in an objective divinity.—As mentioned (note to title-page), Kierkegaard knew Strauss's views and he had obtained Feuerbach's central work in the second edition (1843; Ktl. 488) on March 20, 1844 (cf. *Pap.* v a 14 with note), and read it concurrently with the writing of *Philosophical Fragments.* Apparently Kierkegaard takes a stand here in relationship to the Danish Strauss-disciple A. F. Beck's *Begrebet Mythus eller den religiöse Aands Form,* which appeared in 1842 and which he knew (Ktl. 424). Kierkegaard also had a bone to pick with Beck for his review of *The Concept of Irony* and had polemicized against him in the newspaper *Fædrelandet* (June 12, 1842; cf. sv xiii, 436 and 439ff.). In opposition to the left-wing Hegelians, Kierkegaard maintains in this part of *Philosophical Fragments* that with reference to his New Testament characterization of the revelation of God in Jesus Christ there can be no thought of human poetizing, since it could occur to no human being to poetize God's personal revelation in this very way: God who reveals himself in his opposite, in debasement. Cf. p. 47 and note.

This thought did not arise in my own heart. Kierkegaard's   *p. 45, l. 1* whole development of the conclusion to this chapter is based on I Corinthians 2:7-10.

COMMENTARY TO CHAPTER III

The Absolute Paradox. To explain the absolute paradox,   *p. 46, title* which by definition is inexplicable, is to explain it away. Here it is only a matter of sketching what Kierkegaard means by the expression itself, which has a long history in his thought and is frequently discussed in Kierkegaard studies, and why he uses it.

As usual in *Philosophical Fragments*, Kierkegaard takes his point of departure in the Socratic, that is, in the highest possibility within the purely human. Here it appears that even Socrates, symbolic of the highest among men, could not achieve contradiction-free self-knowledge. His own expressions concerning himself betray a fundamental lack of clarity. This, for an Idealistic view (which, as developed earlier, is basically optimistic and maintains that man in himself possesses the possibility of complete self-understanding), appears at a point which is particularly crucial. This lack of clarity can only be designated as something which "seems to be a paradox," because man Christianly viewed in his actual situation does not have the possibility of self-knowledge. It is lost in sin, for which man himself bears the responsibility. In man's actual situation human thought, characterized as pathos or passion, strives to reach out beyond its limits, seeks what it cannot master, what cannot be contained in its categories—the unthinkable. The fact which human thought, bound in sin and therefore within its own limitations, recoils against and can stumble over (in offense) is God in human form, Jesus Christ, the wholly other, whose total difference from every other human being cannot be elucidated in any way. Therefore Jesus Christ, the God-man, is called the absolute paradox, primarily because as true God and true man he is that very fact which human thought cannot contain, although its loftiest striving is precisely for the ungraspable, which can also be defined as the limit of thought, and, secondly, because he cannot be known as he is unless there be given the condition which he alone can provide. God and man are absolutely unlike, and the difference lies in that man is in the state of sin and God is not. Inasmuch as all human thought must proceed out of man's actual situation, with the presupposition of sin, and out of linguistic possibilities given in the actual situation, the fact adduced here (in *Philosophical Fragments*, in accordance with the method of the work, it is presented in the form of a hypothesis) can only be designated as the absolute paradox, the utterly strange, the ungraspable, the miracle which breaks into the world in the Moment, which must be understood first of all as the point in time when the Christ-revelation took place and, secondly, as the moment when faith is given to the single individual human being. The absolute paradox is Jesus Christ, who came to this world and yet appeared as if he were of this world, and who by his presence places man in the position of the choice, in the possibility of offence or Faith.

As stated, Kierkegaard's concept of paradox has frequently been the object of study. Special mention may be made of Hermann Diem, *Philosophie und Christentum bei Sören*

Kierkegaard, pp. 176ff. and 210ff.; T. Bohlin, *Kierkegaards dogmatiska åskådning*, pp. 256ff.; E. Hirsch, *Kierkegaard-Studien*, II, 768ff. (which gives particular consideration to the *Postscript*) and *passim*; J. Himmelstrup, *Terminologisk Register til Sören Kierkegaards Værker* (sv xv, 1936), pp. 658ff.; V. Lindström, *Stadiernas teologi*, particularly pp. 315ff.; T. Bohlin, *Kierkegaards tro*, pp. 78ff.; Hermann Diem, *Kierkegaard's Dialectic of Existence*, pp. 43ff., 55ff.; Sören Holm, *Sören Kierkegaards Historiefilosofi, passim*; Per Lönning, *Samtidighedens Situation*, particularly pp. 120ff.

reflection upon the nature of such beings etc. In Plato's *p. 46, l. 6*
Phaedrus (229-230) Socrates objects to the young Phaedrus's speculations about the possible historical core of a legend: "Now I quite acknowledge that these allegories are very nice, but he is not to be envied who has to invent them; much labour and ingenuity will be required of him; and when he has once begun, he must go on and rehabilitate Hippocentaurs and chimeras dire. Gorgons and winged steeds flow on apace, and numberless other inconceivable and portentous natures. And if he is sceptical about them, and would fain reduce them one after another to the rules of probability, this sort of crude philosophy will take up a great deal of time. Now I have no leisure for such enquiries; shall I tell you why? I must first know myself, as the Delphian inscription says; to be curious about that which is not my concern, while I am still in ignorance of my own self, would be ridiculous. And therefore I bid farewell to all this; the common opinion is enough for me. For, as I was saying, I want to know not about this, but about myself: am I a monster more complicated and swollen with passion than the serpent Typho, or a creature of a gentler and simpler sort, to whom Nature has given a diviner and lowlier destiny?"

mediation. A parody of the dialectical concept-development *p. 47, l. 2*
according to Hegel: the gentleman stands (thesis); he falls

(antithesis), but he thereby makes progress and comes to stand again (synthesis). Therefore standing and falling are mediated in walking, a forward movement.

p. 47, note   *this theocentric age.* From Kierkegaard's later comments it is clear that he is thinking here of Hegelianism. We find, for example, in *Stages on Life's Way* (Princeton: Princeton University Press, 1945; p. 166): "There are various kinds of eccentricity; the theocentric kind has a reasonable claim to be assigned to the place that belongs to it. But in fact speculation is theocentric, and theocentric is the speculator, and theocentric the theory. So long as it goes no further than that, and the theocentric confines itself to being theocentric three times a week from four o'clock till five in the professor's chair, but for the rest of the time is a citizen and a married man and a good fellow like all the others, one cannot say that the temporal has been unfairly dealt with. Such a theoretical digression three times a week, an incidental occupation, may be expected to have no further consequences." In the *Postscript* (p. 190): "If speculative philosophy wishes to take cognizance of this, and say as always, that there is no paradox when the matter is viewed eternally, divinely, theocentrically—then I admit that I am not in a position to determine whether the speculative philosopher is right, for I am only a poor existing human being, not competent to contemplate the eternal either eternally or divinely or theocentrically, but compelled to content myself with existing. So much is certain, however, that speculative philosophy carries everything back, back past the Socratic position, which at least comprehended that for an existing individual existence is essential; to say nothing of the failure of speculative philosophy to take time to grasp what it means to be so critically situated in existence as the existing individual in the experiment." A very significant explanation of the thought and language is found in *Pap.* VIII[1] A 414, November 20, 1847: "The fundamental derangement at the root of modern times (which branches out into logic, meta-physics, dogmatics, and the whole of modern life) consists of this: that men have removed the deep qualitative chasm from the distinction between God and man. Because of this there is in dogmatics (from logic and metaphysics) a depth of blasphemy which paganism never knew (for it knew what blasphemy against God is, but precisely this has been forgotten in our time, this theocentric age) and in ethics a brash un-concern or, more accurately, no ethics at all."—Hegel himself seems not to have used the expression *theocentric*.

criterion of the Truth. In *Pap.* iv c 50 it appears that Kierke-   *p. 47, l. 6*
gaard knew the Greek Sceptics' view of the currently advanced (especially by Democritus) criterion of truth from Tenne-mann's *Geschichte der Philosophie*. See the next note.

Sextus Empiricus. Kierkegaard had the works of the Greek   *p. 48, l. 1*
sceptical philosopher in J. A. Fabricius's edition (with parallel translation in Latin) of 1621 (Ktl. 146); but as far as can be ascertained he did not know I. Bekker's edition which appeared in 1842. Kierkegaard's comments on Sextus Empiricus here and elsewhere do not, however, seem to be based on an inde-pendent study of his works. In any case, Kierkegaard's read-ing of the primary sources does not seem to have been espe-cially comprehensive. Yet he had carefully gone through the copious, documented presentation in Tennemann v, 267-396, and had read Hegel's shorter and clearer critical treatment in *Vorlesungen über die Geschichte der Philosophie* (W.a.A., xiv, 538-86; J.A., xviii, 538-86; *History of Philosophy*, ii, 328-73). It is, however, doubtful that he had read the corresponding portion in Hegel's *Phänomenologie des Geistes* (W.a.A., ii, 154ff.; J.A., ii, 162ff.; *Phenomenology of Mind*, pp. 246ff.). It is definite that he did get some details from *Diogenes Laertius*, ix.—The source of Kierkegaard's rendition (in the note) of Sextus Empiricus' objection to Democritus is Tenne-mann, v, 302, note 40, which reads: "Man cannot be the cri-

terion of the truth. . . . If . . . man, who is supposed to recognize the truth, is an incomprehensible being, then the truth itself must be inscrutable. Among those who examined this concept, Socrates at once declares himself to be ignorant. I do not know, he says, whether I am a man [human being] or another changeable animal such as Typho [the reference is to *Phaedrus*, 229-30]. Democritus, it is true, undertakes to develop the concept, but he could say no more about it than any ignorant man knows. Man is what we all know. For we all know what a dog, a house, a plant is, but none of them is man. Sextus at this place chides Democritus, and it becomes even more obvious in his *Outlines of Pyrrhonism*, [II, 23; Loeb Classics, Vol. I, 167] where he takes a statement in which Democritus declares a definition to be unnecessary to be a definition in itself, and then draws among other things the conclusion: we all know what a dog is; therefore man is a dog."—Two modern major works are Karl Deichgräber, *Die griechische Empirikerschule, Sammlung der Fragmente und Darstellung der Lehre* (1930) and Léon Robin, *Pyrrhon et le Scepticisme Grec* (1944).

p. 48, l. 1   *the transition involved in "teaching."* Sextus Empiricus poses the problem thus in *Outlines of Pyrrhonism* (III, 253; Loeb Classics, vol. I, 495): that which is to be taught is either true or false; if it is false, it would not be taught, for falsehood is non-existent and of non-existents there can be no teaching; neither would it be taught if one maintained its truth, because the truth cannot be discovered. Since, therefore, neither the false nor the true can be taught, nothing can be taught.

p. 48, l. 3   *Protagoras.* The Greek Sophists' theory of knowledge was that "man is the measure of all things, of things which are, that they are, and of what is not, that it is not"—the so-called "man is the measure" doctrine. Universally valid truth is impossible according to this doctrine, a total subjectivism and relativism in epistemology. In his *Vorlesungen über die*

Geschichte der Philosophie, II (W.a.A., XIV, 30; J.A., XVIII, 30; *History of Philosophy*, I, 373) Hegel translates the Greek in this way: " 'Man is the measure of all things; of that which is, that it is; of that which is not, that it is not.' " Hegel goes on to explain that *man* can be understood as individual man (as by Protagoras) or as universal man (as by Socrates and Plato). If the proposition is understood as Protagoras himself understood it, then, says Hegel, "all is self-seeking, all self-interest, the subject with his interests forms the central point; and if man has a rational side, reason is still something subjective, it is 'he.' But this is just the wrong and perverted way of looking at things which necessarily forms the main reproach made against the Sophists—that they put forward man in his contingent aims as determining; thus with them the interest of the subject in its particularity, and the interest of the same in its substantial reason are not distinguished." Kierkegaard quotes incorrectly here, but it appears later that Kierkegaard understands the line in its original meaning and therefore also as Hegel interprets it.

Reason stands still, just as Socrates did. In Plato's *Symposium*   *p. 48, l. 11*
(p. 220) Alcibiades relates: "One morning he was thinking about something which he could not resolve; he would not give it up, but continued thinking from early dawn until noon —there he stood fixed in thought; and at noon attention was drawn to him, and the rumor ran through the wondering crowd that Socrates had been standing and thinking about something ever since the break of day. At last, in the evening after supper, some Ionians out of curiosity (I should explain that this was not in winter but in summer) brought out their mats and slept in the open air that they might watch him and see whether he would stand all night. There he stood until the following morning; and with the return of light he offered up a prayer to the sun, and went his way."

lies as the ground . . . or is the ground in which all . . .   *p. 48, l. 18 perishes* (Danish: *ligger til Grund for eller gaaer til Grunde i*). The expression must be understood against the background of Hegel's use of it in *Wissenschaft der Logik* where he says (W.a.A., iv, 156; J.A., iv, 634; *Science of Logic*; New York: Macmillan, 1951; p. 137): "The Appearing World has its negative unity in the Essential World; it perishes in it, and passes back into it as its Ground." Therefore the meaning of the expression is that something, seen from one side, is destroyed and, seen from the other, is perfected. The term *aufheben* in Hegel has a double meaning most clearly expressed in Latin: *tollere* and *conservare*. In his *Ledetraad ved Forelæsningerne over Philosophiens Philosophie eller den speculative Logik* (1831-1832), J. L. Heiberg explains the expression in this way (para. 71ff., especially para. 74; quoted from *Prosaiske Skrifter*, 1861, i, 172): "The transition of being to its underlying ground consists . . . in this, that it is destroyed; it is destroyed because it is simultaneously abrogated and preserved [*ophævet*]." This is further explained in a comment: "Whenever one says that something is destroyed, he thereby says that its being is abrogated by a transition to its underlying ground. That a building is destroyed means that it sinks down to the ground, whereby its being is abrogated and preserved and the ground at the same time ceases to be ground for the mediate being; it remains only as the result of the immediate; but as long as the ground is left, the building can be raised on it again or immediate being can develop itself anew."

p. 48, l. 23   *love his neighbor as himself.* Mark 12:31.

p. 48, l. 26   *so say the poets.* In the draft (*Pap.* v b 5, 2) it appears that Kierkegaard is thinking of the count's chief page, Cherubin, in Beaumarchais, *Le Mariage de Figaro*, i, 7 (translated into Danish by N. T. Bruun, 1817, 1821-1822).

p. 49, l. 3   σκοπῶ οὐ ταῦτα. . . . See translation from *Phaedrus*, 230, in note for p. 46. Kierkegaard has forgotten the words "than the serpent Typho" in the Greek text.

For if the God does not exist. Here Kierkegaard, without p. 49, l. 15
making a distinction between *existence* and *being*, takes a position in relationship to the classic proofs of the existence (being)
of God, especially the ontological proof. Most likely he gained
his first acquaintance with these proofs in the lectures by Martensen in 1837 mentioned above. In Kierkegaard's notes we read
(*Pap.* II c 22, p. 336): "It is remarkable that the above proofs
[cosmological and teleological] were known in the ancient
world; whereas this one [ontological] first appeared in the
Christian world. Anselm: [in *Proslogium*] the highest I can
think must be, for if it were not, I could [not] think it, and
then I could [not] think of it as that which is, but this would
be a higher thought etc. By this is not meant that because I
think God, God therefore is, but that because the thought
of God is in me, I therefore must think God. This was later
advanced by Leibniz [*Monadology*, 45] and by Wolff [*Theo-
logia naturalis*, I, 8]: the highest being must possess all attributes; it must possess eternal blessedness, but this involves
being a unity, *cuius essentia existentia*." Kierkegaard returns
(see note on Spinoza below) to this Spinozistic expression.
Likewise he here expressly gives consideration to Kant's well-
known criticism (*Critique of Pure Reason*; London: Macmillan, 1950; pp. 495ff.) to the effect that existence is not a
consequence of the definition of a concept, and to Hegel's
recurrence to the proofs of God's existence and to a criticism
of Kant's objections, in *Anhang zu Vorlesungen über die Philosophie der Religion* (W.a.A., XII, 359-593; J.A., XVI, 359-553;
Philosophy of Religion, III, 155-367) and in *Vorlesungen über
die Geschichte der Philosophie*, III (W.a.A., XV, 583ff.; J.A.,
XIX, 583ff.; *History of Philosophy*, III, 452ff.) where Hegel
affirms that: "Kant does not attain to the comprehension of
that very synthesis of Notion and Being, or in other words, he
does not comprehend existence, i.e., he does not attain to the
establishment of it as Notion; existence remains for him

something absolutely different from a Notion."—Emanuel
Hirsch points out in his Commentary (p. 175) that Schelling
in his Berlin lectures, according to the previously mentioned
report by H. E. G. Paulus, expressed himself in a way very
much like Kierkegaard's here. In Paulus' work (p. 475) it reads
as follows: "The existence of God cannot be proven, only the
divinity of the Existent, the divinity of the eternal being existing by his own act, and even this only *a posteriori*." As mentioned earlier, there is no indication that Kierkegaard knew
Paulus' book, and as is well known he had not been particularly
attentive to Schelling's lectures as they progressed. Therefore
there is no compelling reason to assume that Kierkegaard
exhibits here any strong influence from the Berlin lectures.—
Concerning Hegel's view of proofs of the existence of God,
see, for example, Erik Schmidt, *Hegels Lehre von Gott* (1952),
pp. 111-41.

p. 50, l. 10   *existence an accessorium or the eternal prius.* Existence as an
addition or the eternal presupposition. The draft (*Pap.* v B 5, 3)
reads: "The relationship, therefore, is quite different from what
Kant supposed, that existence is an *accessorium* . . . , although
he undeniably has an advantage over Hegel in that he is not
confused." In the margin is the addition: "eternal presupposition," which in the text becomes "the eternal *prius*." *Accessorium* means something which is added. In Kant the concept
is one thing and existence [being] is something added, an
accessorium, as Kierkegaard calls it, using a term not employed
by Kant. The concept of God is one thing, and the being of
God is something else; they are related to each other as possibility to actuality. In Hegel (*The Science of Logic*, II, 177)
possibility and actuality are *aufgehoben* in "mere Being or
Existence" (that which Hegel in the quotation in the previous
note calls *Existenz*), which consequently can be called the
eternal presupposition, "the eternal *prius*" ("The contingent
therefore is necessary because the Actual is determined as

Possible, whereby its immediacy is transcended and cast off into Ground [or Being-in-Self] and Grounded, and also because this its Possibility—the Ground-relation—is simply transcended and posited as Being." *Ibid.*, p. 178). This expression, "the eternal *prius*," does not seem to have been used by Hegel but rather, as Hirsch maintains, by Schelling, who in his Berlin lectures (according to Paulus's report, pp. 217ff. and *passim*) had affirmed ideas similar to those of Kierkegaard here.

God is not a name but a concept. Kierkegaard formally makes an Hegelian distinction (concerning *concept* in Hegel see note to p. 4, in Commentary, pp. 158-160) but not essentially, since for Kierkegaard the concept is definitely superior to the mere designation *name* but the two are not as deeply contrasted as in Hegel.   *p. 51, l. 5*

essentia involvit existentiam. Cf. Spinoza, *Ethics*, Part I, Def. I, Prop. 7, 11. The essence, or logical content, involves existence.   *p. 51, l. 7*

Spinoza. Most likely Kierkegaard first became acquainted with Spinoza's philosophy through the previously mentioned lectures by H. L. Martensen (*Pap.* II C 22, 3; cf. *Pap.* II B 19). A single passage in the drafts of *Either/Or* (*Pap.* III B 179, 63, p. 208; cf. *Either/Or*; Princeton: Princeton University Press, 1944; I, 31) where Spinoza is mentioned does not suggest special study. It is clear (cf. *Pap.* IV A 190) that in 1844 Kierkegaard read *Tractatus theologico-politicus* in *Opera philosophica omnia*, ed. A. Gfroerer (1830; Ktl. 788), and in connection with the writing of *Johannes Climacus, or De Omnibus Dubitandum Est* (*Pap.* IV 13, 1-17) he read *Tractatus de intellectus emendatione*, as well as *Cogitata metaphysica* (*Pap.* IV C 13). An entry for the *Concept of Dread* (*Pap.* V B 55, 17) in which Spinoza's doctrine of substance is mentioned is manifestly connected with his reading of Karl Rosenkranz's book on Schelling (see Commentary on page 12, note). It was not before the autumn of 1846 that Kierkegaard read Spinoza's   *p. 51, note*

Ethics (cf. *Pap.* VII[1] c 1). In the passage at hand (p. 32) quotation is made only from *Principia Philosophiae Cartesianae*.

p. 51, note　*quo res sua natura* etc.: The more perfect a thing is by virtue of its nature, the more being it has and the more necessary is the being which it has; and conversely, the more necessary the being included in a thing by virtue of its nature, the more perfect it is. *Quod hic non loquimur*: that we do not here speak of beauty and other perfections, which men have called perfections from superstition and ignorance. But by perfection I understand only reality or being (*esse*).

p. 51, note　*distinction between factual being and ideal being.* In this note Kierkegaard explains his use of Platonic language: *factual being* or existence here means mere earthly mutable existence; *ideal being* or *essence* signifies ideal, immutable substance. In like manner Hegel distinguishes between *Seyn* and *Wesen*. Cf. Sören Holm, *Sören Kierkegaards Historiefilosofi*, pp. 21-29.

p. 51, note　*meaningless to speak of more or less of being.* Kierkegaard clearly opposes the doctrine of grades of being which has its origin in Plato—the doctrine of Eros, particularly as developed in the *Symposium*, is the best example—and as formulated by Plotinus (see, for example, W. R. Inge, *The Philosophy of Plotinus*; New York: Longmans, 1923; *Plotinus*; New York: Oxford, 1934, which includes a bibliography) in his emanation theory, which is continued in Spinoza, against whom Kierkegaard expressly directs his polemic, and by Hegel, whose *Phenomenology of Mind* presents a graded cosmos (*Stufenkosmos*) in which phenomena in a series of levels participate in the Idea and thereby progressively unveil the Spirit as the development proceeds further, in the individual as well as in world-history.

p. 51, note　*the dialectic of Hamlet.* Hamlet's question in Shakespeare's *Hamlet*, III, 1: "To be or not to be, that is the question." Kierkegaard owned and extensively read the translation of Shakespeare by A. W. von Schlegel and Ludwig Tieck, I-VI (1841; Ktl. 1883-86).

upon the very face of things. Without suggesting any influ- *p. 52, l. 6*
ence or borrowing from Pascal, we can note a clear parallel
between this and Pascal's view as it is expressed in the *Pensées*
(para. 229): "Nature presents to me nothing which is not a
matter of doubt and concern. If I saw nothing there which
revealed a Divinity, I would come to a negative conclusion;
if I saw everywhere the signs of a Creator, I would remain
peacefully in faith. But seeing too much to deny and too little
to be sure, I am in a state to be pitied. . . ." The relationship
between Pascal and Kierkegaard has frequently been treated
in shorter studies such as Harald Höffding, *Religiöse Tanke-
typer* (1927), pp. 70-97, and H. Fuglsang Damgaard, "Pascal
og Kierkegaard" in *Dansk teologisk Tidsskrift* (1941, pp.
212ff.) and in the large work by Denzil G. M. Patrick, *Pascal
and Kierkegaard* (London: Lutterworth Press, 1948).

Leibniz. In *Epistola ad Hermannum Conringium de Cartesi-* *p. 52, note*
ana demonstratione existentiae Dei (1678, G. G. Leibnitii,
Opera philosophica, ed. J. E. Erdmann, 1840, 1, 78; Ktl. 620),
Leibniz writes, *"quod Deus necessario existat, si modo possi-
bilis esse ponatur."*

by virtue of confidence in him. This is expressly said by *p. 53, l. 3*
Anselm in *Proslogion,* the beginning of Chapter II.

Cartesian dolls. Kierkegaard here has in mind a round- *p. 53, l. 8*
bottomed, low-center-of-gravity doll which rights itself when
pushed over. The so-called Cartesian Devil, however, is a hol-
low glass figure which is placed in a container partially filled
with water and covered by an elastic sheet. When one presses
upon the sheet, the figure moves.

Chryssipus. The Stoic philosopher, who died 207 B.C. shortly *p. 53, l. 22*
after the birth of the Sceptic Carneades in 213 B.C. In *Acade-
mica,* II, 29 (Loeb Classics, pp. 585ff.) Cicero compares them,
but Kierkegaard does not draw upon this. As appears from
the draft (*Pap.* VB 5, 5), his source is Tennemann IV, 344,

where it reads: "Carneades had good reason to laugh at the escape (to hesitate with his answer) which Chryssipus had thought of under pressure of the question of the first link of the relationship in a series of relative things. As far as I am concerned, he said, you may not only rest but sleep, too. What good does it do you? There will follow another who wakes you with the question: 'At what number do you stop?'" A *sorites* (from σῶρος, a heap, usually of grain) is a logical chain of reasoning which the Sceptics used to demonstrate the impossibility of knowledge. They posed the question: how many grains must there be to make a heap? Then one added a grain at a time (in a progressive *sorites*) and asked each time, is this now a heap? Or one began with a heap and took away a grain at a time and continually asked, is it still a heap (a retrogressive *sorites*)? —Kierkegaard polemicizes here, since he sides with Carneades and together with him satirizes Chryssipus and also Hegel, who affirms a continuous transition between various qualities (for example, a number of grains—a heap); whereas Kierkegaard affirms discontinuity, a chasm, over which a qualitative transition is possible only by "a leap."

p. 53, l. 23   *a break in its quality*. The appearance of a new quality.

p. 54, l. 5   *reservatio finalis*. Ultimate reservation.

p. 54, l. 9   *the fool says in his heart*. Psalm 14:1 and 53.2.

p. 54, l. 19   *Socrates . . . , who is credited* etc. In his *Vorlesungen über die Beweise vom Daseyn Gottes* (W.a.A., xii, 517-18; J.A., xvi, 517-18) Hegel says of the teleological proof of God's existence, which argues from the fitness of things in nature: "Kant has criticized this proof, too, as well as the other proofs of the existence of God, and it was chiefly owing to him that they were discredited, so that it is now scarcely worth while to look at them closely. And yet Kant says of this proof that it deserves to be always regarded with respect. When, however, he adds that the teleological proof is the oldest he is wrong. The first determination of God is that of force or power, and the next in order is that of wisdom. This is the proof we meet with first amongst the Greeks also, and it is stated by Socrates (Xenophon, *Memorabilia*, at the end of Book First)." In the pertinent passage Xenophon (*Memorabilia* I, 4; Loeb Classics, p. 55) lets Socrates refute the atheists by pointing out the fitness in animal nature, in the body and soul of man, explained by the fact that a divine providence governs the world for man's good.

what an excellent subject etc. In the place of this short note *p. 54, note* Kierkegaard originally had one substantially longer (*Pap.* v b 40, 11): "I am, after all, no poet and to that extent dare not credit myself with having an opinion, but nevertheless would it not work a madly comical effect if one let a man imagine that he could prove the existence of God—and then have an atheist assume this in virtue of the other's proof. Both parts are equally fantastic; for no more than anyone has proved God's existence has there ever been an atheist [again a striking agreement with Anselm's comments in *Proslogion*, Chapter II], however many there have been who did not want to let what they knew (that God exists) get power over their minds. It is the same with immortality. Suppose that one became immortal through the proof of another [in the margin: (just as Nille became a stone and Degnen a rooster) suppose there was a medicine-man who went around, opened his book, proved the individual's immortality for a fee, just as if one sold indulgences, so that only the individual whose immortality *he* proved became immortal], would it not be infinitely ridiculous? Therefore there has never been anyone who did not believe it, but there have been many who have not wanted to let the belief conquer in their souls, have not wanted to be *convinced*, for what I am convinced of exists only when I immerse myself in it.—With respect to the existence of God, immortality, etc., in short, with respect to all the problems of immanence, recollection holds true; it exists altogether in each man, only he does not know it. But again it follows that the conception can be very deficient."

p. 54, l. 30   *distracts him.* Kierkegaard deleted the following (*Pap.* v b 40, 12) from the final copy: "Too bad that the Sophists did not have anything to do with such a person, because it would have been very rewarding to later ages if Socrates had introduced a little discipline. If Socrates could have known all the many professors and embryonic teachers who prove God's existence, I believe that out of joy over all this magnificence he himself would have sent out an invitation just to have the opportunity of conversing with these wise men."

p. 55, l. 11   *To say that it is* etc. An allusion to the saying of the Sophist Gorgias, which Kierkegaard knew from Tennemann, i, 363: Gorgias seeks to prove that "Nothing genuinely is . . . , and if something genuinely were, it could not be known, and . . . if it were knowable, it could not be communicated through language."

p. 55, l. 17   *via negationis or via eminentiae.* The way of negation or the way of idealization, terms used for two ways of defining the attributes of God employed in theology, particularly by orthodox Lutheran dogmaticians of the seventeenth century. The first is done negatively by denying God all finite and imperfect qualities and the second positively by attributing to God all absolute and perfect qualities. Kierkegaard knew these two modes of approach through lectures in dogmatics covering standard material and most likely through Karl Hase, *Hutterus redivivus*, para. 59, where the argument is summarized.

p. 56, l. 4   διασπορά. Literally, *dispersion.* The expression is most frequently used of the Jews living outside Palestine.

p. 56, l. 8   *an arbitrary act.* Emanuel Hirsch refers in his Commentary (p. 178) to "ähnliche Gedanken" in Hegel's *Vorlesungen über die Beweise vom Daseyn Gottes* (W.a.A., xii, 387-88; J.A., xvi, 387-88; *Philosophy of Religion*, iii, 181-82), but in the relevant portion Hegel attacks the consequences of making immediate knowledge and feeling decisive indications of the nature and characteristics of God.

it has itself produced the God. Kierkegaard calls this thought   *p. 56, l. 10*
madness. He probably is thinking, as on page 43, of Feuer-
bach's theory. Concerning Feuerbach, special reference is made
to Y. Ahlberg, *Kristendomskritiken hos Ludwig Feuerbach*
(1947), with complete bibliography.

there exists an individual etc. From 1843 and on Kierkegaard   *p. 56, l. 21*
touches upon this problem in many *Journal* entries (see *Pap.*
IV A 47, 62, 103, c 84). The earliest parallel to the formulation
here is found in *Pap.* IV A 62, which reads: "That the Son of
God became man is certainly the highest metaphysical and
religious paradox, but it is nevertheless not the deepest ethical
paradox. The appearance of Christ contains a polemic against
existence. He became a human being like all others, but he
stood in a polemical relationship to the concrete ethical elements of actuality. He went about teaching the people; he
owned nothing; he had no place to lay his head . . . Christ's
life was related negatively-polemically to church and state.
The highest ethical paradox would be that God's Son entered
into the whole of actuality, became part of it, bowed himself
under all its pettiness. . . ."

live like the birds of the air. Matthew 6:26ff.   *p. 56, l. 26*

But what can this unlikeness be? Aye, what can it be but   *p. 58, l. 12*
sin. . . . As earlier in the work, Kierkegaard here points out
that man is "untruth," is in sin, by his own guilt. Therefore
there is no basis for discussing the justification of the interpretation, given especially by T. Bohlin (in *Kierkegaards dogmatiska åskådning*, pp. 204-24, and in *Kierkegaards tro*, pp. 94ff.),
according to which the concept of sin here should not be
oriented "on the basis of personal experience of sin and grace
unless it is a consequence of the doctrine of Christ as the
absolute paradox" (*Kierkegaards dogmatiska åskådning*, p.

219). For Kierkegaard the concept of sin is not oriented on the basis of personal experience, for this would *eo ipso* not be a Christian concept of sin, but on the basis of the Gospel, which Kierkegaard does not understand as a doctrine about Christ but as Christ himself present in faith, a presence which in the language of Platonic Idealism (which Kierkegaard purposely employs here) can only be termed paradoxical in conflict with the Platonic and thereby with merely humanly possible categories.

p. 58, l. 21 *The connoisseur in self-knowledge.* Socrates. Cf. note to page 46 with a quotation from Plato.

p. 60, l. 1 *spolia opima.* In ancient Rome the prize war-booty.

p. 61, title *The Offended Consciousness.* (Note by David Swenson.) The writings of Nietzsche, in their relation to and antagonistic criticism of Christianity, exemplify on a grand scale most of the characteristics here ascribed to the passion of offense; they constitute a reaction-phenomenon, tend toward the end to be pervaded by what amounts to an unfree obsession, and borrow from Christianity the chief category in which the attack on Christianity is launched. "Man is something that must be surpassed," *i.e.,* "all things have become new."

p. 61, subtitle *An acoustic illusion.* It seems as if offense came from Reason; whereas it actually is due to the Paradox.

p. 61, l. 1 *the Paradox and the Reason.* (Note by David Swenson.) The thoughtful reader will already have noted that "Reason," as used in this chapter and throughout, is not to be taken in any abstract-intellectual sense, but quite concretely, as the reflectively organized common sense of mankind, including as its essential core a sense of life's values. Over against the "Paradox," it is therefore the self-assurance and self-assertiveness of man's nature in its totality. To identify it with any abstract intellectual function, like the function of scientific cognition, or of general ideas, or of the a priori, or of self-consistency in thinking, etc., is wholly to misunderstand the

exposition of the *Fragments*. Specifically, Kant's distinction
between Reason and Understanding, or any other similar distinction, is wholly beside the point. The Danish word here
translated "Reason" is *Forstanden*, but this should not mislead
anyone into thinking that it ought to be translated by "Understanding" and interpreted in contradistinction to "Reason."

All offense is . . . passive. Danish *lidende*, meaning *suffering*,   *p. 61, l. 13*
is well translated *passive* here, in contrast to *active, acting,*
productive.

σκανδαλίζεσθαι. In C. G. Bretschneider, *Lexicon manuale*   *p. 62, note*
in libros Novi Testamenti (2nd ed., 1829; Ktl. 73-74), II, 411,
the term is explained thus: "σκανδαλίζω (a σκάνδαλον) . . .
offendiculo sum, offendere facio, passiv. offendor, . . . de statu
animi, et ita semper in N.T., ubi est: animum alterius offendo,
einem zum Anstoss gereichen."

index sui et falsi. Indication and criterion of both itself and   *p. 63, l. 4*
of the false. In his *Ethics*, II, Prop. 43, Spinoza says: "sicut lux
se ipsam et tenebras manifestat, sic veritas norma sui et falsi
est." Kierkegaard undoubtedly has drawn upon F. H. Jacobi's
Spinoza-Briefe, Werke (1819) IV, 1, 69, where it reads: "est
enim verum index sui et falsi."

index and judex sui et falsi. Indication and criterion.   *p. 63, l. 11*

constantly about to come. (Note by David Swenson.) Cf.   *p. 65, l. 4*
the following lines from Emerson's "Song of Nature":

> But he, the manchild glorious—
> Where tarries he the while?
> The rainbow shines his harbinger,
> The sunset gleams his smile.

* * *

> I travail in pain for him,
> My creatures travail and wait;
> His couriers come by squadrons,
> He comes not to the gate.

Twice have I moulded an image,
And thrice outstretched my hand,
Made one of day and one of night
And one of the salt sea sand.

One in a Judean manger,
And one by Avon stream,
One over against the mouths of Nile,
And one in the Academe.

I moulded kings and saviors
And bards o'er kings to rule;
But fell the starry influence short,
The cup was never full.

* * *

Let war and trade and creeds and song
Blend, ripen race on race,
The sunburnt world a man shall breed
Of all the zones and countless days.

See also the following passage from Emerson's *Journals*,
(Boston and New York: Houghton Mifflin, 1911), pp. 188-89,
an entry dated April 6, 1842: "The history of Christ is the
best Document of the power of Character which we have . . . .
He did well. This great Defeat is hitherto the highest fact we
have. But he that shall come shall do better. The mind requires
a far higher exhibition of character, one which shall make
itself good to the senses as well as to the soul; a success to the
senses as well as to the soul. This was a great Defeat; we
demand Victory. More character will convert judge and jury,
soldier and king; will rule human and animal and mineral
nature; will command irresistibly and blend with the course
of Universal Nature."

p. 65, l. 9   *quia absurdum.* Because it conflicts with reason. Tertullian
says in *De carne Christi*, v: "Mortuus est dei filius; credibile

est, quia ineptum est. Et sepultus resurrexit; certum est, quia impossibile." (*Corpus scriptorum ecclesiasticorum latinorum*, LXX, p. 200.)

Comedies and romances etc. In a letter dated July 16, 1759,   *p. 65, l. 20*
Johann Georg Hamann writes to his brother: "Is it not an old notion which you often heard from me: Incredible but true? Lies and romances must be probable, hypotheses and fables; but not the truth and fundamental doctrine of our faith." (*Schriften*, edited by F. Roth, 1821, I, 425. Kierkegaard had this edition. Ktl. 536-44.)

truth in the mouth of a hypocrite, etc. In a letter dated   *p. 65, l. 28*
October 12, 1759, Hamann writes to his friend, J. G. Lindner: ". . . frequently I hear with more joy the word of God in the mouth of a pharisee, as a witness against his will, than out of the mouth of an angel of light." (*Ibid.*, p. 497.)

vitia splendida. In *Institution. Divin.*, VI, 9, ed. O. F. Fritzsche   *p. 66, l. 2*
(1844), II, p. 19, Lactantius says, "non est dubium, quin impius sit, quisquis deum non agnoverit, omnesque virtutes eius, quas habere, aut tenere se putat, in illa mortifera via reperiuntur, quae est tota tenebrarum." Undoubtedly he who does not acknowledge God is in error, and all the virtues which he has or thinks he has belong to the way which leads to death and are one with the darkness.

our philosophers etc. Shakespeare's *All's Well that Ends*   *p. 66, l. 6*
Well, II, 3: "They say, miracles are past; and we have our philosophical persons to make modern [common] and familiar, things supernatural and causeless." In Schlegel and Tieck's translation, *Ende gut Alles gut*, which Kierkegaard owned and used (1840; Ktl. 1883-88) and refers to here, reads as follows: "Man sagt, es geschehn keine Wunder mehr, und unsre Philosophen sind dazu da, die übernatürlichen und unergründlichen Dinge alltäglich und trivial zu machen."

a blockhead and a dunce. Luther does not seem to have used   *p. 66, l. 11*
these particular expressions concerning reason (cf. J. C. Irmi-

scher, *Sach-Register über M. Luthers sämmtliche Schriften*, 1857, II, 284-87), but the view of reason expressed here is found in numerous places in Luther—as well as views quite complimentary. See Philip Watson, *Let God Be God* (London: Epworth, 1947), pp. 86-88.—Before 1846 Luther is mentioned in only a few places in Kierkegaard's *Journals*, and by the time he wrote *Philosophical Fragments* he did not have basic, firsthand knowledge of Luther's own works. He owned Otto von Gerlach's ten-volume edition of Luther's main works (Ktl. 312-16) and the large Luther concordance, *Geist aus Luthers Schriften*, I-IV, eds. F. W. Lomler, G. F. Lucius, J. Rust, L. Sackreuter, and E. Zimmermann (1828-1831; Ktl. 317-20), but the expression Kierkegaard uses here does not seem to be in these works. He also owned Jörgen Thisted's Danish translation of Luther's *Huuspostil* (1828; Ktl. 283) but seems to have used it after 1846.—Kierkegaard owned Tertullian both in Latin, *Opera*, ed. E. F. Leopold, I-IV (1839; Ktl. 147-50) and in German, *Q. S. F. Tertullians sämmtliche Schriften*, translated by F. A. von Besnard (1837; Ktl. 151). In *Pap.* II A 467, it appears that Kierkegaard got the expression (*credo*) *quia absurdum* from W. M. L. de Wette, *Lærebog i den christelige Sædelære og sammes Historie*, translated by C. E. Scharling (1835; Ktl. 871), in which Lactantius is also quoted frequently. —Kierkegaard owned *F. Lactantii Opera*, ed. O. F. Fritzsche, I-II (1842-1844; Ktl. 142-43). He is not mentioned in the *Journals*, but in *Either/Or* (I, 104) there is a freely formulated expression from *Institutiones*; so it may be deemed probable that Kierkegaard refers to Lactantius in *Philosophical Fragments* from and on the basis of what he had read, for example, in Wette, an assumption strengthened by the expression "is frequently quoted."—Kierkegaard read Shakespeare constantly (usually in Schlegel and Tieck's German translation); in the same way he read Hamann (particularly after the autumn of 1836) and was very partial to Hamann's letters, which he had in F. Roth's edition (Ktl. 536-44). The expression used here ("romances and lies") Kierkegaard had already quoted in *Pap.* I A 237. In German the only monograph is W. Rodemann, *Hamann und Kierkegaard* (1922); see also Thulstrup, "Incontro di Kierkegaard e Hamann" (*Studi Kierkegaardani*; Brescia: Morcelliana, 1957). In English there is Ronald Gregor Smith, *J. G. Hamann*, with selections and bibliography (New York: Harper, 1960).

Yes and no to the same thing! Lear's reply in *King Lear*, IV, 6: "They flattered me like a dog; and told me I had white hairs in my beard ere the black ones were there. To say 'aye' and 'no' to everything I said!—'Aye' and 'no' too was no good divinity." In Schlegel and Tieck's translation (XI, 101, 1840): "Ja und Nein zugleich, das war keine gute Theologie."   *p. 66, l. 12*

halb zog sie ihn, halb sank er hin. Goethe, *Der Fischer.*   *p. 67, l. 29*
Kierkegaard owned *Goethes Werke*, vollständige Ausgabe letzter Hand, I-LV (1828-1833; Ktl. 1641-68).

COMMENTARY ON CHAPTER IV

we resume our story. In the draft (*Pap.* V B 6, 3) it appears that Kierkegaard had originally thought of including the passion of Christ. Emanuel Hirsch (*Kierkegaard-Studien*, II, 706, note) explains the change by saying that it must have been impossible for Kierkegaard to present Christ's passion and death on the cross as a story (Danish: *Digt*).   *p. 68, l. 2*

the God's servant-form . . . not . . . disguise. Cf. p. 39 where also the distance from Docetism is emphasized.   *p. 68, l. 11*

not a parastatic body. Not a temporary, merely apparent body.   *p. 68, l. 12*
send someone before him. John the baptizer.   *p. 68, l. 25*
He humbled himself. The expression is from Philippians 2:7.   *p. 69, l. 15*
soft raiment. The expression is from Luke 7:25.   *p. 69, l. 24*
legions of angels. Matthew 26:53: " 'Do you think that I cannot appeal to my Father, and he will at once send me more than twelve legions of angels?' "   *p. 69, l. 25*

p. 69, l. 31   *not concerned for his daily bread, like the birds.* Cf. Matthew 6:26ff.

p. 70, l. 1   *neither has nor seeks a shelter or a resting place.* Cf. Matthew 8:20.

p. 70, l. 15   *stopping wherever evening overtakes him.* Perhaps based on Luke 24:29.

p. 70, l. 27   *serene security of the lilies.* Cf. Matthew 6:28.

p. 71, l. 10   *The learner is his brother and sister.* Cf. Matthew 12:49: "And stretching out his hand toward his disciples, he said, 'Here are my mother and my brothers.'"

p. 71, l. 12   *Wherever . . . the crowd gathers.* See, for example, Matthew 4:25 and other passages.

p. 71, l. 16   *one . . . sought him out secretly.* Reference to Nicodemus who "came to Jesus by night." John 3:2.

p. 71, l. 28   *the Eternal.* Cf. p. 16 and note. Here the Eternal is defined as the qualitatively new, the transcendent, that is, the divine intrusion into the immanental.

p. 71, l. 30   *permitted . . . born in an inn.* See Luke 2:7ff.

p. 72, l. 12   *an historical point of departure* etc. Cf. title-page and note.

p. 73, l. 8   *Faith . . . must be the condition . . . which the Paradox contributes.* See p. 17 and note.

p. 73, l. 15   *the contemporary learner. . . . In the immediate sense.*

p. 74, l. 13   *he can wash his hands.* Cf. report on Pilate, Matthew 27:24. "So when Pilate saw that he was gaining nothing, but rather that a riot was beginning, he took water and washed his hands before the crowd, saying, 'I am innocent of this man's blood. . . .'"

p. 74, l. 16   *every word of instruction that fell from his lips.* The expression is taken from Matthew 4:4.

p. 74, l. 23   *no more than Plato was a disciple of Socrates* etc. No more a disciple of *this Teacher* than Plato was a disciple of Socrates, who in the accidental relationship to his pupils taught them to bring forth what they actually possessed. See Chapter I and notes.

As over against an eternal understanding of oneself. A   p. 75, l. 4
"Socratic" understanding.

romancing and trumpeting. Kierkegaard manifestly alludes   p. 75, l. 18
here to Alcibiades' praise of Socrates in Plato's *Symposium.*

as he himself says. Cf. p. 13 (reference to *Theaetetus,* 150).   p. 76, l. 9

Faith is not a form of knowledge. Since Faith is already de-   p. 76, l. 20
fined (p. 73 and earlier on pp. 16-17) as "the condition of which
we have spoken, which the Paradox contributes," it follows
that in *Philosophical Fragments* Faith cannot be characterized
as a subjective human achievement or act, neither an act of
knowing nor an act of willing. The Christian Faith is not
merely the substantiation and acceptance of a natural state
but is the divine gift which constitutes the fellowship between
God and the single individual human being, and therefore
Faith when seen from man's side has a definite content, the
redemptive revelation in Jesus Christ, the God-man, God's
self-communicating which constitutes the fellowship, as has
been developed in the foregoing presentation. In this passage
it is also apparent that human reason is regarded as created,
fallen in sin, and actually incapable of grasping, of knowing
anything other than ideal and actual objects ("knowledge of
the eternal . . . purely historical knowledge"), but not the
revelation of God in the Moment, a fact which transcends
reason, and therefore it is "set aside" in the act of Faith. If
the miraculous content of Faith is to be defined and described,
it is humanly possible to do this only with the aid of inadequate
human language, the possibilities of which collapse with those
of reason; therefore it needs to be designated as paradoxical,
something which reason really cannot think and express (see
p. 46, "something that thought cannot think"). Inasmuch as
Kierkegaard says (p. 73) that "Reason sets itself aside," the
presupposition for this act is revelation.—Kierkegaard's concept of Faith has been frequently discussed, usually in connection with his concept of sin, as in T. Bohlin, *Kierkegaards*

dogmatiska åskådning, especially pp. 261ff. In addition to the literature mentioned in the notes to page 19, reference is also made to Marie Thulstrup, "Forstanden contra troen, en bemærkning til Kierkegaards problemstilling" (*Dansk teologisk Tidsskrift,* 1954, pp. 89-97). Of the many recent works on dogmatics which deal with the concept of faith, the following may be mentioned: Emil Brunner, *Revelation and Reason* (Philadelphia: Westminster, 1946) and R. Hauge, *Gudsåpenbaring og troslydighet, om forholdet mellom det objektive og det subjektive i den kristne tro* (1952). —Since Kierkegaard in *Fear and Trembling* (Princeton: Princeton University Press, 1945; p. 104) and in *The Concept of Dread* (p. 10) combats F. H. Jacobi, who in *David Hume über den Glauben oder der Idealismus und Realismus* (*Werke,* 1815, II, 155ff. and 164ff.) had defined faith as the immediate, the innate (that Kierkegaard actually combats Jacobi and not Hegel has been pointed out by T. Bohlin, *Kierkegaards dogmatiska åskådning,* pp. 380ff.), it is doubtful that he here aims his polemic directly against Hegel, who uses the term *faith* (*Glaube*) with various meanings, including the sense of knowledge in imperfect form. On this, in addition to the literature cited on Hegel's philosophy of religion in connection with page 13, see G. Dulckeit, *Die Idee Gottes im Geiste der Philosophie Hegels* (1947), especially pp. 84ff.

p. 79, l. 22   *All romancing and trumpeting.* Surely this sortie has some particular object, but just what it is has not been found.

p. 80, l. 16   *what he has seen and his hands have handled.* The expression comes from I John 1:1: "That which was from the beginning, which we have heard, which we have seen with our eyes, which we have looked upon and touched with our hands, concerning the word of life—the life was made manifest, and we saw it, and testify to it, and proclaim to you the eternal life which was with the Father and was made manifest to us. . . ."

walked some distance. This quite certainly refers to the   *p. 80, l. 21*
walk to Emmaus, Luke 24:13ff.

the traveler. As early as 1835 Kierkegaard had made a note   *p. 80, note*
of this (*Pap.* I 55): "The position of one who follows the
commentators is frequently like that of the traveler to London;
the road does in fact lead to London, but if one wants to go
there, he must turn around."

within the framework of this miracle. No person can give   *p. 81, l. 16*
faith to another.

I ate and drank etc. The expression is from Luke 13:26ff.   *p. 84, l. 2*

he taught in our streets etc. Luke 13:26ff.   *p. 84, l. 3*

knows him even as he is known. The expression is taken   *p. 84, l. 16*
from I Corinthians 13:12.

Mithridates. Kierkegaard must have remembered from his   *p. 85, l. 8*
schooldays the story of King Mithridates the Great of Pontus
(111-63), who is supposed to have known twenty-two languages and the names of all his soldiers.

every successor must receive the condition from the God   *p. 85, l. 24*
himself etc. By this is said what is later developed more fully
in Chapter v: there is no disciple at second hand.

a brief. A signed résumé.   *p. 86, l. 11*

sub poena præclusi et perpetui silentii. Under penalty of   *p. 86, l. 15*
being excluded and not being heard again. A judicial expression.

autopsy of faith. According to faith's own view.   *p. 87, l. 6*

the false Smerdes. Kierkegaard may have read Herodotus's   *p. 87, l. 11*
story (III, 61-71; Loeb Classics, II, 77-93) of the false Smerdes
(who pretended to be Smerdes, the brother of King Cambyses,
and seized the throne of Persia in 522 B.C.) in K. F. Becker's
popular *Verdenshistorie* (I-XII, 1822-1829; Ktl. 1972-83) tr. by
J. Riise (1841), I, 129: "If Smerdes the pretender had been a
brother of Patizethes, he would easily have been recognized
by the fact that he had no ears, which he had lost because of a
crime during Cyrus's reign. Among the women of the harem

there happened to be a daughter of one of these nobles [who thought Smerdes was not what he claimed to be], and it was easy for her to find out while he slept whether or not the ears were missing."

p. 87, l. 29   *game of seeing somebody to "grandmother's door."* In this child's game one of the players asks the others where grandmother's door is and receives impertinent misleading answers. Afterwards they must go along to "grandmother," who tests them.

p. 87, l. 31   *runs only with the lime-rod.* Goes on a wild-goose chase.

COMMENTARY ON THE INTERLUDE

p. 89, title   *Interlude.* Kierkegaard uses the designation *interlude* in the same sense which *diapsalmata* has in the Greek translation (Septuagint) of the Old Testament—that is, as a resting-point in the thought-development. The designation is not without irony, since the Interlude must be regarded as being among the most difficult parts of Kierkegaard's writings. —For an understanding of the accounting with Hegel and Speculative Idealism which directly or indirectly takes place in *Philosophical Fragments*, it is important to note that the relevant portion of the draft (*Pap.* v B 14 and 41) not used in the book contains a very sharp blow against Hegel's "absolute method," which is supposed to be usable both in logic and in the historical sciences. Certainly Hegel was a great logician, it says, "but along with this he had a partiality for logical gimcrackery," and in the final version of the Interlude this "gimcrackery" receives an even more devastating judgment: complete rejection. —The issues in the Interlude have been studied especially by: Charles R. Magel, *An Analysis of Kierkegaard's Philosophical Categories* (ms. of doctoral thesis, University of Minnesota, 1960, concentrating on *Philosophical Fragments* and particularly on the Interlude); Hermann Diem, *Philosophie und Christentum bei Sören Kierkegaard* (pp. 3ff., although primarily concerned with Kierkegaard's later discussion in the *Postscript*); Sören Holm, *Sören Kierkegaards Historiefilosofi* (particularly pp. 34ff.); and Johannes Slök, *Die Anthropologie Sören Kierkegaards*, pp. 35-52. See also Gregor Malantschuk, "Frihedens Dialektik hos Sören Kierkegaard" in *Dansk teologisk Tidsskrift* (1949), pp. 193-207. Only Slök has expressly noted that the issues for Aristotle, Hegel, and Kierkegaard are not the same, despite similarities in terminology, and that Kierkegaard, despite shifting language-usage, has here, and especially in *The Sickness unto Death*, one and the same theme, that of anti-Idealism. A characteristic of Kierkegaard's mode of approach here is that in order to attack his real opponents in the work, the Speculative reconciliation of Christianity and Idealism, he goes back not only to the creator of Idealism, Plato, but also to the master of classical logic, Aristotle, and not to the great sceptic of modern philosophy, Hume, who nevertheless was not unknown to Kierkegaard, but to ancient scepticism, and that he goes back to these thinkers in order to clarify the Christian categories in their uniqueness.— Of importance for the understanding of Kierkegaard's view of doubt are the draft *Johannes Climacus eller De omnibus dubitandum est* (*Pap.* IV B 1-17) and the relevant portions of the *Postscript* (especially pp. 282ff.) and of *The Sickness unto Death* (Garden City, N.Y.: Doubleday, 1954; especially pp. 168ff.).

Kierkegaard owned the Aldine edition of *Aristoteles' Opera*, I-XI (1562), J. T. Buhle's edition, I-V (1791-1797), and the first two volumes of I. Bekker's Akademi edition (1831), as well as various other translations, such as I. Bekker's in Latin (1831). Of the special editions of Aristotle's various works he had F. A. Trendelenburg's edition of *De Anima* (1833) and a stereotype edition of the *Rhetorica*. In German he had Karl Zell's translation of *Topica* and of *Analytica*, A. Heydemann's of *Categoriae*, C. H. Weisze's of *Physica*, Christian Garve's of

Ethica Nicomachea, I-II, C. H. Weisze's of *De anima* and *De mundo*, Christian Garve's of *Politica*, 1-2, C. L. Roth's of *Rhetorica*, C. Waltz's of *Poetica* (also in M. C. Curtius' older German translation), E. Hepner's of *De somno et vigilia* and *De insomnis et de divinatione somnum*, and L. Spengel's of *Rhetorica ad Alexandrum* (Ktl. 1056-95). Of the general histories of ancient philosophy Kierkegaard had used for orientation in Aristotle the copious works of Tennemann and Hegel. But he also knew Poul Möller's draft of lectures on ancient philosophy (printed in *Efterladte Skrifter*, IV), just as he had used G. O. Marbach, *Geschichte der griechischen Philosophie* (1838; Ktl. 642) and H. Ritter, *Geschichte der Philosophie alter Zeit*, 2nd printing, I-IV (1836; Ktl. 735-38). In February, 1843, Kierkegaard had obtained A. Trendelenburg, *Elementa Logices Aristotelicae* (1842; Ktl. 844) and *Erläuterungen zu den Elementen der aristotelischen Logik* (1842; Ktl. 845; see note to *Pap.* IV A 40). The first volume of Trendelenburg's *Geschichte der Kategorienlehre* came out in 1846 and therefore does not come into the discussion here, likewise with E. Zeller, *Die Philosophie der Griechen*, I-IV (1844-1852; see *Pap.* X⁶ C 6, 1; Ktl. 913-14), which Kierkegaard apparently did not obtain until 1852. In addition to the basic knowledge we must assume Kierkegaard had of Aristotle's philosophy and especially of Aristotelian logic, he also heard Aristotle discussed in the previously mentioned lectures by Martensen under the title, *Prolegomena til den speculative Dogmatik* during the winter semester, 1837-1838 (see *Pap.* II C 20), and in 1841 he read K. F. Hermann, *Geschichte und System der platonischen Philosophie* (1839; see *Pap.* III A 107). In 1842 he read Garve's above-mentioned translation of *Ethica Nicomachea* (*Pap.* III A 209) and of *Politica* (*Pap.* IV A 8), and in 1842-1843 he studied Tennemann's (vol. III) exposition of Aristotle (*Pap.* IV C 45 and elsewhere). In the draft of a polemical piece against J. L. Heiberg's review of *Repetition* (*Pap.* IV B 117) he appeals to Aristotle's understanding of the relationship between possibility and actuality, a problem which is also taken up here in *Philosophical Fragments*. Aristotle is frequently discussed in the works, not least in *Fragments*, where it is clear that Kierkegaard had studied the works on logic (for more detail, see notes on particular passages). —Aristotle is frequently considered in research on Kierkegaard, but there is no full study of the subject.

repeating the same things, "about the same things." Callicles   *p. 89, l. 22*
in Plato's *Gorgias* (490): "How you go on, always talking in the same way, Socrates!" To which Socrates replies: "Yes, Callicles, and also about the same things. . . . See now, excellent Callicles, how different my charge against you is from that which you bring against me, for you reproach me with always saying the same; but I reproach you with never saying the same about the same things. . . ."

coming into existence. For this section Kierkegaard mani-   *p. 90, l. 12*
festly read Tennemann III, 125-27, where Aristotle's doctrine of motion is presented, but it is clear in various parts of the Interlude that Kierkegaard went back to the primary sources. For comparison the relevant portions from Tennemann are given: "The word κίνησις had been used by Plato already, in a broader and narrower sense, namely, for any change and for motion in space. Aristotle uses it in the broader sense. He, of course, could designate all changes with one word, *motion*, because he really treats the science of natural entities which exist in space, and their changes occur in space. Therefore he declares that motion in space is the basis of every other motion. . . . It should not appear strange that he sometimes considers production and passing away (γένεσις, φθορά) as kinds of motion. . . . Change takes place only with actual objects. Everything which is, is either possible or actual, and the actual is conceived as substance with a certain quantity and quality etc. within the remaining categories. Everything changing

changes either with regard to the subject or with regard to its quantity and quality or with regard to place. There are no other kind of changes. Because in everything possibility and actuality are distinguishable, the change, then, really is the actualization of the possible. . . . The transition, then, from possibility to actuality is change, κίνησις. One could express this more accurately by saying: change, motion is the actualization of the possible, insofar as it is possible. Therefore Aristotle uses the expressions ἐνέργεια and ἐντελέχεια, both of which mean actualization as action in which something becomes actual."

p. 90, l. 13   κίνησις. *Motion*, used by Aristotle for all kinds of change.

p. 90, l. 14   ἀλλοίωσις. *Qualitative change.* Here Kierkegaard, as well as Tennemann, stays close to Aristotle's *Physica* (*Works*, 11, 200ᵇff.) in which motion and qualitative change (both translated by Kierkegaard as change; Danish, *forandring*) are treated together.

p. 90, l. 21   μετάβασις εἰς ἄλλο γένος. Transition to another (conceptual) sphere. The expression is taken from Aristotle's *Analytica Posteriora* (*Works*, 1, 75ᵃ), which states that proofs in one science cannot straightway be transferred to another— for example, geometrical truths cannot be demonstrated arithmetically. Here the question has to do with the shift from coming into existence to another kind of change. Kierkegaard frequently uses the expression later.

p. 91, l. 2   *This coming-into-existence kind of change, therefore, is not a change in essence, but in being.* Cf. Kierkegaard's note on pp. 51-52 and the Commentary. *Essence* here designates the unchangeable, *being* (mode of being) the changeable.

p. 91, l. 7   *"subject of coming into existence remains unchanged in the process of coming into existence."* The source of this quotation has not been located. It may simply refer to the expression used earlier on the same page.

the change involved in coming into existence is the transi-   *p. 91, l. 16*
tion from possibility to actuality. Aristotle's *Physica* (*Works*,
II, 200^{b}ff.). See note above.

Is not necessity then a synthesis . . . ? In his *Wissenschaft der*   *p. 91, l. 31*
Logik (W.a.A., IV, 207ff.; J.A., IV, 685ff.; *Science of Logic*, II,
178ff.), where he discusses "Relative Necessity, or Real Actuality, Possibility, and Necessity," Hegel comes to the same
conclusion which Kierkegaard gives here.

the Aristotelian principle. In *De Interpretatione* (*Works*, I,   *p. 92, l. 11*
21^{b}ff.) Aristotle discusses logical contradictions and shows that
the contradictory of the proposition "it may be" (it is possible
that something is) is *not* "it may *not* be" (it is possible that
something is not), since this proposition is compatible with the
first and thus prevents the possible from being necessary (22^b);
rather, the contradictory of "It is possible" etc. is "It is impossible." When Kierkegaard says that this reasoning "tends only
to confuse the issue here, since it is essence and not being which
is reflected upon," such a remark is manifestly due to Kierkegaard's supplementing Aristotle's formal logical reasoning
at this point with a Platonic metaphysical view (the distinction
between essence, the eternal, and unchangeable Idea, and
temporal being, the changeable world of phenomena).

Epicurus. In his exposition of Epicurus's philosophy, Tenne-   *p. 92, l. 13*
mann says (III, 407): "Judgments (δόξαι) can be either true
or false. The criterion of their truth is sensory perception:
negative, if no sensory perceptions contradict the judgment;
positive, if actually confirmed by experience. If experience is
contrary, the judgment is false."

Aristotle's doctrine. In *De Interpretatione* (*Works*, I, 22^{a}ff.)   *p. 92, l. 25*
Aristotle argues (22^b) that unless necessity implies possibility,
it must imply either impossibility or possibility of the opposite;
but neither of these hypothetical implications is compatible
with necessity; whence by a *modus tollens*, necessity does imply
possibility. But on the other hand, inasmuch as possibility is

compatible with the possibility of the opposite, which latter is not compatible with necessity, there is a new difficulty, which Aristotle solves by assuming two forms of possibility, one compatible and the other incompatible with the possibility of the opposite.

p. 93, l. 1   *The change involved in coming into existence is actuality.* Actuality is here understood as empirical, historical actuality.

p. 93, l. 8   *All coming into existence takes place with freedom etc.* Kierkegaard solves the problem posed in the Interlude by means of a postulate which derives its significance only from the basic Christian position in the work. Therefore he can say, "Nothing comes into existence by virtue of a logical ground, but only by a cause. Every cause terminates in a freely effecting cause [God]," and he thereby turns the polemic against Hegel, who by identifying logic and metaphysics clearly identifies logical ground and cause (and both with God as active). The objection can be formulated in this way: Hegel identifies his thought (conception of existence) with being (God's essence and activity in existence).

p. 93, l. 27   *simultaneous coming into existence.* By *Nebeneinander, Space,* reference is made to Hegel's view that nature is the unfolding of the Idea in Space, which is "das ganz ideelle Nebeneinander" (*System der Philosophie*; W.a.A., VII, 1, p. 45; J.A., IX, 71), and history is the unfolding of the Idea in Time.

p. 94, l. 2   *an ingenious speculation.* Probably has to do with the romantic philosophy of nature as expressed by Schelling or Steffens, according to which nature forms a series of levels. This view is not notably developed in the works of Schelling (see note to page 13) nor in the philosophical works of Henrich Steffens in Kierkegaard's possession (*Carricaturen des Heiligsten*, I-II, 1819-1821; *Anthropologie*, I-II, 1822; *Christliche Religions-Philosophie*, I-II, 1839; Ktl. 793-98), but romantic nature-philosophy was widely known, and Kierkegaard may, for example, have found it in C. L. Michelet's *Geschichte der letzen Systeme der Philosophie in Deutschland* (1837; Ktl. 678-79).

a dialectic with respect to time. Falling within the category of temporality.   *p. 94, l. 9*

the perfection of the Eternal to have no history. The Eternal is here defined in the same way as before (see, for example, p. 15 and note).   *p. 94, l. 15*

Chrysippus . . . Diodorus. Kierkegaard read about Chrysippus in Tennemann, IV, 273: "Chrysippus had a dispute with the Megarian Diodorus and with his teacher Cleanthes about the possibility of the future and the necessity of the past. He asserted against the one that everything past, inasmuch as it cannot be changed, is necessary, and against the other that even that which will not happen is possible." In the same work (II, 155-56) there is this about Diodorus: "He claimed that only that is possible which actually is or which actually will happen. Nothing happens which does not happen out of necessity, and whatever can possibly happen is either already actual or will become actual. Just as the truth about what has happened cannot become false, it is also impossible that the truth about the future becomes false. What has happened cannot be made to have not happened. Here the necessity and the unchangeability is so obvious that nobody can deny it." In David Swenson's note on Chrysippus we read: "Chrysippus taught that many possibilities would never become actualities, Diodorus identifies the possible with present or future actuality. The former doctrine assigns reality to the concept of a 'might have been'; the latter makes such a thought meaningless. Cicero, in *De fato*, Chapters VI, VII, IX, concludes from the principle of Diodorus that the future is as unchangeable as the past, only that we do not see it in the future as we do in the past. Compare also Bertrand Russell's remark, that 'we all regard the past as determined simply by the fact that it has happened; but for the accident that memory works backward and not   *p. 95, l. 2* forward, we should regard the future as equally determined by the fact that it will happen.' *Mysticism and Logic,* pp. 201-02. Similarly, Diodorus argued from the impossibility of the unrealized alternatives *after* the event, to their impossibility *before* the event, on the principle that the impossible cannot arise out of the possible. He thus abolished the concept of the possible except as identical with the actual. Chrysippus is credited with the counter-proposition that even if the ring on his finger never happened to be broken, it is nevertheless breakable, thus distinguishing between the possible and the actual." It appears in *Pap.* IV c 34 that Kierkegaard read about this basic disagreement also in paragraphs 169-70 of Leibniz's *Theodicée,* which he studied during 1842-1843 in J. C. Gottsched's German translation of 1763 (Ktl. 619), and also about Cicero's and Pierre Bayle's discussion of it.

p. 96, l. 22   *freedom would be witchcraft etc.* An illusion to Holberg's comedy, *Hexerie eller blind Allarm.*

p. 96, note   *The Absolute Method, Hegel's discovery.* Hegel says in *Vorlesungen über die Philosophie der Religion* (W.a.A., XI, 59; J.A., XV, 75; *Philosophy of Religion,* I, 59): "There can be but one method in all science, since the method is the self-unfolding Notion (Begriff) and nothing else, and this latter is only one." Since the unfolding of thought in Speculative Philosophy is identical with the unfolding, through dialectical development, of the highest being, of the Idea, of God, Hegel can call the method he uses the absolute method. It is based upon the concept (in Hegel both an entity of thought and an entity of being) which contains opposites which "flop over and over" (see note to page 5). Especially at the close of *Wissenschaft der Logik* (W.a.A., V, 327-53; J.A., V, 327-53; *Science of Logic,* II, 466-86) Hegel explains what he means by the expression "the absolute method" (p. 468): "Accordingly, what must now be considered as method is no more than the movement of the Notion itself, whose nature has already been understood. This meaning, however, is now added, that the Notion is everything, the self-determining and self-realizing movement. Hence the method must be recognized to be universal without restriction, to be a mode both internal and external, and the force which is utterly infinite, which no object can resist insofar as it presents itself as external and as removed from and independent of reason, while also it can neither have a particular nature as against it nor fail to be penetrated by it. The method therefore is both soul and substance, and nothing is either conceived or known in its truth except insofar as it is completely subject to the method; it is the peculiar method of each individual fact because its activity is the Notion." Since the Idea advances through the dialectical development of the concepts, it becomes, as it says, "immer reicher und konkreter" (p. 349; "richer and more concrete"; English translation, II, 482) through the absolute method. It must be noted, as Kierkegaard does not, that "konkret" and "concretion" in Hegel do not mean "palpable" or "physical" etc. but mean "put together" (cf. *concresco, grow together*), without particular reference being made to the elements themselves which are put together. That this is the case is emphasized among Hegel scholars, particularly by I. Iljin, *Die Philosophie Hegels als kontemplative Gotteslehre* (1946).—In a provisional draft of the Interlude Kierkegaard writes (*Pap.* VB 14) with an unrestrained irony and mockery of Hegel's method. For example (pp. 70-71): "There is a phrase, which when uttered, pierces the soul with awesome solemnity; there is a name to which, when uttered with the phrase from which it is inseparable, one bows down, takes off his hat; even one who does not know the man takes his hat off, long before he sees the man, and stands with hat in hand without seeing the man; it is a phrase which signifies something and a name which signifies something—they are the Absolute Method and Hegel. The Absolute Method is now at home not only in logic but also in the historical sciences. O worldly greatness, whatever you are, O most beautiful rose, however sharp your thorns! I would never want to be the Absolute Method but only have such a dwelling as Hegel has prepared for it in logic, not to mention in the historical sciences. To be obliged to take flight in word-play and witticisms, to fill up holes with blotting paper, to have to decorate with tinsel and remain silent about its all not hanging together properly—O, it is costly to be the Absolute Method even when the trumpet fanfare proclaims its majesty."

p. 97, note   *China and Persia.* A reference to Hegel's *Vorlesungen über die Philosophie der Geschichte* (W.a.A., IX; J.A., XI; *Philosophy of History*), which is divided into four main sections: the Oriental World, the Greek World, the Roman World, and the German World. The first section deals with China, India, and Persia.

p. 97, note   *Geert Westphaler.* In Holberg's comedy by the same name there are four monarchies, divisions of world-history, suggested by Nebuchadnezzar's dream (Daniel 2).

p. 97, note   *many a Hegelian Geert Westphaler's tongue.* Kierkegaard obviously refers to the Danish jurist C. M. Weiss (1809-1872), strongly influenced by Hegel, who in 1838 in J. L. Heiberg's journal *Perseus* (to which Kierkegaard subscribed) published his paper (pp. 47ff.) "Om Statens historiske Udvikling." There it says that Hegel "conceived of the formations of the advancing movement of the state in four main stages, his so-called world-historical monarchies. . . ." In an unused draft for a literary "Nytaarsgave" (1844) by the pseudonym Nicolaus Notabene, Kierkegaard writes (*Pap.* IV B 131) that the idea of the four world-historical monarchies "has been taken up now in our time and one hears it everywhere, and at times it is spoken of in such a way that one would think Geert W. to be the source."

might have been cleared up. Might have been but had not.   *p. 97, note*

write three volumes. Hegel's *Wissenschaft der Logik* (*Sci-   p. 97, note*
ence of Logic*).

The essentially historical . . . has . . . actuality. Something   *p. 97, l. 5*
has in fact occurred, has taken place.

A manifestation theory. A reference to Schelling (not to   *p. 98, l. 15*
Hegel, as Drachmann maintains in his note to this passage),
who in his Berlin lectures (1841-1842) had employed the expression in speaking of the created world as a manifestation
of the will of God the creator. (Cf., for example, H. E. G.
Paulus' report, referred to earlier, p. 611.) Hegel does not
seem to have used the phrase (cf. Kierkegaard, *Concept of
Dread*, pp. 10-11, and Hegel, *Philosophy of Religion*, pp. 59,
81, 83, 207), although he does with similar meaning speak of
the manifestation, self-realization, or revelation of the Idea by
itself (*Encyklopädie* . . . , W.a.A., vii, 2, pp. 29ff.; J.A., x,
33ff.; *Encyclopedia of Philosophy*; New York: Philosophical
Library, 1959; pp. 147, 153). By "construction" Kierkegaard
also points to Schelling, who in an earlier work (1803),
Vorlesungen über die Methode des academischen Studium
(which Kierkegaard owned in the third unaltered edition,
1830), had used the expression as a technical term (p. 92,
1830 edition).

If the past became necessary etc. The past understood as   *p. 98, l. 28*
having occurred by necessity.

Boethius. In the provisional draft (*Pap.* v b 15, 8), Kierke-   *p. 99, l. 4*
gaard quotes Boethius (*De consolatione philosophiæ*, v, 4;
Kierkegaard owned the Agriæ edition, 1758, Ktl. 431) in Latin:
"*nam sicut scientia præsentium rerum nihil his quæ fiunt, ita
præscientia futurorum nihil his, quæ ventura sunt necessitatis
importat.*" That is, "Just as knowledge of the present does not
impart necessity to the present, so foreknowledge of the future
imparts no necessity to that which will happen."

no knowledge . . . has anything of its own to give. This can   *p. 99, l. 6* hardly be termed a direct criticism of Kant, whose position in Critical Philosophy is that in our apprehension existence is determined but in reality it is free.

p. 99, l. 8   *historico-philosophus . . . a prophet in retrospect.* This is a reference to an expression in Carl Daub's paper in *Zeitschrift für spekulative Theologie*, ed. Bruno Bauer, 1 (1836), "Die Form der christlichen Dogmen- und Kirchen-Historie" (p. 1): "The act of looking backwards is, just like that of looking into the future, an act of divination; and if the prophet is well called an historian of the future, the historian is just as well called, or even better, a prophet of the past, of the historical."—Kierkegaard owned this periodical (Ktl. 354ff.) and had already read (*Pap.* II A 72) in the summer of 1837 Daub's copious study, which had been occasioned by D. F. Strauss's *Leben Jesu.* Kierkegaard always mentions Daub with respect, but there is hardly adequate basis to attribute (as does Hirsch, *Kierkegaard-Studien*, II, 539-51 etc.) deep and lasting significance to Kierkegaard's study of Daub's thought. Hirsch says (p. 549) that "Daub's problems, unresolved according to the formal principles for the history of the Reformation period and thereby also according to the relationship between doctrine and revelation, historical on the other side and historical faith for us, are precisely the problems which Kierkegaard takes up with new means in *Philosophical Fragments.*" This is correct, but it is not the whole truth about *Philosophical Fragments* and its issues. The direct impetus for Kierkegaard's writing *Fragments* was not Daub's study but was undoubtedly Strauss's *Die christliche Glaubenslehre* (see note to title-page). —Of Daub's works Kierkegaard owned, in addition to the one mentioned above, *Philosophische und theologische Vorlesungen*, ed. by Marheineke and Dittenberger, I-VII (in eight volumes, 1838-1844; Ktl. 472-72g), but oddly enough not his main work, *Judas Ischariot oder das Böse in Verhältniss zum Guten* (1816-1818).

Leibniz. In his *Theodicy* (especially para. 406-16), in con-   *p. 99, l. 13*
nection with Boethius, Leibniz develops the distinction be-
tween God's foreknowledge and predestination and concludes
that of the infinite number of possible worlds God chose to
produce the best possible.—As mentioned in the note to page
99, Kierkegaard read Leibniz's *Theodicée,* Gottsched's German translation, in 1842-1843 (*Pap.* IV C 29-41). For a study
of Kierkegaard and Leibniz see Kalle Sorainen, *Kierkegaard
und Leibniz* (*Eripainos Ajatus,* XVIII; Helsinki: 1952), pp.
177-86.

nam necessarium etc. For the necessary necessarily presup-   *p. 99, l. 15*
poses itself. The source has not been located.

Plato, Aristotle. Socrates says to Theaetetus (*Theaetetus,* 155):   *p. 99, l. 27*
". . . wonder is the feeling of a philosopher, and philosophy
begins in wonder." Aristotle says in *Metaphysics* I, 2 (*Works,*
VIII, 982^b): "For it is owing to their wonder that men both
now begin and at first began to philosophize. . . ." *Pap.* III A
107 (from 1841) reads: "Aristotle's thought that philosophy
begins with wonder is a positive point of departure for philosophy, not as in our day with doubt. . . ." It appears from an
added remark that Kierkegaard read the above-quoted line
from Aristotle in K. F. Hermann, *Geschichte und System der
platonischen Philosophie* (1839), I, 275, note 5 (Ktl. 576). It
is striking that in the Danish text corresponding to the end
of page 99 of *Fragments* Kierkegaard uses the Danish *Beund-
ring* (translated more accurately as *admiration*), rather than
Forundring (*wonder*), as the beginning of philosophy. As
Hirsch remarks in his Commentary, this can be explained
through the influence of F. von Baader (who is mentioned
three lines below Plato and Aristotle), who in *Fermenta cognitionis* (which Kierkegaard owned and read; see note to page 12,
note) speaks of admiration as the life-giving principle of
thought, and through the influence of Schelling's Berlin lectures, in which, according to H. E. G. Paulus's report (p.

450) he said, "Initium philosophiae est admiratio, oder noch bestimmter nach Plato: τὸ πάθος τοῦ φιλοσόφου ἔστὶ το θαυμάζειν." In a draft of *De omnibus dubitandum est* (*Pap.* IV B 13, 23) Kierkegaard comments: "Descartes teaches that wonder (*admiratio*) is the only passion of the soul which has no opposite—therefore one recognizes the correctness of making this the point of departure for all philosophy." Therefore it is most reasonable to assume that Kierkegaard has in mind this statement but by a shift of memory attributes it here to Plato and Aristotle.

p. 99, l. 30   *Baader.* The expression has not been located.

p. 100, l. 1   *Method . . . word . . . concept.* The Greek μέθοδος means a following after, pursuit, especially pursuit of knowledge.

p. 100, l. 2   *progress . . . teleological.* Governed by purpose.

p. 100, l. 4   *wonder stands in pausa.* In expectation. Most likely Kierkegaard got the expression from Hebrew grammar, in which a longer interval between words (noted by a distinctive marking) is called *Pausa* (cf. J. C. Lindberg, *Hebraisk Grammatik*, 2nd printing, 1828, p. 13, which Kierkegaard owned and had used in preparation for examination; see *Pap.* II A 404 with note.)

p. 100, l. 6   τέλος, end, purpose.

p. 100, l. 9   *immanent progression.* The reference is to the movement of the Idea in Hegel's philosophy. He says, for example, "If it is considered that progress is a return to the foundation, to that origin and truth on which depends and indeed by which is produced that with which the beginning was made, then it must be admitted that this consideration is of essential importance; and it will be more clearly evident in the Logic itself." (W.a.A., III, 64; J.A., IV, 74; *Science of Logic*, I, 83.)

p. 100, l. 21   *Immediate sensation . . . cannot deceive.* As appears in this and the next paragraph, this is said in agreement with ancient Greek sceptical philosophy.

p. 101, l. 11   *Faith believes what it does not see.* Cf. Hebrews 11:1: "Now faith is the assurance of things hoped for, the conviction of things not seen." Here Kierkegaard uses the term *faith* more as a sense for the historical, for coming into existence, not in the Christian meaning (cf. pp. 104, 107-110, and notes).

Greek scepticism. Concerning Kierkegaard's knowledge of Greek sceptical philosophy, see notes to pp. 21-22 and pp. 47-48.   *p. 101, l. 29*

Hegelian doctrine of a universal doubt. In his exposition of   *p. 102, l. 4*
Socrates in *Vorlesungen über die Geschichte der Philosophie* (W.a.A., xiv, 69; J.A., xviii, 69; *History of Philosophy*, i, 406), which Kierkegaard knew well from the time he worked on *Om Begrebet Ironi*, Hegel says: "Philosophy must, generally speaking, begin with a puzzle in order to bring about reflection; everything must be doubted, all presuppositions given up, to reach the truth as created through the Notion." Further, in the presentation of Descartes in the same work (W.a.A. xv, 335ff.; J.A., xix, 335ff.; *History of Philosophy*, iii, 224ff.), it reads: "Descartes expresses the fact that we must begin from thought as such alone, by saying that we must doubt everything (*De omnibus dubitandum est*); and that is an absolute beginning." Even if Kierkegaard had in mind such expressions in Hegel or a portion in *Phänomenologie des Geistes* (W.a.A., ii, 63ff.; J.A., ii, 71ff.; *The Phenomenology of Mind*, p. 135) concerning doubt, he nevertheless was thinking first and foremost of the Danish Hegelians Martensen and Heiberg. Martensen, in his review (*Maanedskrift for Litteratur*, xvi, 1836, pp. 515-28) of Heiberg's "Indledningsforedrag til det i November 1834 begyndte logiske Cursus paa den kongelige militaire Höiskole," wrote that according to modern philosophy, which begins with Descartes, "doubt [is] the beginning of wisdom" (p. 518), but, continues Martensen, "the requirement: 'de omnibus dubitandum est' is not as easily fulfilled as it is said to be, for the demand is not for limited doubt, not for some popular doubt about this or that, from which one has withheld something not to be cast in doubt," and Hegel himself

in "the infinite abstraction of thought from all particularity" intended "to carry through this dialectical doubt" (p. 521). Heiberg in his review of W. H. Rothe, *Læren om Treenighed og Forsoning* in *Perseus, Journal for den speculative Idee* (I, 1837, p. 35), says that "doubt is . . . the beginning of the philosophical system." Also in his thesis, *De autonomia conscientiae sui humanae* (1837, p. 19) Martensen maintains that philosophy begins with doubt. In *Johannes Climacus or, De omnibus dubitandum est* (English translation, pp. 115ff.) Kierkegaard analyzes the content of this proposition.

p. 102, l. 10   ἐποχή. Holding oneself in check. The Greek Sceptics used the expression to designate an attitude distinguished from the positions of the dogmatic philosophers. Kierkegaard was acquainted with the expression from Tennemann (II, 175 and 179; V, especially pp. 94ff.), Hegel (W.a.A., XVI, 96-97, and XIV, 519; J.A., I, 241-42 and XVIII, 519; *History of Philosophy*, II, 314), and from *Diogenes Laertius* (IX, 61 and 104; Loeb Classics, II, 475 and 515); cf. *Pap.* IV B 10, 16, and 10, 17. Kierkegaard calls this form of doubt *retiring*, since in the end it withdraws from the dogmaticians' positions so that doubt becomes total and its result negative. Cf. *Pap.* IV B 13, 21, where it is contrasted with "inquiring doubt," which is merely a method which has a positive result.

p. 102, l. 11   *refusal to give assent* (Danish: *nægte Bifald*). B. Riisbrigh translates *Diogenes Laertius* (IX, 107) into Danish as follows: "Maalet, hvortil Skeptikerne sigte, er . . . Bifalds Tilbagehold, der har Sinds Rolighed i Fölge med sig." According to *Pap.* IV B 13, 13, Kierkegaard read this portion in translation, which is not accurate. The Loeb translation reads as follows (II, 517-18): "The end to be realized they hold to be suspension of judgment, which brings with it tranquillity like its shadow." The Greek for "suspension of judgment" is again ἐποχή (see note above).

p. 102, l. 12   μετριοπαθεῖν. Kierkegaard gives an inaccurate rendering of μετριοπάθειαν, which means "moderate feeling" or "moderate affection." Most likely Kierkegaard remembered the expression, which Sextus Empiricus uses (*Outlines of Pyrrhonism*, I, 25-30; Loeb Classics, I, 19-20) from Hegel's exposition of Scepticism in *Vorlesungen über die Geschichte der Philosophie* (W.a.A., XIV, 551, note; J.A., XVIII, 551; note, in Greek, omitted in *History of Philosophy*, II, 341), where it is quoted. See *Pap.* IV B 10, 19.

every Greek sceptic etc. Cf. *Diogenes Laertius* (IX, 103; Loeb   *p. 102, l. 14* Classics, II, 515): ". . . we recognize that it is day and that we are alive, and many other apparent facts in life; but with regard to the things about which our opponents argue so positively, claiming to have definitely apprehended them, we suspend our judgment because they are not certain, and confine knowledge to our impressions. For we admit that we see, and we recognize that we think this or that, but how we see or how we think we know not."

If my senses, for example, etc. The following discussion is   *p. 102, l. 24* manifestly developed on the basis of *Diogenes Laertius* (especially IX, 107-08; Loeb Classics, II, 517), which first gives an account of the dogmatic philosophers' criticism of Sceptic epistemology: "Against this criterion of appearances the dogmatic philosophers urge that, when the same appearances produce in us different impressions, e.g., a round or square tower, the Sceptic, unless he gives the preference to one or other, will be unable to take any course; if, on the other hand, say they, he follows either view, he is then no longer allowing equal value to all apparent facts. The Sceptics reply that, when different impressions are produced, they must both be said to appear; for things which are apparent are so called because they appear." *Diogenes Laertius*, IX, 105 (Loeb Classics, II, 515) reads: "We see that a man moves, and that he perishes; how it happens we do not know. We merely object to accepting the unknown substance behind phenomena."

p. 102, l. 30   *in suspense.* Undecided, in uncertainty.

p. 102, l. 32   φιλοσοφία ζητητική, *etc.* Aspects of Scepticism called Zetetic,
Aporetic, Sceptic. The expressions, which go back to Sextus
Empiricus, *Outlines of Pyrrhonism* (1, 7; Loeb Classics, 1, 5),
do not seem to be quoted by Tennemann or by Hegel in the
above-mentioned presentations of Scepticism. Kierkegaard most
likely got them from *Diogenes Laertius* (ix, 69; Loeb Classics,
ii, 483; he owned a Greek stereotype edition published in
Leipzig, 1833; Ktl. 1109) where all these terms are used: "All
these were called Pyrrhoneans after the name of their master,
but Aporetics, Sceptics, Ephectics, and even Zetetics, from their
principles, if we may call them such—Zetetics or seekers because they were ever seeking truth, Sceptics or inquirers because they were always looking for a solution and never finding one, Ephectics or doubters because of the state of mind
which followed their inquiry, I mean, suspense of judgement,
and finally Aporetics or those in perplexity, for not only they
but even the dogmatic philosophers themselves in their turn
were often perplexed."

p. 103, l. 5   θετικῶς. Positively, categorically. (*Diogenes Laertius*, ix, 75;
Loeb Classics, ii, 489.)

p. 103, note   *Plato and Aristotle.* In Plato's *Theaetetus* (195) Socrates says:
"... I do not know what to answer if any one were to ask me:
—O Socrates, have you indeed discovered that false opinion
arises neither in the comparison of perceptions with one another nor yet in thought, but in the union of thought and
perception? Yes, I shall say, with the complacence of one who
thinks that he has made a noble discovery." From *Pap.* iv b
13, 7 and 13, 22 it appears that Kierkegaard in his view of
Aristotle's thought here stays close to the presentation of Poul
Möller in *Udkast til Forelaesninger over den aeldre Philosophies Historie* (quoted here from Möller's *Efterladte Skrifter*,
3rd ed., 1856, iv, 211). In the section "Aristoteles's Logik eller
Metaphysik" it reads: "Aristotle makes the right relationship

of the words the object of his inquiry because the single conception cannot be either true or false but only the relationship
of conceptions in propositions. The conceptions are the result
of the impressions similar things have made upon men . . . ;
but the true and the false first appear when man links such
conceptions with the concept of being or non-being."

Descartes. In the draft (*Pap.* v B 15, 11) Kierkegaard quotes   *p. 103, note*
the relevant passage from Descartes' *Principles of Philosophy*
(XXXI, XLII): ". . . errors do not depend so much on our intellect
as on our will. . . ." ". . . there is a great deal of difference
between willing to be deceived and willing to give one's assent
to opinions in which error is sometimes found." Kierkegaard
owned Descartes' *Opera Philosophica* (Amsterdam, 1678; Ktl.
473). The first references to Descartes, whom he always calls
by his Latinized name Cartesius, in the *Journals* (*Pap.* I A 328,
II B 18, C 18—the latter two obviously in connection with
Martensen's lectures mentioned earlier) do not suggest much
firsthand knowledge. Only when working on *De omnibus
dubitandum est* (*Pap.* IV B 1-17) did Kierkegaard begin to read
Descartes' works.

The conclusion of belief is not . . . conclusion . . . resolution   *p. 104, l. 9*
(Danish: *Troens Slutning . . . Beslutning*). In the Interlude
Kierkegaard uses the word *belief* (*Tro*) "in a direct and
ordinary sense, as the relationship of the mind to the historical"
(p. 108) and therefore here as a sense for coming into existence.
[David Swenson distinguishes in translation between *Tro* as
belief and *Tro* as *Faith* in the Interlude.] In the Supplement
(pp. 107-110) he moves to a consideration of *Faith* (*Tro*) "in an
eminent sense" (p. 108), that is, Christian Faith. In this passage
(p. 104) it is stated that the conclusion of belief (*Tro*) is "not
. . . a [logical] conclusion," since a logical conclusion would
mean that historical knowledge is within the same category as
logical knowledge.

Jacobi. Kierkegaard owned F. H. Jacobi's *Werke*, I-VI (1812-   *p. 104, l. 19*

1825; Ktl. 1722-28). In 1844 he began to read Jacobi (see *Pap.* v a 21, 31, and c 13). Jacobi maintains (in opposition to Mendelssohn concerning proofs of God's existence and other points) that we can understand only what we can construe and prove only what we can deduce from higher principles; but this does not hold true of actuality, because we can neither understand nor prove that something exists; this must be believed. Likewise every conclusion from effect to cause is a matter of belief, since the causal relation must be believed, not being subject to proof or understanding. (See especially *Von den göttlichen Dingen und ihrer Offenbarung, Werke*, iii, 367ff.) It is curious that Kierkegaard does not take Hume's epistemology into consideration here. Martensen had spoken (*Pap.* ii c 18-19) about Hume in his lectures, mentioned previously, and in his reading of Hamann Kierkegaard could not have avoided awareness of Hume (see *Pap.* i a 100 and 237).

p. *104, l. 32* *making things ambiguous, dis-putare. Dis* indicates a separation, and *puto* means literally to calculate, estimate, consider.

p. *105, l. 17* φιλοσοφία ἐφεκτική. Sceptical philosophy, the principle of which is reserved (cf. pp. 102-103 and notes).

p. *107, note* *nisus.* Pressure, urge. In his *Wissenschaft der Logik* (W.a.A., iv, 69; J.A., iv, 547; *Science of Logic*, ii, 67-68) Hegel says of contradiction in the concepts: "And similarly, internal or self-movement, or impulse in general (the appetitive force or nisus of the monad, the entelechy of absolutely simple Essence) is nothing else than the fact that something is itself and is also deficiency or the negative of itself, in one and the same respect. . . . Something therefore has life only in so far as it contains Contradiction and is that force which can both comprehend and endure Contradiction." In the Introduction to *Vorlesungen über die Philosophie der Geschichte* (W.a.A., ix, 70; J.A., xi, 92; *Philosophy of History*, p. 108) the same thought is explained in this way: "Here we have only to indicate that Spirit begins with a germ of infinite possibility, but *only* possibility—containing its substantial existence in an undeveloped form, as the object and goal which it reaches only in its resultant—full reality. In actual existence Progress appears as an advancing from the imperfect to the more perfect; but the former must not be understood abstractly as *only* the imperfect, but as something which involves the very opposite of itself—the so-called perfect—as a *germ* or impulse." Therefore, what takes place occurs, according to Hegel's view, with logical (metaphysical) necessity, which resides in the concepts' plenitude of contradiction. Kierkegaard, however, maintains that there certainly is contradiction in existence, but not as *nisus* or the impulsive power of becoming, but as the impulsive power in wonder.

Faith . . . in a direct and ordinary sense . . . in an eminent sense. The decisive distinction in the concept of Faith (cf. note to p. 104). *p. 108, l. 13*

Socrates did not have Faith etc. Inasmuch as his God-relationship was not in relationship to something historical. See *Pap.* VI B 45 for explicit qualification of the categorical distinction made here. *p. 108, l. 21*

Every time the believer makes this fact an object of his Faith. The believer is clear that the fact under consideration is an historical fact. *p. 109, l. 20*

COMMENTARY ON CHAPTER V

The Disciple at Second Hand. This includes all disciples other than the contemporary disciples, or, as is stated on pp. 112-113, all are essentially on the same plane. Now the difference between Kierkegaard's view and Lessing's, for example, becomes quite apparent: there is no disciple at second hand. *p. 111, title*

sorites. See note to page 53. *p. 113, l. 7*

spatium. Distance, interval. *p. 113, l. 32*

we do not speak historically but algebraically. Systematically, in principle. *p. 114, l. 2 p. 115, l. 10*   *seventy interpreters.* In the spurious Aristeas-letter, allegedly a report from Aristeas to his brother Philocrates, written during the reign of Ptolemy Philadelphus of Egypt (285-246 B.C.), which tells how Aristeas, on instructions from the Alexandrian librarian Demetrius of Faleron in accordance with the King's wishes, travelled from Egypt to Jerusalem to obtain a copy of the Jewish law. He was accompanied by scholars who were to translate it into Greek for the royal library. The seventy-two translators, after seventy-two days, achieved a clear translation which was approved by representatives of the Jewish congregation in Alexandria. The number seventy-two was later rounded off to seventy and has given the name to this Alexandrian translation, *The Septuagint*, often written LXX. Kierkegaard obviously knew the more legendary report, according to which the translators were locked up and each one translated the entire Old Testament into Greek. When they were ready, it turned out that their translations agreed exactly.

p. 115, l. 32   *not a simple historical fact.* Rather a fact in which the divine and the human are joined paradoxically in the Christ-revelation.

p. 117, l. 12   *the decision . . . is fearful.* Faith or offense. Whereas Kierkegaard (especially pp. 16-17 and 73) previously defined Faith as "the condition . . . which the Paradox contributes," he now speaks of man who must choose between Faith and offense.

p. 119, note   *ob meliorem informationen.* For having been better informed.

p. 119, note   *Epicurus.* In a letter to Menoeceus, found in *Diogenes Laertius* (x, 125; Loeb Classics, II, 651) Epicurus says: "When we are, death is not come, and, when death is come, we are not."

p. 119, l. 19   *the advantage of the consequences would seem to lie.* But actually it does not.

p. 119, l. 20   *Naturalization. Pap.* V A 10: "If Christianity could be naturalized in the world, every child would certainly not need to be baptized, for then a child in being born of Christian parents would already be a Christian by birth. Meanwhile men have really wanted to naturalize Christianity. Martensen's famous theory of baptism points, perhaps unconsciously, toward this. The consciousness of sin is and continues to be the *sine qua non* for all Christianity, and if any one could be exempted from this, he could not become a Christian. . . ." Therefore Kierkegaard is here clearly opposed to Martensen, who in *Den christelige Daab* (1843), p. 23, maintains that "It is clear in and for itself that in the period when the essential task was to establish the church in the world, much had to take forms different from those in later times when the church had put out its firm roots in the world where God's kingdom had become just like nature . . . where it had become an indwelling in the folk-spirits."

the protection of . . . a professor. A fling at Martensen. · *p. 120, l. 12*
Faith may indeed become the second nature in a man etc. · *p. 120, l. 14*
Cf. pp. 22-26 on the new birth.

left it behind. The Socratic view. · *p. 120, l. 26*

non plus ultra. Extreme or ultimate. · *p. 121, l. 1*

Recollection. See pp. 11ff. and notes. · *p. 121, l. 4*

the barber in The Busy Man. Ludwig Holberg's Comedy, · *p. 121, l. 13*
I, 6: "A sailor-wife in the Neuen Buden [Nyboder, since 1631 quarters for naval personnel] had at one time brought thirty-two children into the world and was nevertheless no stouter than an ordinary pregnant woman. How can your grace comprehend this? . . . I can tell the story with details; the children were all baptized but straightway died."

both natures. The natural man and the man of Faith. · *p. 121, l. 18*

Apollonius. In Flavius Philostratus the Elder's *Life of Apollonius of Tyana* (vi, 21; Loeb Classics, ii, 91) it says that · *p. 121, l. 28*
Apollonius "related to them how I [Apollonius] had once been the captain of a large ship, in the period when my soul was in command of another body. . . ."

the life of the race . . . in continuity with the first. According · *p. 122, l. 8*
to Hegel's deterministic philosophy of history Christianity is

a necessary element in the dialectical development of the (human) spirit in time (W.a.A., IX, 387-408; J.A., XI, 409-30; *Philosophy of History*, pp. 407-27) and provides a presupposition of the subsequent history of the race.

p. 123, l. 19   *the quantitative is confined.* For Kierkegaard variations within a qualitative concept are merely quantitative.

p. 123, l. 23   *that sister of Destiny.* The Greek-Roman mythological goddess of Fate, Klotho, spins the thread of life, Lachesis determines the length, and Atropos cuts it off.

p. 125, l. 3   *an accommodation to a less exact usage.* Here Kierkegaard expressly states that the terminology in the philosophical portions of *Philosophical Fragments* is not adequate for the Christian categories.

p. 125, l. 12   *a "casus" in life.* Kierkegaard uses here a terminology drawn from Hebrew grammar. *Casus* is the form which governs a word's relationship to another. If a noun does not govern anything else it is said to be in *status absolutus*; whereas it is in *status constructus* if it governs another word.

p. 127, l. 2   *the total difference.* The Socratic: that a human being owes nothing essential to another human but owes everything essential to himself; the Christian: that a human being owes nothing essential to another human being but owes everything to God.

p. 127, l. 4   *the above meaningless consequence.* That a contingent human being should be able to play the role of God for another person.

p. 128, l. 9   *the believer . . . is always in possession of the autopsy of Faith.* First-hand view, not a report by another.

p. 128, l. 21   *folly to the understanding.* See I Corinthians 1:23.

p. 128, l. 29   *this content exists only for Faith.* Because human knowledge can grasp the Christ-revelation event only as another natural historical event and cannot see in it anything extraordinary.

p. 129, l. 10   *requirement that man must renounce his reason.* Cf. pp. 72ff. and notes.

p. 129, l. 14   *many good and upright people living here on the hill.* The reference is to Holberg's *Erasmus Montanus*, especially IV, 2. Emanuel Hirsch in his Commentary does not understand that *the hill* (*Bjerget*) is the name of the town in which the comedy takes place.

the credibility of a contemporary. The problem is dealt with *p. 129, l. 24* from a somewhat different point of view in the *Postscript* (especially pp. 25ff.).

it would be more than enough, "algebraically" speaking or *p. 130, l. 27* in principle. Kierkegaard has said expressly that "if the contemporary generation had left nothing behind them but these words," etc., and he thereby expresses the hypothetical character of the entire development of thought in the work. Therefore he could write here: "it would be more than enough."

just as Saft always ended up in the pantry. In Oehlen- *p. 132, l. 8* schläger's *Sovedrikken* (1808), surgeon Branse says of his amanuensis Saft: "How the devil he twists and turns so that he ends up either in the pantry or in the wine-cellar."

profitable for the disciple that the God should again leave *p. 132, l. 12* *the earth*. John 16:7: "Nevertheless I tell you the truth: it is to your advantage that I go away."

intermediate situation. Temporary situation. *p. 132, l. 26*

the barber in ancient Greece. According to Plutarch's *Lives* *p. 133, l. 12* (*Nicias*, 30), a barber from Piræus brought the first report of the defeat in Sicily (413 B.C.) to Athens, where he was put on the rack as a spreader of false rumors. Kierkegaard apparently has confused this with another story learned in school about the Athenian warrior who ran from Marathon to Athens to bring news of the victory (490 B.C.) at Marathon and who thereupon fell dead.

the testimony . . . has the prohibitive form of Faith. A form *p. 133, l. 26* which does not directly communicate the content but a form which has a deterring effect.

not filling so many books. Cf. John 21:25: "But there are *p. 133, l. 30* also many other things which Jesus did; were every one of them to be written, I suppose that the world itself could not contain the books that would be written."

p. 133, l. 32   *until the word goes forth that it is finished.* Cf. John 19:30: "When Jesus had received the vinegar, he said, 'It is finished'; and he bowed his head and gave up his spirit."

p. 134, l. 21   *looked upon my project . . . as a godly one.* Little by little Kierkegaard gives an explanation of the purpose of the work until on pages 137-138 he openly says what he has really been discussing, Christianity in distinction from philosophic Idealism.

p. 135, l. 9   *the happy generation.* In the ordinary terminology of dogmatics, the Church triumphant: *ecclesia triumphans.* Here and following, Kierkegaard points to the understanding of Christianity held by N. F. S. Grundtvig and his followers.

p. 135, l. 22   *translation . . . by a not unknown genius.* A reference to Grundtvig's translation of Ephesians 5:19 in *Christelige Prædikener eller Söndags-Bog* (1830; Ktl. 222-24), III, 614: "saa der hos eder er Sang og Klang [RSV: "singing and making melody"] af Hjertens-Grund for Herren." —In the authorship Kierkegaard's sharpest criticism of Grundtvig appears in the *Postscript* (pp. 35ff.). In 1835 (*Pap.* I A 60ff.) he had already taken toward Grundtvig's theological views a basic critical position from which he did not depart later. —The principal points of relationship between Kierkegaard's and Grundtvig's understandings of Christianity are touched upon in many works, but there is no thoroughgoing study. An investigative survey is given by C. Weltzer in *Grundtvig og Sören Kierkegaard* (1952), pp. 12-23. The most recent contribution is Sören Holm, *Grundtvig und Kierkegaard* (Tübingen: Katzmann, 1956).

p. 135, l. 30   *nature-tones on the island of Ceylon.* The German naturephilosopher G. H. von Schubert, in *Die Symbolik des Traumes* (2nd edition, 1821, p. 38; Ktl. 776), writes of the "Naturstimme, der Luftmusik auf Ceilon, welche im Tone einer tiefklagenden, herzzerschneidenden Stimme, furchtbar lustige Menuetten singt" (quotation located by Arild Christensen). In the draft of a letter to P. W. Lund (*Breve og Aktstykker*, I, 35) Kierkegaard refers to this work by Schubert.

Faith is always militant. In the customary language of dogmatics: *ecclesia militans.* p. 136, l. 2

abracadabra. Nonsense. Manifestly an allusion to Holberg's comedy of the same name. The term itself, which was used as an incantation against fever, is of uncertain, possibly Hebraic, origin and meaning. p. 136, l. 13

repudiation of the principle of contradiction. In his *Metaphysics* (*Works*, VIII, 1005^b) Aristotle says: "the same attribute cannot at the same time belong and not belong to the same subject and in the same respect. . . ." —As is known, Hegel in *Wissenschaft der Logik* (W.a.A., IV, 57ff.; J.A., IV, 535ff.; *Science of Logic*, II, 58ff.) asserts that the principle of contradiction has been repudiated. In Denmark this position was transferred from logic to theology by J. A. Bornemann (1813-1890) and Martensen, in that they maintained that both rationalism and supernaturalism had been abrogated as "obsolete points of view." J. P. Mynster, however, protested first of all, although F. C. Sibbern had already attacked J. L. Heiberg's Hegelian treatment of this logical principle. Concerning this question, see V. Kuhr, *Modsigelsens Grundsætning* (1915). Cf. p. 5 and note in present volume. It is clear that Kierkegaard, not only here but consistently, affirms the validity of the principle of contradiction both in formal logic and in philosophy and theology, even though, as emphasized by J. Himmelstrup, he usually has the principle of exclusion in mind. p. 136, l. 32

the next section of this piece. Refers to *Concluding Unscientific Postscript*, which was published February 28, 1846. p. 137, l. 11

to promise the System is a serious thing. Kierkegaard possibly has Rasmus Nielsen in mind, who as the newly appointed professor of philosophy began in 1841 to publish sectionally p. 137, l. 20

his never-to-be-completed *Den speculative Logik*. It may be, as is often the case in Kierkegaard's writings, that Martensen is the one referred to.

p. 138, l. 3   *it did not arise in the heart of any man.* See I Corinthians 2:7-9: "... we impart ... hidden wisdom of God. ... 'What no eye has seen nor ear heard, nor the heart of man conceived. ...'"

p. 138, l. 15   *"that great thinker ..."* A freely quoted and employed expression from J. G. Hamann's letter to Lavater (January 18, 1778): "to me ... the wisest writer and most obscure prophet is the executor of the New Testament, Pontius Pilate."

p. 138, l. 22   *ex cathedra.* The expression means: from the bishop's seat or from the professor's lectern. The latter is more suitable here inasmuch as it is directed to the Hegelians Rasmus Nielsen and Martensen.

Other Titles in Mythology, Philosophy, and Religion Also Available in Princeton and Princeton/Bollingen Paperbacks

THE ANCIENT NEAR EAST: *An Anthology of Texts and Pictures*, edited by James B. Pritchard (#10), $2.95

ARCHAEOLOGY AND THE OLD TESTAMENT, by James B. Pritchard (#137), $2.95

ATTACK UPON "CHRISTENDOM," by Søren Kierkegaard, translated by Walter Lowrie (#116), $2.95

CHRISTIAN DISCOURSES, by Søren Kierkegaard, translated by Walter Lowrie (#225), $2.95

THE COGNITIVITY PARADOX: *An Inquiry Concerning the Claims of Philosophy*, by John Lange (#196), $1.95

THE CONCEPT OF DREAD, by Søren Kierkegaard, translated by Walter Lowrie (#90), $1.95

CONCLUDING UNSCIENTIFIC POSTSCRIPT, by Søren Kierkegaard, translated by David F. Swenson and Walter Lowrie (#140), $3.95

EITHER/OR (Volume I), by Søren Kierkegaard, translated by David F. Swenson and Lillian Marvin Swenson with revisions and a foreword by Howard A. Johnson (#253), $2.95

EITHER/OR (Volume II), by Søren Kierkegaard, translated by Walter Lowrie with revisions and a foreword by Howard A. Johnson (#254), $2.45

ELEUSIS AND THE ELEUSINIAN MYSTERIES, by George E. Mylonas (#155), $4.95

ESSAYS ON A SCIENCE OF MYTHOLOGY: *The Myth of the Divine Child and the Mysteries of Eleusis*, by C. G. Jung and C. Kerényi (P/B #180), $2.95

FEAR AND TREMBLING *and* THE SICKNESS UNTO DEATH, by Søren Kirkegaard, translated by Walter Lowrie (#129), $1.95

FOR SELF-EXAMINATION *and* JUDGE FOR YOURSELVES! by Søren Kierkegaard, translated by Walter Lowrie (#115), $2.45

THE GREAT RELIGIONS OF THE MODERN WORLD, edited by Edward J. Jurji (#81), $2.95

KARL JASPERS: *An Introduction to His Philosophy*, by Charles F. Wallraff (#197), $2.95